SOLDIERING FOR FREEDOM

Joseph G. Dawson III, General Editor

Editorial Board
Robert Doughty
Brian Linn
Craig Symonds
Robert Wooster

SOLDIERING FOR FREEDOM

A GI'S ACCOUNT OF WORLD WAR II

Herman J. Obermayer

TEXAS A&M UNIVERSITY PRESS   COLLEGE STATION

LIBRARY OF CONGRESS CATALOGING-IN-PUBLICATION DATA

Obermayer, Herman J.
    Soldiering for freedom : a GI's account of World War II /
  Herman J. Obermayer.
        p. cm.—(Texas A&M University military history series ; no. 98)
    Includes index.
    ISBN 1-58544-430-8 (cloth : alk. paper)
    ISBN 1-58544-406-5 (pbk. : alk. paper)
    1. Obermayer, Herman J.—Correspondence. 2. Obermayer,
Leon—Correspondence. 3. Obermayer, Julia—Correspondence.
4. United States. Army. Combat Engineer Battalion, 1291st. 5. Army
Specialized Training Program (US) 6. World War, 1939–1945—
Regimental histories—United States. 7. World War, 1939–1945—
Personal narratives, American. 8. World War, 1939–1945—Western
Front. 9. Military engineers—United States—Correspondence.
I. Title. II. Texas A&M University military history series ; 98.
D769.3351291st.O24 2005
940.54'8373'092—dc22   2004019329

All photographs in this book were taken by the author
(or with the author's camera), except those of the
2131st ASTP Unit. They are reprinted with permission
of the *Alumni Gazette of the College of William
and Mary in Virginia* 11, no. 1 (October, 1943).
The author's photographs are courtesy the Eisenhower Center for American Studies, Metropolitan College, University of New Oreleans, and its
affiliate the National D-Day Museum.

FOR

BETTY NAN

WITH LOVE

•

ABIDING, EVERLASTING

OFFICE·OF·U.S.·CHIEF·OF·COUNSEL

APO 403 U.S. Army

15 December 19[_]
letter #167

Dear Folks:

Someday years from now when a dinner partner of mine looks at me with that stop-boring-me look I'll pull the rabbit out of the hat and tell her how I watched Goering and Hess and Jodl squirm and make faces during the Nurnberg Trials. Yesterday afternoon I spent three hours watching and listening to the trial and really spent three of the most interesting hours I can remember.

You'll probably have to prove less about your identification and background to get into the holy of holies or the swankiest club of Newport than you do to get into the trials.

Contents

AIR 6 CENTS MAIL

UNITED STATES OF AMERICA

FROM Pfc Herman Sherman Jr.

Med Det — 124 Eng C Bn

APO 17404, % P.M. N.Y.

APO N.Y.
1945
POST

VIA AIR MAIL

⑪

Mrs Leon J. Sherman

821 Westview Avenue

Philadelphia 19, P

PASSED BY

U 50843 S

ARMY EXAMINER

Lt Robert E. Reed

PREFACE

The Past Is Prologue

I anticipated that reading my World War II letters after sixty years would be an enjoyable exercise in nostalgia—and little more. But I was surprised. I found much more. I discovered a striking number of harbingers of the major happenings that have dominated the news media during the twenty-first century's early years.

In the spring of 2003, the governments of France and the United States waged a war of words against each other over Iraq. On both sides of the Atlantic, pundits and foreign-affairs experts saw the breach as something profound. They saw it as the beginning of the end of a historic international partnership, a relationship based on mutual aspirations and philosophies with their origins in the American Revolution.

But popular reaction was quite different. The rupture brought to the surface long dormant, but deeply felt, hostilities. Hundreds of thousands of people participated in anti-American rallies in Paris and Marseilles. Billboards vilifying President George W. Bush became part of the French landscape. American wine and cheese shops doubled and tripled their sales by aggressively advertising that they did *not* sell French products. American tourists boycotted France. In March, 2003, only 260 Americans, compared with 895 in the previous year, registered at Ste. Mère Église's information office, an important stop on Normandy beach military-cemetery tours.

The dichotomy between the lamentations of diplomats and journalists on the deterioration of Franco-American relations and the bitter hostility demonstrated by the working classes was not a new phenomenon for me. I had seen it before. Like today's ordinary person in the street, the GIs with whom I served in World War II did not share the establishment's romanticized version of American-French relations. The "f—king frogs," whose country we occupied, despised us—and the feeling was mutual.

From the day in January, 1945, when I waded ashore in the bomb-ravaged port of Le Havre, I was dubious about journalistic portrayals of France's enthusiasm for America. Why would residents of a city that Germany's Luftwaffe had spared but Britain's Royal Air Force had devastated welcome us as friends? In 1940, the population of Le Havre was approximately 190,000. Before the port city fell to the Allies, 5,000 civilians were randomly killed and 12,500 buildings destroyed. Aerial bombs kill anonymously, but they have return addresses. This is not a statement about the morality or efficacy of mass bombings. It is intended only to help explain why anti-American feelings in much of France were deep. In every large city in Normandy almost every resident knew an innocent civilian who had been killed or maimed by Allied bombs. We were seen as hostile murderers, not generous liberators.

While awaiting a combat assignment at a reinforcement encampment in Normandy, I visited Rouen, one of the region's largest cities and the capital of Upper Normandy province. In 1940 its population was about 109,000. In one week in June, 1944, Allied bombs killed more than 1,500 civilians and made 40,000 people homeless there. During the same month, the Allies demolished Rouen's ancient cathedral, the site of Joan of Arc's fifteenth-century trial. The number of French noncombatants who were killed in the city that week is approximately twice the number of American soldiers who died on the Normandy beaches on D-Day.

Americans on the home front rarely saw newsreel footage or newspaper stories about the destruction U.S. bombers wreaked on France's midsized cities. This is largely attributable to tight censorship, one of whose objectives was to keep articles about the ever-growing American-French hostility from appearing on hometown front pages. Additionally, stateside readers and moviegoers chiefly wanted three kinds of war reportage: big-picture explanations of the war's progress, military commanders' strategic decisions, and boy-next-door, combat-zone stories about lonely, miserable, but brave GIs. Even today the facts are not readily available.

After France's capitulation and surrender in 1940, the Nazis treated the country as a friendly constituency of the "Thousand-Year Reich" that would extend from the Atlantic to the Volga. The German attitude toward France was long-term. Ours was short-term. We needed France's infrastructure and land to pursue our enemy across the Rhine. Our objective was to defeat Hitler—not to develop France into a future American state. Our Army commandeered most of the country's railways, roads, harbors, hotels, and hospitals. Our Air Force rained bombs on strategically important cities. During the four years that Hitler's bureaucrats governed Normandy, they enhanced its agricultural and industrial infrastructure. In contrast, we ruined much of it.

The gasoline pipeline roustabout crew, of which I was a part, considered our French neighbors "the enemy." Our job was to keep to a minimum French sabotage of the U.S. Army's above-ground gasoline pipeline. The flow of vital gasoline to combat troops was seriously impeded as a result of daily pipeline ruptures caused by French peasants tampering with the line. We had no way of knowing whether the saboteurs were big-time black-market operators, petty thieves, or Berlin-sponsored, anti-American secret agents, but we knew that, regardless of intent, the result was the same. They were aiding Nazis, who were killing American GIs. And they were fully cognizant of the fact that they were impeding the American war machine in a major way. Our daily experience made us detest the local peasantry.

Biographers of General George S. Patton Jr., the flamboyant leader whose Third U.S. Army spearheaded the Allies' successful dash across France, have written about his rage when General Dwight D. Eisenhower halted his advance forty miles west of the Rhine because the movement of essential supplies, particularly gasoline, could not keep up with his tanks. Gasoline-distribution problems probably delayed the war's end by six months. Europe's political map for the next fifty years would have been vastly different, if the Allies had entered Germany half a year before the Russians. If American and British troops had taken Berlin before the Russians, America's NATO allies—Poland, Hungary, and the Czech Republic—would probably never have been absorbed into the USSR's Communist sphere.

In his war memoir, *Crusade in Europe,* Gen. Dwight D. Eisenhower describes the stalled Allied advance and identifies the chief problem. "From the beaches, gas and oil were pumped forward to main distribution points through pipelines laid on the ground. . . . Regardless, however extraordinary the efforts of the supply system, this remained our most acute difficulty. All along the front the cry was for more gasoline." Eisenhower further explains, "A reinforced division consumed 600 to 800 tons of supplies per day. When battling in a fixed position, most of this tonnage is represented by ammunition; on the march the bulk is devoted to gasoline and lubricants." The official Corps of Engineers' report on Europe's gasoline pipeline notes that "frequent breaks" were a major problem. It does not take a military-supply analyst to conclude that only human hands can open steel couplings and push aside rubber gaskets. Regular pipeline breaks in a war zone are almost always the result of deliberate hostile actions.

Stephen E. Ambrose, in *Citizen Soldiers,* says of the gasoline pipeline, "Thousands of gallons of gasoline . . . were syphoned off each day. The gasoline pipeline running from the beaches to Chartres was tapped so many times that only a trickle came out at the far end."

GIs had fun in Paris. But many GIs—maybe most—were dismayed by the opulence Paris enjoyed when it was the Third Reich's second most important city: well-manicured golf courses, elaborately mounted operas, thoroughbred–horse racing. American soldiers instinctively disliked Parisians who were living it up while their GI buddies were being killed a few miles away. I was probably typical. I enjoyed Paris's cultural and entertainment opportunities as well as its architectural beauty. But my comrades and I often discussed how the only explanation for Paris's good fortune was that its citizens rarely, if ever, harassed their Nazi overlords. French bureaucrats in Paris docilely executed orders from Berlin. They issued the directives that sealed the fate of France's Jews: between 75,000 and 100,000 were executed in Gestapo death camps. The legal, aggressive, open solicitation of soldiers by Paris's licensed prostitutes (semiofficially sanctioned by the U.S. Army) perplexed and offended many. We were products of a post-Puritan culture where movies could not be exhibited with socially unacceptable, four-letter words, nudity, or soulful kissing.

Journalists and historians have consistently misinterpreted the absence of open hostility toward GIs in Paris and other large French cities during World War II. Soldiers in victorious armies are almost always treated deferentially and courteously (often with feigned enthusiasm), particularly when they participate in triumphal parades and public displays of the conqueror's superiority, such as pulling down Saddam Hussein's statue.

News stories adjacent to the photos of American soldiers being kissed on the Champs Élysées in August, 1944, would have been enhanced, if they had included caveats about history's long chronicle of public welcomes for conquering warriors. Two millennia earlier, Roman legions were welcomed in Gaul when Caesar himself was leading the troops. However, most of his seven-year campaign there was spent quelling rebellions and insurrections that developed after his best warriors had moved on.

One day after landing in France, I was one of the medics assigned to administer to the needs of several hundred American soldiers who were badly injured when, as a result of sabotage, an American troop train crashed through a large brick railroad terminal near the largest reinforcement camp in Normandy. Approximately two hundred GIs were killed outright. Tight censorship prevented Americans on the home front from learning about this and many other acts of sabotage by the French in 1944 and 1945. This book includes photographic confirmation of that event sixty years after the fact. Today, the Iraq war's liberal military censorship standards plus cell phones and satellites make big news of a single American death as a result of a roadside bombing. In stark contrast, journalists were forbidden to report on anti-American activities by the many nonuniformed Nazi sympathizers who were part of the French landscape during World War II.

As America's current leaders struggle to find a proper balance between harshness and liberality in rehabilitating Iraq and Afghanistan, my experience as a member of the Allied Army of Occupation in its earliest days has contemporary pertinence. American troops entered German cities as conquerors—not liberators. The official brochure, signed by a lieutenant general, that was distributed to all GIs with their first pay as members of the occupying army included this advice: "Don't believe there are any good Germans. Don't believe it was only the Nazi government which brought on the war. People have the governments they want and deserve. German women have been trained to seduce you." On this victor–vanquished relationship rests one of history's most successful nation-building programs.

On a more personal level, in the months following the end of hostilities, the Army of Occupation programs that I saw were characterized more by trial and error than well-considered strategy. The unrealistic nonfraternization policy that prohibited all social contact between GIs and German civilians caused gigantic morale problems among our troops. A typical example involved a high-school classmate of mine who was promoted from private to sergeant for his bravery under fire. He was then reduced to private in June, 1945, because he had spent a night with a German girl. When I unexpectedly met him in Paris the following month, he was bitter to the point of being disloyal to America. He, however, viewed his hostility as nothing more than reciprocal disloyalty. He pointed out that his commanding officer could not have cared less if he had spent the night with a French girl on the west bank of the Rhine—rather than a German girl on the east bank.

In a report to Congress on the Allied military government in Germany, Congressman Albert Gore (father of Vice President Albert Gore Jr.) said, "Non-fraternization has taken on an importance to which it is not logically entitled. The treatment meted out to Germany must be based on something more than the assumption of unnatural attitudes by our occupying troops."

Questions about the efficacy and appropriateness of war crimes tribunals are still being asked today in Brussels, the Hague, Baghdad, and Washington. International legal scholars see a precedent in the trial at Nuremberg, where the twenty-two Third Reich cabinet officers, party officials, editors, generals, and admirals who composed Hitler's inner circle were tried (and half were executed).

I attended the Nuremberg trials. There I had a unique opportunity to look true evil in the face and record my observations while they were still fresh. My letters include a detailed description of the courtroom and the tribunal's environment, as well as observations on how Hitler's top lieutenant, Hermann Goering, demonstrated leadership qualities even in the prisoner's dock, where he was stripped of his medals and badges of rank. Few persons are still alive who spent a day with the "masters of the master race."

I was a twenty-one-year-old sergeant in December, 1945, and most of the visitors were at least twenty years older than I was. Only ten Americans were admitted each day to the visitors' gallery. Most of the seats were assigned to prominent judges, legal scholars, politicians, and officials of smaller Allied nations. I had learned that a thirty-year-old lawyer, a friend from Philadelphia, was working on Justice Jackson's prosecutorial staff. Between us, we arranged for me to have the credentials necessary to attend. By a quirk of good fortune, I was in Nuremberg's courtroom on a historic day. On December 14, 1945, the prosecution presented to the court—and the world—the first documented confirmation that the Nazis had killed six million Jews.

With America once again facing enormous challenges on the world stage, my World War II family letters are timely. Unvarnished opinions and candor distinguish intimate communications from objective journalism, carefully crafted political commentary, and broad-perspective history. I did not pretend to see the big picture. I did not try to cover up my biases. I assumed that after one or two readings my letters would be destroyed. It is this original presumption of transience that validates the fresh insights that can be gleaned from long-forgotten wartime correspondence.

The letters herein have been edited for clarity and ease of reading.

SOLDIERING FOR FREEDOM

CHAPTER 1

DRAFTED AT EIGHTEEN

LIVING IN CLOSE PROXIMITY to death was part of growing up in America in the early 1940s. It was a scary time. Never achieving middle age was every young man's deep, unexpressed fear. My locker mate, the baseball captain, and the band leader in Philadelphia's Central High School class of 1942 did not live to celebrate their nineteenth birthdays. Out of 596 men who matriculated with me at Dartmouth in the fall of 1942, 20 never reached voting age. Another six died while still in their early twenties, most of them from war wounds.

World War II engaged the entire American society. Except for two diabetics, every man I knew between eighteen and thirty years of age was in military service. In March, 1944, the entire civilian enrollment at Dartmouth College was 174, many of them wounded veterans. This was the lowest enrollment since 1819. Although there were more than eight times as many undergraduates in 1940 as there were during the Mexican War (1846–1848) and the Civil War (1861–1865), the war experience on campus was less pervasive. More young men attended Dartmouth during America's nineteenth-century wars than during World War II.

In 1999, I visited the Eisenhower Center for American Studies in New Orleans, a major World War II archive affiliated with the National D-Day Museum. Would they accept a gift of several hundred letters I had written during World War II? Apologetically, I explained that they did not describe acts of bravery or valor. They dealt instead with training, reinforcement depots, tedious assignments, occupation-army tensions, the ways soldiers found to relax, and French acts of sabotage. My offer was accepted with enthusiasm. Only a tiny percentage of sixteen million U.S. servicemen experienced frontline combat. The Eisenhower Center has many combat memoirs but few contemporaneous letters about my more typical kind of war experience. This book was born at that meeting. The fact that professional archivists at a research institution associated with America's most important World War II museum thought my correspondence and photos historically worthy was exhilarating—and flattering. I immediately began reviewing book formats in which letters, photos, and essays were coordinated.

When I arrived in the European Theater, the last great battle on the western front—the Battle of the Bulge—still hung in the balance. High casualties and the need for immediate replacements put my combat engineer battalion on the first troopship to travel directly from the United States to France. We waded ashore at Le Havre in subfreezing weather in January, 1945. Several weeks passed before my feet stayed warm and dry for more than a few hours, with the result that, even now, my feet are unusually sensitive to temperature changes. Many soldiers on my troopship saw frontline action during the war's waning months. I earned a combat campaign star but was never close enough to a battlefront to hear or see booming guns.

Every letter in this collection was written to my parents, whom I loved deeply. It was my way of sharing a high-risk, patriotic adventure. Regular correspondence between the same people over an extended period defines a relationship. It reveals biases, beliefs, aspirations, passions, and loves. This was a two-way correspondence. Mother wrote me daily and Daddy weekly. Unfortunately, only half of this wartime correspondence survives. Still, these letters disclose much about my parents' character and personality traits—as well as my own.

Leon and Julia Obermayer were well-educated, practical intellectuals. My father graduated from the University of Pennsylvania Law School in 1908, my mother from Columbia University in 1921 with a bachelor of science degree. Both articulated strongly held convictions about politics, religion,

Family picture taken during my last U.S. furlough, November, 1944. *Top row:* Daddy, Mother, and Uncle Hen; *bottom row:* Arthur, Helen, and me.

and morals. Nevertheless, they were always respectful of the opinions of others, particularly those of their three children.

After college, Mother became one of America's first female research bacteriologists at Mt. Sinai Medical Center in New York City. As was common in that era, she gave up her career to become a successful attorney's proper spouse. In that role, she drafted Daddy's speeches, reviewed carbon copies of the day's law-office correspondence each evening, entertained clients, and managed a large household. She also found time to help my brother, Arthur, and me with our Latin and my sister Helen with her piano lessons. Daddy won honorary degrees and headed several important boards, but these were always considered extracurricular activities. To his dying day, he retained an almost boyish pride in being a "Philadelphia lawyer."

For nearly thirty-five years, the Obermayer family lived in a large stone house in the Germantown section of Philadelphia. Besides my parents, the family unit included my younger brother and sister, as well as Uncle Hen, my father's bachelor brother, who lived with us. At 6:30 P.M. each weekday evening, the six of us ate dinner together. We children were expected to arrive punctually with hands washed, hair combed, and, for the boys, tie pulled up. At mealtime, Daddy and Uncle Hen never shed their business suits, including vests. Only an exceptional conflict was allowed to interfere with this ritual. During dinner each of us was expected to talk in turn about the day's activities. There was an implicit challenge to make our contributions interesting and to respond to questions. Daddy described his trial preparations and his law partners' idiosyncrasies. He often bowdlerized luncheon-club jokes. Mother reported on neighborhood gossip, books she was reading, and conversations with her own parents, who lived in New York City. Uncle Hen, who owned a pants factory in nearby Hatfield, Pennsylvania, was not very talkative. Still, he participated. He discussed his disputes with union organizers, the vaudeville shows that he regularly attended, and the stock market. We children, in turn, reported on school and scouting activities, dancing classes, sports, and what our friends were up to. We knew a great deal about each other.

The Obermayers did many things together. In the summer of 1941, a year after the fall of France and the London blitz, all of us, except Uncle Hen, traveled across the country by car on a thirty-eight-day vacation. Gasoline was still plentiful, and hotels were crowded. Notwithstanding the fact that most Americans doubted the country would get involved in "Europe's war," Congress approved drafting men aged twenty-one to twenty-seven into the Army and supplying Britain with aging airplanes and battleships under the Lend-Lease Act. While we were visiting Yellowstone National Park, British Prime Minister Winston Churchill and President Roosevelt signed the Atlantic Charter aboard a warship off Newfoundland. That winter, in the midst of the national trauma following Pearl Harbor, the family jointly wrote a 150-page journal describing the preceding summer's trip. Mother drafted the text on yellow legal pads. In the afternoons she read it aloud so we could suggest appropriate additions or deletions. Then Daddy did the final editing. His secretary typed the official version with three carbons. The original, with maps and exhibits, was displayed on a living-room table. We children each had a bound copy with our own name embossed on the cover. My copy still enjoys an honored place in my library.

I was a Great Depression child, but only in a chronological sense. Although beggars rang our doorbell several times a week—and we always gave them a dime (the inflation-adjusted equivalent is $1.40) plus a hot meal—that cataclysmic event affected me only marginally. While I attended public schools, my social life revolved almost exclusively around affluent Jews, mostly children of my parents' friends. I spent six happy summers at a camp in Maine, where all of the campers came from homes similar to mine. On weekends I played sports at a Jewish country club with the same boys I learned canoeing and riflery with in the summers. Once a month I attended a black-tie cotillion whose invitation list was compiled by a committee of the mothers of the same boys. When I went to Dartmouth this social pattern changed—superficially. In the early 1940s Dartmouth was one of the few major colleges where most of the gentile fraternities admitted one or two token Jews. I was proud to have been asked to join Sigma Chi, an old and prestigious club. As a member I was warmly welcomed, and I never heard an anti-Semitic remark in the fraternity house. Yet, when I returned to Philadelphia on holidays or vacations, my social life reverted to its old pattern—segregated by both religion and economic class.

High school was one of the intellectual high points of my life. Founded in 1836, Philadelphia's Central High School is America's second-oldest public high school (Boston Latin is the oldest; Baltimore City College, which was founded in 1839, is third.) As the "people's college" it was authorized by the Pennsylvania legislature to grant university degrees. I earned a bachelor of arts degree before I entered Dartmouth. Superior grades and a high IQ were the only conditions for admission to the boys-only institution. No other public high school offered courses in Greek, ethics, astronomy, philosophy, and

Obermayer family home at 821 Westview Street, Philadelphia, from 1929 to 1962.

economics. Its privately endowed, thirty-thousand-volume library was more than twice as large as the library in any other public high school in Philadelphia.

All of my letters home were signed "Obe." Long before I could talk I acquired my nickname. Daddy wanted me named Herman for his father, who had fought as a Confederate infantryman in the Battle of Antietam. Mother, on the other hand, thought it unfair to burden me with a knockwurst-and-sauerkraut name since things German were unpopular in the years following World War I. So a compromise was struck. I would be named Herman, but I would be known as Obe—the first three letters of my last name. For eight decades the nickname has stuck.

Although we were not a particularly pious family, our Jewish faith was important to us. Religious practice was structured so that it did not intrude in our social lives. We celebrated only the most important holidays, and we observed dietary proscriptions mainly in the breach. Yet, Friday Sabbath dinner began with the lighting of candles, followed by a brief service in which each family member had an assigned part. Daddy brought home flowers every Friday evening. Each spring, the extended family gathered at our home for a Passover Seder. Rosh Hashanah and Yom Kippur were paid holidays at Uncle Hen's factory, notwithstanding the fact that he had no Jewish employees.

My life as an easygoing college student ended one month after my eighteenth birthday. On October 17, 1942, during halftime at a Harvard-Dartmouth football game, a loudspeaker blared out the news that the House Military Affairs Committee had approved the drafting of eighteen- and nineteen-year-olds. Suddenly war stopped being an abstraction. I knew that soon I would be in uniform and that my life might be shortened. That night I got drunk for the first time.

An event per month quickly moved me from Harvard's football stadium to active military duty. In November, President Roosevelt signed the draft act for eighteen- and nineteen-year-olds. In late December, I registered at my draft board. In January, I passed the Army physical. In February, I was classified 1-A. In March, I was notified to prepare for induction. In May, I became a soldier. In June, 1943, I reported for active duty.

It was no accident that I was processed through the military conscription system with alacrity. Daddy chaired the neighborhood draft board. His position could have posed an ethical dilemma for both of us, but we both understood that I had to be on the board's fast track. For most draftees the interval between registration and induction was eight to ten months. For me, it was five. In World War II there were no "student deferments." That term first became part of the national lexicon during the Vietnam War.

My happy home life ended abruptly on June 12, 1943. Early that morning, I boarded an Army train for the New Cumberland Army Reception Center near Harrisburg, Pennsylvania. By midafternoon I had exchanged my civilian clothes for a private's uniform. I saluted officers. I said "Yes, sir" to sergeants as well as to lieutenants. In subsequent days I took a battery of intelligence and skill tests while attending seemingly endless lectures and movies on military courtesy, venereal disease, patriotism, and reasons I should hate the Germans and Japanese. Until I received orders that sent me to the Army Specialized Training Program (ASTP), much of each day was spent becoming acquainted with the most basic soldiering skill: how to cope with long intervals of enforced idleness. In wartime as in peacetime, soldiers are like firefighters. They must be skilled and brave. But they must also be patient.

When the United States started drafting eighteen-year-olds, the Allies were losing on every front. America had been humiliated in the Philippines. The Japanese had conquered all of Southeast Asia, including the British stronghold of Singapore. Nazi legions occupied most of Europe. Then, in the autumn of 1942, the "hinge of fate" (Winston Churchill's phrase) began its slow swing toward the Allies. The British victory at El Alemein kept the Germans from seizing the Suez Canal, and American combat troops landed in North Africa.

Like my letters, my photos were intended for family consumption only. They had the same singular purpose as my letters: to share my soldiering experience with my loving parents. I have never thought of myself as a photojournalist. My Kodak folding camera used 120 film, which had to be processed in civilian photo shops in France before I could send the prints home—and then only after censorship ended.

From the time I arrived at the New York Port of Embarkation staging area until a few days after the Nazi surrender in May, 1945, every letter I wrote was read—and often redacted or destroyed—by my commanding officer, who knew me well. I hated this censorship. Since I was not privy to vital military information or strategic secrets, I perceived his review of my correspondence as little more than voyeuristic eavesdropping.

I also deeply feared that censorship would isolate me from my loved ones in my hour of greatest need. Wounded GIs in Army hospitals (many of whom languished for long periods) were not allowed to tell their loved ones where they were, the nature of their injuries, or how they had gotten wounded. Our close family decided that—even if it meant taking some risks—we would find a way to communicate with each other in times of crisis. Fully aware that I risked court-martial, I helped develop a family code to circumvent Army censorship. It worked smoothly.

Whenever I had classified information to transmit, I referred to "Aunt Eva" (there was no Eva in our family). In the following paragraph, the first letter of every third word spells out a message. For example, after citing the nonexistent Aunt Eva, I disclose my move to the Chartres Reinforcement Depot as follows: "Daddy's letter **m**entioned my friend **O**scar and his **v**ery good grades, **e**tc. It was **d**ecided by our **c**rowd that regardless **h**ow little he **a**pplies himself to **r**esearch or tries **t**o play the **r**egular guy he **e**nds up the **s**tar student" (my family read this as "MOVED CHARTRES"). Mother acknowledged receipt of a coded message by referring to "Uncle Tom" (there was also no Tom in our family) in a letter's final paragraph. A family with a literary bent used names from Harriet Beecher Stowe's *Uncle Tom's Cabin* to dodge oppressive censorship.

The formula was not original. A few weeks before my final furlough, the Philadelphia newspapers reported a daring—and successful—prison break. The fugitive and his outside accomplices had discussed escape plans through family letters in which the first letter of every third word spelled a message. I figured that if this method had fooled jail officials, many of whom are specially trained to scrutinize small volumes of mail, it would probably also deceive my commanding officers, who had little training in—and even less enthusiasm for—their censorship job. Not one of my coded letters was excised or stopped.

As a soldier I was not ambitious to achieve military rank. Still, I always wore my uniform with pride. I understood that democracy and freedom came with a price tag. Sixty years ago I believed that soldiering in defense of America and its values was important and noble work. I still do.

CHAPTER 2

BACK TO COLLEGE AS A SOLDIER

TWO MONTHS after I left Dartmouth I was back on a college campus—this time in uniform. I was assigned to the Army Specialized Training Program (ASTP), the country's first purely merit-based experiment in higher education. To be accepted, enlisted soldiers who had graduated from high school had to meet only two criteria: They had to obtain a high score on the General Classification Test (the Army's IQ test) and be between eighteen and twenty-two years of age.

Created by a special act of Congress, the ASTP was different from college-based Navy programs, which were designed to train officers. Upon graduation, all participants in the Navy's college plans were commissioned. The ASTP was not an officer training program. It was created to fulfill the Army's need for a pool of educated enlisted men to draw on for technically demanding assignments. Thus, between April and November, 1943, approximately 150,000 GIs were assigned to ASTP units at 222 colleges and universities around the country.

Before being assigned to a particular institution for training in engineering, foreign languages, or medicine—the three areas of ASTP study—soldiers were screened at Specialized Training and Reassignment (STAR) units. So it was that over a three-week period I took a battery of tests at a STAR unit at Virginia Polytechnic Institute (VPI) in Blacksburg, Virginia. At first I was considered a candidate for Oriental language study because I had done well in a language-aptitude test. However, I was subsequently rejected because I did not speak at least one foreign language fluently. In the end I was chosen to study civil engineering because

I earned high grades on the algebra and geometry portions of the test.

In August, 1943, I arrived at the College of William and Mary in Williamsburg, Virginia, to study civil engineering. We were taught basic courses, similar to those in the freshman curriculum at engineering colleges (calculus, English, history, physics, chemistry, mechanical drawing, and geography). In addition to our scholastic endeavors, we were required to adhere to a strict military schedule. Each week soldiers in the program received a minimum of twenty-four hours of classroom and laboratory work, twenty-four hours of supervised study hall, six hours of physical training, and five hours of military instruction—a fifty-nine-hour work week. The haste with which ASTP was organized required the recruiting of faculty with limited academic credentials. Oliver Freud, a prewar railway engineer in Europe and the son of Austrian psychoanalyst Sigmund Freud, taught mathematics at William and Mary in such heavily accented English that soldiers rarely understood him. Since most of the young males who, under normal circumstances, would have applied for entry-level faculty positions had already been drafted into the military, the bulk of the specially recruited ASTP faculty were women who had recently graduated from college. There was considerable socialization between the young female instructors and the soldiers, particularly since coeds were restricted by curfews, visitation regulations, and alcohol consumption prohibitions.

Chartered in 1693 by King William III and Queen Mary II of England, the College of William and Mary is America's second oldest institution of higher learning. It severed formal ties with Britain in 1776 and became coeducational in 1918. The school boasts that it has sent its sons into every armed American conflict since the colonies came to Britain's aid in the French and Indian War. Yet, not until 1943 did it have any experience in housing U.S. soldiers—and it proved ill equipped for that task. Most of us were billeted in a 1920s gymnasium with more than 250 men sleeping in double-decker bunks arranged on a 94-by-50-foot basketball court. The toilet facilities were designed for

William and Mary's Blow Gym housed 250 soldiers. There were no foot-lockers. All personal possessions, including books, were stored in barracks bags or hung from pipe racks. *Courtesy College of William and Mary*

brief usage during sporting-event intermissions, not for several hundred men who needed to shave and shower before breakfast. Still, we did not complain. We were envied throughout the Army because we were out of harm's way. *Yank,* the Army's weekly magazine, said ASTP stood for "All Safe Till Peace," and its motto was "Victory in '44 or Fight."

Prior to the war, William and Mary had enrolled more men than women students. But by 1943, the ratio of women to men was three to one. The girls rolled out the welcome mat for the ASTP's college-age, uniformed soldiers. Jukeboxes boomed the refrain of the Lucky Strike Hit Parade's top song, "They're Either Too Young or Too Old," a lilting lament about the scarcity of eligible men.

Everywhere in the United States, soldiers were treated with respect and even affection in 1943. I rarely traveled by bus or train on weekend passes. Motorists regarded it as their patriotic duty to give uniformed hitchhikers a ride. Soldiers planning to spend the weekend in Washington did not have to worry about hotel accommodations. Several churches made their pews and pulpits available to GIs on Saturday nights. Typical of the sentiments that bound civilians and soldiers during the war was the understanding by Washington's pastors that a simple offer of pew cushions, blankets, and pillows, plus coffee and doughnuts on Sunday morning helped make the nation's capital an enjoyable place to visit. One Sunday morning I was thanking a pastor for his kindness when he introduced me to a soldier whose "wife" had come to Washington, supposedly at great sacrifice. When they were unable to find a reasonably priced hotel room, he generously allowed the couple to occupy his office. As it happened, the young man he introduced me to was a William and Mary friend. I did not let on that I knew he had a wife in Kansas City. War sentiment extended even to men's restrooms. Fashionable restaurants, as well as gas stations and pool halls, displayed Hitler, Mussolini, and Hirohito decals on the back of urinals.

Most of my stateside military career was spent not far from Richmond, Virginia, the old Confederacy's capital. Then, and later on when I was part of a redneck pipeline crew in France, I saw only isolated evidences of racial prejudice while serving in the Army. That was not because it did not exist. Rather, it was because racial segregation was so complete and pervasive that I almost never came into direct contact with black troops. Although there were several hundred black soldiers on the large troopship on which I crossed the Atlantic, they were segregated in the bowels of the ship. Except during lifeboat drills, we never saw each other. When black GIs exercised and got fresh air on the main deck, white enlisted soldiers were confined to quarters.

African American soldiers constituted approximately 0.5 percent of the ASTP, but none of the 789 blacks in the program were sent to Southern colleges. Their presence there would likely have been disruptive, if not a breach of established segregation laws. A 1948 Army study titled "The Employment of Negro Troops" describes black soldiers' chances of being accepted for the ASTP as slim. Only 2.5 percent of those between eighteen and twenty-two had Army General Classification Test scores that were high enough to qualify them for admission. Of that group, many lacked the necessary high-school diploma.

Although I saw little racial discrimination during my Army career, I constantly chafed under the many forms of discrimination enlisted men faced. Throughout the European Theater, hotels, bars, restaurants, and barbershops routinely discriminated against enlisted men—black and white alike. U.S. military police enforced the "officers only" signs that French proprietors placed in front of their drinking establishments. Many upscale American resorts turned away enlisted men. Although owned by a Rockefeller-controlled, tax-exempt foundation, the Williamsburg Inn made its main dining room off limits to enlisted soldiers until the autumn of 1943.

All ASTP soldiers received a private's basic pay of fifty dollars a month. For many ASTPers this was a comedown. They were noncommissioned officers who allowed their rank to be reduced to private in order to attend college. The Army believed that, for its purposes, engineering specialists could be fully trained in two years. At the end of each twelve-week period, the host institution reported to the Army on each student-soldier's progress. Those who did not pass muster were sent to battle-ready units. At the end of the first grading period, 24 out of approximately 350 William and Mary soldiers were assigned to combat troops: 8 went to the 87th Infantry Division, 10 to the 37th Infantry Division, 5 to the 14th Armored Division, and 1, with civilian-life expertise, to the Aberdeen Proving Ground.

Although not technically William and Mary students, ASTP soldiers were a major factor on campus. After protracted negotiations, the Army brass decided that the commanding officer would appoint an Army editor of the college weekly newspaper, *The Flat Hat.* The Army editor was to report on unit activities, write occasional editorials, and attend regular staff meetings. I was selected for the job. Prior to publication, everything the Army editor wrote had to be approved by the unit commanding officer. I recall my disappointment when an editorial with absolutely no military significance was killed. It questioned the fairness of Virginia's alcoholic beverage law, which prohibited the sale of liquor to minors—even though the Army regularly commissioned teenagers as battle-unit commanders and bomber pilots.

The ASTP was too good to last. From conception to death, it existed less than a year. By February, 1944, the Pentagon brass decided it could no longer afford to have 150,000 able-bodied, bright soldiers attending college. They were needed in combat units, especially for the upcoming Normandy invasion.

Even though the Allies had begun to win victories during the ASTP's short life, in the spring of 1944 the Axis powers still controlled most of Europe, and the Japanese occupied all of Southeast Asia. While the Germans had surrendered and evacuated North Africa, Sicily, and much of Italy, the Allies suffered heavy casualties on the road to Rome. Battling the Japanese for control of small—but strategic—islands was costly in terms of both men and morale.

In March, 1944, William and Mary's ASTP unit was summarily transferred to the 95th Infantry Division at Indiantown Gap, Pennsylvania. Approximately half of the Williamsburg contingent stayed with the 95th Division, which took heavy casualties seven months later in the siege of Metz, a French city near the German border. Eight William and Mary ASTPers are known to be buried in the U.S. Military Cemetery outside Metz. This number takes on significance when one realizes that only about 150 William and Mary men stayed in the 95th Division. Others are buried elsewhere in France. Some probably still languish in Veterans' Administration hospitals.

In *Citizen Soldiers* Stephen E. Ambrose, author of more than ten World War II histories, laments the fact that the ASTP led to the death of some of the country's best and brightest. "More than half the ASTPers got sent into rifle companies, as replacements," Ambrose observes. "The Army promised them a free education, then changed its mind and put them into front lines, where most of them never would have ended up, if they had declined the offer to enter the program." He explains that, because of the overwhelming need for frontline, foot-soldier replacements in the spring of 1944, even base-camp education programs were abandoned. In the normal course of events, military training's natural-selection process would have made ASTPers into company clerks, meteorologists, headquarters orderlies, artillery calculators, and mapmakers—all assignments less hazardous than a combat infantryman's.

Company F
3310 Service Unit (STAR)
VPI, Blacksburg, Va.
July 9, 1943

Dear Folks:

This letter is being written from a college dormitory exactly one year after I began my first class at Dartmouth. I begin my Army college career with the same high hopes.

This morning I realized I was in the South when we stopped for fifteen minutes in Roanoke, Va. Although some colored people were in the railroad-station waiting room, I nonchalantly walked in and discovered that there are two separate waiting rooms for white and colored people. The boys got quite a laugh out of my ignorance. The trip on the Norfolk and Southern Railroad was very enjoyable. Our train was on time all the way to Christiansburg. The mountain scenery was some of the most beautiful I have ever seen.

When we arrived at Blacksburg we were met at the station by our company commander, a dignified, gray-haired officer with a thick southern accent. He immediately took us to chow and ate with us in a fine clean mess hall where we had tablecloths, paper napkins, and waiter service. Immediately after lunch we were assigned to barracks, where we will remain during our stay at VPI. Our room has two double-decker bunks and three desks but is otherwise devoid of furniture.

At four o'clock all of the soldiers went out and drilled on the main parade ground. It was then that I thought I had met my Waterloo. I know nothing about drilling and stood out like a sore thumb. The sergeant gave me hell and thought I was a moron. I just meekly smiled and said, "Yes, sir." I am expecting a rough time with the drilling for a little while. [Most soldiers were assigned to the ASTP only after completing basic training. I was sent directly from the New Cumberland (Pennsylvania) Army Reception Center, where we "walked" to meals in formation but were not instructed in close-order drill.]

At six o'clock, when we were supposed to stand for "retreat," it was pouring. We stood in the rain for almost half an hour and formed ranks and generally wasted time while the noncoms tried to make up their minds what to do with us. It was one of the damn dumbest displays of Army discipline I have yet seen. For no good reason everyone got their clothes wet, and we have only one or two suits to begin with.

Blacksburg, Va.
July 13, 1943
1:30 P.M.
Dear Folks:

This letter is being written while I'm doing what I have done most of in the Army—wait. I'm not quite sure what I'm waiting for, but I'm sure I'm waiting.

This morning at eight o'clock I took the language-aptitude test. Now I must have an interview with the STAR board before I can find out whether I will study languages. If they advise me not to study languages, I will try to get into Basic, which is the equivalent of the first year in an engineering college. I believe Basic I will be relatively easy for me, while the language study will be quite difficult. However, I still want to go into language study, if the Army thinks I'm capable.

The language-aptitude test that I took this morning was quite an unusual and interesting test. The adjutant general's department created a language with a system of nouns, adjectives, possessives, and so on and then with that key the soldier was expected in thirty minutes to do as much as he could on a sixty-three-question test (I finished fifty-eight). However, the lieutenant in charge told me that I would have to do brilliantly in order to get in these special classes with my limited linguistic ability and none-too-impressive record.

Blacksburg, Va.
Bastille Day, 1943
Dear Folks:

The VPI auditorium is one of the most beautiful college auditoriums I have ever seen. The whole exterior of the campus is magnificent. But the library is terrible. Even Central High School had a superior one. The science laboratories, which are housed in a magnificent Gothic building, also seemed poorly equipped. That is probably true of many Southern colleges. On the outside they're very impressive looking, but scholastically they're inferior. At Dartmouth our auditorium (Webster Hall) is thirty-five years old and definitely outdated. But the college is built around the library and classrooms.

Blacksburg, Va.
July 16, 1943
Dear Folks:

You would never have believed it two years ago. It now looks like your dear son is going to study civil engineering. Yesterday morning the STAR board turned me down for the study of Oriental languages. They said I had a high mark in the language-aptitude test, but a new directive had just been issued that required all men to have some knowledge of a language before they could study it. They suggested I try French, but I was afraid of entering a class where I would undoubtedly start with two strikes against me. They then recommended me for the algebra and plane-geometry tests, which are the prerequisites for Basic I Engineering. I did not attend physical training or anything else yesterday and reviewed algebra. Today I took the tests. I am quite doubtful about the results, but I tried hard. All I can do now is hope and pray.

Today the twenty-six thousand soldiers stationed here, as well as the three hundred Navy men and the eight hundred men in the VPI Corps of Cadets paraded before the colonel. Although we were sloppy, it was quite an impressive sight. If Hanover, New Hampshire [the site of Dartmouth College] is like Blacksburg is today, it is no longer a college town but an Army camp.

Blacksburg, Va.
July 22, 1943

Dear Folks:

When I left the Henry School **[public grammar school in the Germantown section of Philadelphia]** *at age thirteen, I thought I left old-maid school teachers behind me, but today I attended three classes under the Army. Two were taught by women. My chemistry teacher is physically the image of Miss Weaver* **[a grossly obese older teacher at the Henry School whom the children ridiculed]**. *My refresher courses so far have not been particularly interesting. We have had three different chemistry and math teachers in four days. The only thing we do in drawing is practice lettering. In chemistry everything has been so mixed up we have learned almost nothing. In math we have been reviewing algebraic formulas. With my recent study of math this has been very easy.*

Our original company commander has been transferred. His successor is starting a new regime of discipline, but so far he has been very unsuccessful. With men moving in and out every day, he has very little control over the company. He makes sure that everyone goes to afternoon physical training. Already this week we have gone on a five-mile road march, run over a three-mile steeplechase course, and drilled for two hours. Everybody bitches about it. But it's the kind of training I need. I'm glad of the opportunity to get it at VPI.

I received a very interesting letter from David McDowell telling about life in Hanover in wartime—no beer on the streets or in the dorms. No beer anyplace unless you are twenty-one. No cutting classes. There are only about three hundred civilians left. In classes roll is taken by Navy section leaders; students rise when the professor enters the room and file out in order. It's a funny world! This week's Saturday Evening Post *has an editorial about colleges returning to their prewar status—nothing startling or unusual, just interesting. Talking about magazine articles, I just read Lessing Rosenwald's article on Zionism in* Life. *I liked it very much.* **[Lessing J. Rosenwald (1891–1979) was an art collector and chairman of Sears, Roebuck. He achieved worldwide** *notoriety in the late 1930s and 1940s as head of the American Council for Judaism, America's best known anti-Zionist Jewish organization.]*

Will you please send me another can of Kiwi [shoe polish] and some blotters? [Ballpoint pens were not invented until after the war.] Thanks.

Blacksburg, Va.
July 25, 1943
Dear Folks:

Yesterday I went to classes in the morning. In the afternoon I played bridge. This really isn't the Army. They play more bridge than poker, and there is less profanity than I heard at college. The bridge players were all out of my league, but I had a good time anyway. In the evening I went to the early movie and wrote letters and "batted the breeze" with my new roommate, who just graduated from the Army cooks' school at Camp Lee. The other fellows who live in our room were in Roanoke.

Our new company commander says we fall out too slowly when the whistle or bugle is blown. Last night after supper 250 men of Company F came back to the barracks and practiced coming downstairs quickly when a whistle sounded. The company commander himself came to supervise. He is really going to change this place from a country club to the Army.

About the shoes: As a soldier attending college, I have considerable opportunity to wear civilian shoes. I really think I need another pair. There are three possible ways of getting them; you may decide which is best: (1) After I get permanently settled through my company commander, I may be able to get the equivalent of an 18 coupon. It takes several weeks, and, already owning a pair of dress shoes, I may get turned down. I do not recommend this. (2) You can buy them for me in Philadelphia at the QM [quartermaster] depot with Lt. Morton's letter. This is the cheapest way. (3) You can send me an 18 coupon. [Shortly after Pearl Harbor, in order to ensure the equitable distribution of scarce consumer goods at reasonable prices, the Office of Price Administration (OPA) established a nationwide rationing sys-

tem. Coffee, meat, butter, cheese, and canned milk were among the rationed food items. Rationed products included gasoline, tires, cars, shoes, and typewriters. Stores marked sale items with both the price and the number of ration coupons required for purchase.]

Blacksburg, Va.
July 27, 1943
Dear Folks:

Today I did very well on mail, receiving two packages and two letters from home. Of course, I was glad to read Daddy's letter about Lt. Schoenfeld. I do not know if Lt. Schoenfeld has much authority around here. As a postal officer, he is part of the Adjutant General's dept. I believe that Schoenfeld is a member of Pi Tau Pi. I would appreciate it if you would look him up in the "Pi Tau Pi Roster." At your convenience send me the Pi Tau Pi roster. It is either in my files under "Pi Tau Pi" or in my bookcase, probably the latter. Mother, thank you once again for the money enclosed in your letters. I can always use it. [Pi Tau Pi was a national, noncollege Jewish fraternity. Boys from similar economic and social backgrounds were invited to join, and many remained involved for life. Members attended regional and national conclaves, dances, and sports events where they met their counterparts from other cities—most importantly members' sisters and their female Jewish friends.]

Yesterday we had an hour of close-order drill in the afternoon. Our platoon was drilled by the cadet company commander. Although I am able to do most of it after a fashion, I still don't look like I had basic training. He thought I was just messing things up to be funny. He took my name for some sort of company punishment.

Blacksburg, Va.
July 29, 1943
Dear Folks:

This is probably the last letter I will write you from VPI. I have received orders saying I will be transferred to the 3321st Service

Unit at William and Mary. Although the exact time of departure is not announced in advance, we will probably leave Saturday morning. There are more than 125 men going to William and Mary to study basic engineering. I believe that will be the last group because it was announced today that they have an order on hand for 350 men to be sent to Carnegie Tech in Pittsburgh.

In Mother's letter she said she thought it was pathetic that the Army was paying us for what we're doing. I haven't seen any pay yet, and I don't think I will for quite a while. [**An Army private's pay was $50 per month before deductions for life insurance and war bonds.**] But I have already begun to think about what I will do with my magnificent pay when I get it. Today the colonel said that even if we were in the ASTP our mothers could put Service Stars in the windows. Living the type of life I have up till now, it's kind of hard to believe that I'm a soldier.

Williamsburg, Va.
August 1, 1943
Dear Folks:

As you know, this is the chief tourist attraction of eastern Virginia. Every soldier, sailor, and marine stationed in Virginia has visited here at one time or another. This weekend there must have been three or four times as many men in uniform on the streets as men in civilian clothes. Williamsburg is within fifty miles of Camp Peary, Norfolk Naval Base, Newport News Base, Fort Eustis, Quantico, Richmond Air Base, Camp Lee, Camp Pickett, and probably a few smaller camps.

Every coed—thanks to the Navy—is afraid that every man in uniform has rape in his eyes when he looks at her. Of course, the male civilians don't like us much either. The prices and services in the stores indicate an attitude of "here comes a soldier—soak him while you can." However, I guess before long I will make some friends and find a girl who will trust me or one who won't give a damn.

As for the physical setup of Company A, there are upwards of 300 of us living in a gymnasium, about 250 on half the main *floor and the remainder scattered in handball courts, etc. I am living on the main floor. We have double-decker bunks and poles to hang our clothes on. The rest of our worldly possessions must be kept in a barracks bag.*

Of course, we will not be able to study in the same place we sleep. The arrangement is that we will be marched over to a study hall, where we will be forced to study while monitors walk up and down to make sure.

This week we will have eight hours of physical training a day. By the end of the week, it is assumed we will be in condition. I need that badly. Although I will gripe like hell, I am sure it will do me good.

Williamsburg, Va.
August 11, 1943
6:45 A.M.
Dear Folks:

College never was like this!! This is a most terrific grind. Everyone seems to get a lot more assignments than he has time to complete. I will write the details about my teachers and roster when I get ten minutes to write a letter.

I finished Ambassador Bullitt's novel, which I will send back sometime today. I will write you about it in detail one of these days. I do not think it is anti-Semitic. I believe the Republicans are doing Bullitt an injustice when they use it against him.
[William C. Bullitt (1891–1967), the first U.S. ambassador to the USSR and ambassador to France in 1940 during the time of its surrender to the Nazis, was the 1944 Democratic candidate for mayor of Philadelphia. In his youth he wrote a popular novel about Jews and high society. His political opponents said it proved he was an anti-Semitic aristocrat.]

The way this program looks now, I don't think I'll have much time to worry about girls. Today, my toughest day, I have classes, including physical education, from 8 A.M. until 5:30 P.M. That's a real grind anywhere.

Williamsburg, Va.
August 12, 1943

Dear Folks:

Monday morning at eight o'clock classes began. When I say "began," I don't mean that we had an introduction to our work. We had assignments that would scare the daylights out of a peacetime college student.

It seems that we are part of the College of William and Mary. Our professors treat us like regular students, but nobody knows how we are finally to be graded or tested.

Every place you study you have some good and some bad teachers. This place is no exception. All of my teachers, except my math and physics teachers, are pretty good. My chemistry teacher is tops.

Although I am not in a very good position yet to describe my courses, I can tell you some of the following things about them.

English—at present we are studying parts of speech, sentence structure, etc. Someday we will begin to read selections from a book of patriotic essays and poems, compiled by a West Point professor for the ASTP.

Math—we are studying something in which I am very weak: algebra. Although I have studied mathematics recently, I don't know much algebra. Will have to work hard.

Physics—I have a lousy teacher, but I am working hard.

History—no texts yet.

Geography—this course was the surprise. It is really quite difficult. We spent the first period trying to mathematically prove the sphericity of the earth.

Military—we have lectures four days a week and one drill session. The lectures are on the typical ROTC [Reserve Officers Training Corps] and OCS [Officer Candidate School] subjects. Next week we expect to study property accounting.

The real problem so far has been providing us with studying facilities. They have tried a different system every night. The way tonight's worked out, they will probably try a new one tomorrow.

The thing that really makes this place so damn difficult is the physical training three times a week for two hours. After each workout I feel like a wet washrag, only stiff.

Someday soon I expect to apply for a "social card," which gives you certain privileges with the girls on campus.

Williamsburg, Va.
August 19, 1943
Dear Folks:

I have now spent almost three weeks at a coed school. The more I see of coed colleges, the more I like men's colleges, particularly Dartmouth. When girls are walking around everywhere and you regularly see them in the classroom buildings, the library, and so on, you just can't help thinking about them. When I go to the library to study, I unconsciously brush my hair and sometimes take an extra shave. Then, if a girl should happen to sit next to me, I spend ten minutes trying to think of a way to start a conversation. It's no good. At Hanover I went to the library, took off my shoes and shirt, put my feet on the table, smoked if I wanted to, and put my unshaven face in a book.

In one of your recent letters you asked whether I had been paid. Yes, I was paid $62.17 on August 10. Yesterday I signed the payroll for August 31.

Our military course, although quite interesting, has also turned out to be difficult. This week we heard lectures on quartermaster forms and discussed when officers were "accountable" and "responsible." We are also expected to remember all sorts of form numbers.

All of my other classes are about the same as last week, except that they are getting progressively harder. The English grammar we are learning is quite difficult. This is the first time since Miss Spratt **[English teacher at the Henry School in Philadelphia]** *that anyone has tried to teach me "nominative absolute" or "accusative in indirect discourse" without references to Latin grammar. You have to be a good English teacher to do that.*

Francis Defalco, the soldier who sleeps above me (he went to Boston University before the war), has a brother who was sent to Dartmouth with the V-12 Unit. He hates it. Says it is the loneliest place in the world, with no accommodations for sailors. I guess Hanover, with military restrictions, is not the most wonderful

college town in America. In peacetime I am sure it was.
[Dartmouth hosted several different naval-officer programs be-
tween the summer of 1942 and the autumn of 1945. More than
fifteen thousand men attended college in Hanover wearing Navy
or Marine uniforms.]

Williamsburg, Va.
August 23, 1943
Dear Folks:

The physics exam is over. I did not do very well, but I have
plenty of company. I haven't met a single man who answered all
of the questions or one who thinks all the ones he answered were
right. At any rate, it's behind me. I spent most of yesterday
worrying about it and studying for it.

I don't know how often you read Danton Walker's column in
The Inquirer. *I now read it quite regularly in the* Washington
Times-Herald. *Last week he said he expects all OCS on this side*
of the ocean to be closed in the near future. He says all of the new
officers are going to be chosen from the men who have seen service
in Africa, etc. The only possible exception might be the ASTP.
However you look at it, I'm in the right outfit.

College of William and Mary
August 26, 1943
Dear Folks:

Conditions are getting steadily better here. I don't think it will
be long before some of us will be moved from the gym. This week
we were all issued footlockers, as well as two extra uniforms, both
of which we needed badly.

Our unit has organized a baseball team. Tonight we are hav-
ing our big game with the chaplains. We have already played
some local civilians, as well as the marines at Yorktown. I have
not seen any of the games yet. I feel that I can spend my spare
time a lot more profitably sleeping than watching ball games.
[In addition to the ASTP, the College of William and Mary
was the site of the Navy's school for chaplains. Navy and
Army chaplains were ordained in their particular faith be-

fore they entered the service as officers. Immediately after indoctrination, they were sent to special schools where they learned to minister to the needs—particularly final rites—of soldiers and sailors of other faiths. ASTP soldiers marched to and from meals. A favorite marching song was:

> *The chicken that they feed us,*
> *They say it is the best.*
> *We get the neck and asshole,*
> *The chaplains get the rest.*
> *Oh, I don't want no more this Army life,*
> *Gee, Ma, I just wanna go home.]*

College of William and Mary
September 2, 1943
Dear Folks:

It has been announced that our final exams will be written by the Army and may very likely be administered by Army officers. I am doing quite well in all of my courses except physics. If the professor is charitable, I will probably pass that also (this period). I have one of the highest averages in my math class because I resolved as soon as I got here that I would never let myself get in the position I got in at Dartmouth in math. I do my math the first thing every night. [The only class I flunked in high school or college was freshman calculus at Dartmouth.]

All of the discussion of the draft of fathers has certainly caused resentment here. The men feel it's not right to send 150,000 soldiers with an average age of twenty-one or twenty-two to school for a year or two and then draft fathers. Although I'm reaping great benefits from this program, I agree with the general attitude.

I received the cookies on Monday and thought they were very good. If that's the kind of cookies you make without butter—don't worry about butter in the future. Thank you.

There are lots of very interesting fellows here from all sorts of homes and backgrounds. One of the most interesting is a fellow named Ward, who is a Montana boy. He never used a telephone until he made a call from Fort Eustis about two months ago. He saw only two or three motion pictures in his life before coming into the Army. He hates Roosevelt and national parks. He is a typical independent Western farmer.

A humorous ASTP "anthem" is enclosed.

ASTP Anthem

Take down your service flag, mother,
Your son's in the ASTP.
He won't get hurt by a slide rule
So the gold star never need be.

We're just "Joe College" in khaki,
More Boy Scouts than soldiers are we,
So take down your service flag, mother,
Your son's in the ASTP.

We learn English and banking in pool halls
And by Braille system anatomy
We're getting a broad education
In this glorified ROTC.

The air corps may take all the glory
The infantry may have all the guts,
But wait till we tell them our story,
We sat out the war on our butts.

This is a bridge-playing outfit,
No more poker and dice.
What the hell is the Army
Without beer and whiskey and vice?

We're told that we may be commissioned
After two or three years of hard work,
But who wants a bar on his shoulder
When he spent the war doing WAC's work?

After the war game is over
And grandchildren sit on our knee,
We'll blush when we have to tell them
We fought with the ASTP.

College of William and Mary
September 6, 1943
Dear Folks:

I'm back at work again. This weekend I made a trip of three hundred miles and had a wonderful time—it almost sounds like the real Joe College days when I start taking weekends. At three o'clock Saturday afternoon Gil Hicks, Andy Highduke, and I stood on Richmond Road with our thumbs out waiting for a lift with Washington, D.C., passes in our pockets.

We didn't really expect to go to Washington, but those passes gave us the right to be almost anywhere in northern Virginia. Within two minutes we received a ride on a flat-top truck with forty other servicemen all the way to Richmond. We arrived there about 4:30. We then took a train the rest of the way to Washington and arrived there at nine o'clock. If you had been in Philadelphia, I might have come home.

The evening being half gone, and not knowing where to sleep or where to go, we proceeded to a local bar, where civilians bought most of our drinks. Then a civilian invited several servicemen to his home for some more drinks. After some food at an all-night restaurant we decided to look for a place to sleep. We told a cab driver our plight. He said, "Come along. They always take servicemen at Saint Margaret's Church." At St. Margaret's, after a pleasant greeting, we were shown to a cot in a room behind the altar. In the morning we were given razor blades, etc., as well as coffee and doughnuts. We were told there was absolutely no charge for the service.

That is really a wonderful church. They give parties for the servicemen every Saturday. They will never refuse one a place to sleep. When the rooms behind the altar are filled, they allow the men to sleep in the pews and on the pulpit. In the morning we hitchhiked all the way back to Williamsburg. It took only four hours and thirty-five minutes. We never had to wait more than five minutes for a lift.

The weekend doesn't sound particularly exciting on paper. In the final analysis it wasn't. Still, I had a good time.

College of William and Mary
September 11, 1943
Dear Folks:

Today is one of the really important anniversaries of my life. **[I was bar mitzvahed on September 11, 1937.]** *As I think back six years I realize how wonderful and full my life and all of our lives have been and how full they have been of each other. War and peace, age and youth seem to strengthen our family unit rather than weaken it.*

Thursday night the major was in his glee, for we had a parade in connection with the third war-bond drive. **[Low-interest loans from private citizens and businesses helped finance World War II. Eight war-loan drives between December, 1942, and December, 1945, raised $190 billion. Movie stars, swing bands, and comic-strip artists, as well as soldier units, participated in war-bond rallies. Students and poor people could purchase bonds by buying twenty-five-cent war-bond stamps and pasting them in books until they had enough stamps to buy a twenty-five-dollar (maturity value) bond. Soldiers could buy ten-dollar bonds. In addition to funding the war effort, bond drives psychologically bonded civilians and soldiers.]**

I was not able to take part in the parade, but it was a real success. It proved to some of the people around here that, even if we attended school, we could act like soldiers when we had to. I could not take part in the parade because "graceful Obe" has been excused from marching all week with a taped foot. Instead of scaling the eight-foot wall on the obstacle course, I got to the top and fell off. In typical style, I landed the wrong way. Don't shed any tears over me. I'll be back at work on Monday.

Williamsburg, Va.
September 23, 1943
Dear Daddy:

Another year has passed, and again I'm writing you a letter of congratulations on your birthday. Again I want to take this opportunity to say much more than "Happy Birthday." Every other year I have written you as a son writing to his father, a boy writing to an older man; the first relationship will always exist, but I'm afraid the second will never exist again. Two years ago I was a high-school kid, and last year I was a poor imitation of Joe College. Today I'm a soldier, old enough to shoot and kill and die. This letter is from man to man.

During the past year all of our philosophies and outlooks have changed. Many of our hopes and desires have been frustrated or at least been made to fit a plan that was not ours. Today we are separated by three hundred miles. We are all living under war conditions of stress and sacrifice, but we are thankful, very thankful. If next year oceans should separate us and we must continue the sacrifices of war, we will be even more thankful—we will always offer prayers of thanks.

I've told you this many times before. As each year goes by and external forces seem to separate us more and more, the family seems to mean more and more. One of the relationships that I cherish most highly is our wonderful love and friendship. It may be that distance lends enchantment, but today I feel that it is stronger, if that is possible, than ever before. I only hope that it means to you some small part of what it means to me.

This letter is not complete without a final good wish for all you want this year and forever. Hearty congratulations.

College of William and Mary
September 27, 1943
Dear Folks:

This morning the fall semester started for William and Mary's civilian students. Their coming has certainly made a change in everything around the campus. Many of our teachers have been

*switched around because of the civilians. As a result, I have a new
physics lab teacher and a new math teacher [Oliver Freud]. He
speaks worse English than Paul Kahn [a cousin who emigrated
from Germany in 1935]. We also have a new English teacher and
a new geography teacher. At Dartmouth they made the Navy and
the civilian semesters coincide. I think that is a much better method.*

*Yesterday morning I went to Sabbath services, which were re-
ally wonderful. There were almost seventy-five people there, about
fifteen of whom were girls. I think about twenty-five of the boys
came just because they thought there were going to be girls attending. Most of the girls were very, very disappointing, so it looks like
I'll be meeting most of my Southern Jewish friends in Richmond.
The service was conducted by a Chaplain Cohen of New York
City, but the sermon was delivered by a Chaplain Booth, who is a
gentile Navy chaplain. He served as a chaplain in the last war,
and until he entered the service was a professor of New Testament
literature and head of the Department of Religion at Bethany
College, Bethany, West Virginia.*

*His sermon was magnificent. It's been a long time since any-
thing has affected me the way that sermon did. He spoke on loyalty—loyalty to our homes, our traditions, our ideals. After he
was done, the only thing I questioned was whether our generation
hasn't put loyalty to country on such a pedestal that some of the
more basic and really important loyalties fall by the way. Certainly the Army teaches you that you have only one loyalty.*

College of William and Mary
September 29, 1943
Dear Folks:

*Yesterday the fifty-one who flunked out at the end of the first
four-week period left. They were all sent to replacement training
centers in the branch of service they came from. Nobody went to a
camp farther south than Camp Croft, S.C., or farther west than to
Camp Custer, Michigan. From replacement training centers they
will be sent either to units that are being activated or will be
made cadre there. All of the major's threats about "on the ball or
on the boat" were a little empty.*

College of William and Mary
October 4, 1943
Dear Folks:

Saturday night's dance was an overwhelming success. I think it was one of the best affairs I have ever attended. All of the girls wore evening dresses. You'll rarely see a better-looking group of girls all together in one gym.

On Thursday I went to the Rosh Hashanah services held in the Phi Beta Kappa hall, which were very disappointing. There are no Jewish Navy chaplains here now, and the J.W.B. [Jewish Welfare Board, the USO constituent organization for Jewish soldiers] man never arrived. Some of the fellows made a noble effort to conduct a service, but I found it disappointing. It was certainly not conducive to real prayer. I'm glad I'll be home next Saturday. On Sunday morning Rabbi Greenfield of Newport News did a very good job of conducting the services.

College of William and Mary
October 14, 1943
Dear Folks:

I've just taken my mathematics test. This week my good academic record seems to have collapsed like a house of cards. In the past three days I have taken exams in physics, chemistry, history, and math. All of the results were poor. I've studied hard, but when I went to class I just didn't seem to have the stuff. The coming two weeks are going to be hell. I'm sure I'll be ready for a week's furlough when I'm done.

The first three days of next week we will not have classes because we are going to take two three-hour Army exams every day. Although these exams will not affect our academic standing in any way, it has been impressed upon us that our scores may determine the Army's final decision about our status. As soon as these exams are over, we return to regular classes, where we will take almost nothing but exams. William and Mary has been in the habit of giving three-hour final exams, but since we will not have time for this, they are planning to give us somewhere near the equivalent in regular classroom exams. I only hope I do better then than I am doing now.

The Army brass and The Flat Hat *have finally arrived at a working agreement, by which the ASTP gives them six dollars a week for their paper. One of our men is to be a member of their staff. He will have under him six or eight Army men to whom he makes assignments. The arrangements regarding censorship are still pretty much in the air.*

I have been chosen Army editor. The staff and I met on Tuesday night with the civilian staff. What a meeting! What a half-assed way to run a paper! I may have sworn about the way Junius Hoffman ran The Dartmouth *[**Dartmouth's daily student newspaper**], but he was Joseph Pulitzer himself next to these girls. The meeting was attended by twenty-one girls, one seventeen-year-old boy freshman, and me. The lack of organization and general chaos are hard to describe.*

With regard to my furlough, I feel sure of getting a week, but I'm not exactly sure when I'll leave because they've changed the order three times in the last two days. The difficulty is about pay. We can't get paid until October 31, and several men will have trouble getting home if they don't get paid. However, most of the men don't want to wait for their pay and prefer to get an extra day or two of furlough. The present arrangement is to leave here after our last class on Saturday (2:30) and get a supplementary pay on November 10. Don't plan yet on my being home on Sunday.

Last night we had a parade for the mayor of Williamsburg. Next week we're going to have one for Governor Darden of Virginia. If the major has his way, before long we'll be parading for the local sanitary commissioner. He really loves parades.

College of William and Mary
October 22, 1943
Dear Folks:

On Wednesday I sent you the first issue of The Flat Hat *with my name on the masthead, plus one other boy and about a dozen girls. My first attempt at satire in a newspaper met with all kinds of opinions; most of the coeds and several of the fellows liked*

College of William and Mary ASTP (Army Specialized Training Program) Company A marching to mess. *Courtesy College of William and Mary*

it, but many others said I was trying to be smug and tear down my unit. Certainly I didn't want to do that, but I guess that is all part of being an editor and expressing opinions. After I return from my furlough I expect to write an editorial or feature on why the twenty-one-year-old men in this unit should be allowed to apply for liquor ration books. How about looking for some speeches that were used at the 1932 GOP convention, where Daddy wore a pin saying "My Vote Goes Wet"? [At the 1932 Republican National Convention, the major platform fight concerned the repeal of Prohibition. Those in favor of the GOP's supporting repeal wore "My Vote Goes Wet" buttons. By a narrow vote the Republicans failed to support repeal, while the Democrats endorsed it. Some historians believe the support of repeal was a major factor in the Democratic landslide that year. Although not a delegate, my father attended the convention as an observer and supporter.]

Tyler Hall, Company B
College of William and Mary
November 13, 1943

Dear Folks:

The first five days of Basic II are almost over. The only thing I can say about them is that they've been hell. The major has started a new system of administration. Now this place is being run more like a reform school than either a college or an Army camp. Under this new system, the only thing you officially have time to do is to study and sleep. You don't even get enough of the latter. We are also divided into sections of twenty or thirty men who attend every class together, sleep together, and march to and from classes together.

This does away with all the wonderful freedom we had before, by which a man could walk from one class to another holding a girl's hand. If he came late or early, it was his own responsibility. Under the new system, we cannot march from one class to another until the whole section has formed. Any man who takes the time to talk to a professor after class naturally annoys everybody.

This sort of military discipline, I am sure, accomplishes nothing good when you are sending men to college and putting them through the program we are going through. To add insult to injury, we now have no more free periods. During our "free" periods, we are now forced to go to our rooms or study halls to study. We must get special permission to do anything else, even on campus. Rumor has it that this is going to be changed tomorrow because of consistent objections from everybody—I certainly hope so!

When we returned from our furloughs, all of the grades for the past term were posted on the bulletin board. I was very pleasantly surprised by mine. I received the following grades: history (A), math (B), chemistry (B), English (B), physics (C), geography (C).

I did not have time to figure out exactly where I stood in my class. I feel sure I am in the first 20 percent, maybe in the first 10 percent. Even if I don't stay in the ASTP another day, I have gotten enough college credits (two hours short) to just about complete my sophomore year at Dartmouth.

About forty men flunked out of the unit, and many had no idea they were flunking until they saw their grades on the bulletin board. All of them left Tuesday morning. It didn't make any difference what subject they failed. As long as they had two failures they were out.

Our military classes this term are quite different from last term. On Tuesday we took a four-mile hike. On Thursday we cleaned rifles. That is quite a change from listening to lectures and seeing movies.

College of William and Mary
November 20, 1943
Dear Folks:

*One of our members was sent back to Aberdeen [**Aberdeen Proving Ground, an artillery camp in Maryland**] last week, being guilty of the heinous crime of "not conducting himself as a soldier and a gentleman." He had traveled with a lady of rather questionable character, who is the wife of a Seabee and who sued the Seabee for divorce a few weeks ago. He spent most of his free time with her. She could be seen regularly waiting for him outside the gym. The officers suggested in rather mild language that he slow down this relationship. When he failed to do much about it, he was dismissed. The next day they sent a list of the married men in our unit to the dean of women so that their activities with the coeds would be curbed. (Previous to this they had not been able to get on blind-date lists, etc., anyway.)*

I do not believe that the man who was kicked out was right to do what he did, but I think if you take into consideration the Army's usual approach to the men's sex relationships, this punishment was much too severe.

Two men were also kicked out this weekend for cheating. Although this time the evidence against the men was rather flimsy, in less than forty-eight hours they were back at replacement training centers. After the first two cheating incidents, the major had no choice but to be severe.

For the next two weeks I will be the cadet sergeant who will lead our platoon to and from classes, etc. This is my first try at really commanding men. I am glad to have the opportunity to practice on men I know well, men I'm sure will tolerate my errors.

College of William and Mary
December 9, 1943
Dear Folks:

Yesterday I spent two hours taking the medical aptitude test prepared by the AMA [American Medical Association]. I believe, on the basis of that test, I could probably qualify as a medical student. However, I wrote on my test booklet that I was definitely "not interested." For the first thirty-five minutes we did not even see the test booklets but just read a paper containing a description of some organs of the body and the symptoms of some common diseases, as well as a diagram of the head showing nerves, blood vessels, etc. All were written in highly technical medical terminology and were exceedingly difficult to read. Then these papers were collected and the test booklets distributed. We were quizzed on the information we had read as well as vocabulary, general knowledge, logical thinking, and so on. All told, I believe it was one of the best aptitude tests I have taken. In the past year I've taken more intelligence and aptitude tests than the average psychiatrist's son in peacetime.

College of William and Mary
December 16, 1943
Dear Folks:

Rumors are flying thick and fast these days about the liquidation of the ASTP. There is considerable basis for them. It now seems very likely that my stay in the ASTP will be limited to nine months at William and Mary.

An article appeared in Tuesday's Chicago Tribune *about the ASTP closing. They posted it on the bulletin board with an equivocal denial from the War Department. As the facts have been analyzed by our officers, the quota for the ASTP has been filled. As they did in OCS earlier this year, they have practically closed admissions. Also it is getting harder and harder to get into*

advanced engineering. Even if I don't get into it, I am thankful
that I got into ASTP while it was still possible.

The major would not let me publish my editorial on underage
drinking. Lieutenant Brooks [company commander] liked it.
But his advice was to speak to the major before publishing it.
There is no good to be gained from annoying him when I don't
have to. I would like to write one on how I don't think discipline
and culture can be combined, but I'm afraid the major wouldn't
like that one either.

Sunday morning I went to the Sabbath services in Wren
Chapel, which are conducted regularly by Chaplain Resnikoff of
Camp Patrick Henry. He delivered a poor sermon, but he seemed
like a good man and one whom all the men liked. Afterward they
fed us corned beef, etc., in the Dodge Room of the Phi Beta Kappa
hall. The food is given by the Newport News, Va., USO. It may
also interest you to know that there is another Jewish chaplain at
the chaplains' school here. He is the first one in several months.
Of course, we were all glad to see him. The chaplains' school is al-
most empty these days, as very few preachers wish to join the
Navy in the months just before Christmas.

College of William and Mary
January 11, 1944
Dear Folks:
I have spoken to several of the men who expressed a preference
for medicine and passed the medical aptitude test. Last week they
all had interviews with an AMA doctor from Richmond. The
way Lt. Brooks describes it, it seems that much of the decision as
to who shall study medicine will rest with the AMA. All of the
men I spoke with said the first two questions they were asked were
(1) What is your religious preference? and (2) What does your
father do for a living? Those questions hardly sound like a "demo-
cratic Army."

In class today we had a roundtable discussion on the causes of
American wars: social, political, economic, etc. I spoke on the
principle that the instinct to fight is essential in man. As a result,
wars are inevitable. I quoted from Nietzsche and Darwin. The

professor asked me to come over to see him after classes. He said he did not want to see a man go through life believing that wars are inevitable. He didn't convince me, but we had an interesting and pleasant hour.

The rumor I wrote you about was confirmed Tuesday night when the major had one of his regular bull sessions. He began by saying that he is being transferred to Leheigh University in Bethlehem to take charge of an ASTP unit of more than 2,200 men. He is leaving at the end of this week. The new man from Pennsylvania Military College is due here today. I am very sorry to see the major go. He is a fine man and just lax enough to suit my tastes. The new man from a military college is liable to be very G.I. I don't like any kind of G.I.-ness.

College of William and Mary
January 18, 1944
Dear Folks:

Last night the new major had his first meeting. I cannot say that I left the meeting pleased. He is typical of military colleges where they have lots of discipline and rules just to give the effect— and questionable benefits—of military discipline. We cannot wear fatigues, must always wear hats, and uniform jackets on weekends, etc. None of the things he said are important in themselves, but he definitely wants to give the impression that he is tough. In order to make that impression, he didn't crack a smile or say a pleasant word. However, I'll still reserve judgment about him until he carries out a few of his threats. The only really interesting rumor about him is that his wife is a former "Miss America," but she is still in Philadelphia.

On Sunday I went to Sabbath services, where we had a poor sermon by Chaplain Resnikoff of Camp Patrick Henry, but very good, hot roast-beef sandwiches from the USO of Newport News, Va. The food is so good at Sabbath services that I think of it regularly during the sermon. I feel like an Irishman going to a wake instead of a Jew going to a synagogue.

Saturday afternoon the new major started out with a bang by having a formal personal and room inspection. That was the first inspection I've experienced since I've been in the Army. All of us spent all Saturday morning cleaning our room.

College of William and Mary
January 24, 1944
Helen's birthday
Dear Folks:

Last Tuesday night I took my roommates to the Williamsburg Inn for supper with the money that Daddy sent me after Dartmouth's basketball victory. The dining room in the Williamsburg Inn has only recently been opened to enlisted men. We had a very fine and well-served meal. On behalf of Room 201 in Tyler Hall I say, "Thank you very much."

The GI exams we took this year seemed just as foolish as the ones we took last term. They never seem to be a fair test of what we have studied. I never think objective tests of that type are fair in the natural sciences and mathematics. This year, to add insult to injury, the new major would not give us the nights off before the exams, but continued instead with organized study.

*This week they announced the number of men from Basic III who will go on to advanced engineering. Nine were chosen out of a group of 55. All are to be sent to VMI [**Virginia Military Institute**] at Lexington, Va. Of the group of 9 men, 6 were chosen on the basis of grades alone, while the other 3 were chosen for different reasons. The choice of those 3 is rather hard to explain, although one of them was 36th in his class, but a former VMI student. Another was about 12th, but was an expert draftsman as a civilian.*

The first of a series of purges took place on Thursday, when twenty-six men were called out of classes and told to take seven-day furloughs, as they were being kicked out. We've been told that more will follow.

College of William and Mary
February 8, 1944
Dear Folks:

Yesterday Lt. Brooks explained, in vague, indefinite Army equivocations, what happened to the men who finished basic and were not sent on to advanced training. There is an order (which he was required to read to us) that said that all of those not sent to advanced or to special schools (radar, etc.) would be sent to units in the Army ground forces (infantry, cavalry, artillery). The group from here who just finished went to the following places:

>   *10   VMI for electrical engineering*
>   *12   Temple for premed*
>   *4 Radar school at Madison, Wis.*
>   *8 87th Infantry Division at Camp Butler, N.C.*
>   *10   37th Infantry Division at Fort Jackson, S.C.*
>   *5 14th Armored Division at Camp Campbell, Ky.*
>   *1 Aberdeen Proving Ground at Aberdeen, Md.*

The way most of these men were chosen is very hard to explain, if possible at all. Certainly they were not chosen on the basis of grades alone. There also seems to have been no distinction made between those who went to the armored forces and those who were assigned to the infantry. The one man who went to Aberdeen Proving Ground was supposed to have pull. I guess he went there because some colonel or general requested it. All of these are activated divisions. They will probably go overseas within the next two months. One of the infantry divisions has just returned from three months of maneuvers in Tennessee.

My roster is really quite bad. Before I went home I went to see Lt. Brooks about getting some free periods Saturday morning, but instead of that I got a full Saturday schedule. I went to see him early Monday morning, but he refused to change it. His only excuse was that he was too busy to tend to it. He meant he was too damned lazy.

All of the athletes have a special section with well-spaced free periods and a lot of easy teachers, but they couldn't take care of the people who run the paper. It was bad enough that they gave virtual athletic scholarships in college, but when they do it in the Army, it's too much. To add insult to injury, I got Dr. Freud, the Austrian madman, for math, as well as Miss Philips for physics.

College of William and Mary
February 12, 1944

Dear Folks:

Williamsburg is a soldier's boomtown. There seems to be a shortage of everything ranging from beer and rooms all the way to valentines. Ever since last Monday there has not been a single valentine obtainable in Williamsburg except "to my sweetheart in the Service." I really didn't think that was quite appropriate to send to the folks at home. This is just a short note to tell you that although you won't receive cards with red hearts and Cupid's arrows from "Obe" on St. Valentine's Day, 1944, all my thoughts and love are with you.

During these war years, when most of my friendships and loves seem ephemeral and shallow, my appreciation of family love and unity is multiplied many, many times over. Anything I might write about my love for you would be trite and banal, when all I want to say is that I send all of my love and devotion to you.

College of William and Mary
February 13, 1944

Dear Folks:

On Friday I signed a paper agreeing to have $6.25 each month taken out of my pay for bonds. I named Mother as co-owner. That is something I've wanted to do for a long time, but I never got around to doing it until this week.

The new major was certainly not kidding when he told us that our military classes would be more rigorous and difficult this semester. On Tuesday we did close-order drill. On Thursday we took a six- or seven-mile hike in a little over an hour and a half. Saturdays we now have not only parades but also a barracks and personal inspection.

This week we heard from several of the fellows who flunked out of the program and were sent back to replacement training centers in their respective arms and services. Most of them were sent out on maneuvers within a week after their arrival. They expect to be sent overseas within the next month. Maybe McGinn's original statement of "on the ball or on the boat" was true.

The more I see of the damned English course, the madder I get. It could be a reasonable course because this term we have read some pretty good stuff (Mill, Thoreau, FDR, Wilson, Holmes, etc.), but so far we have had two tests, both of which were in spelling. This English teacher is a bear on spelling and grammar. Nothing annoys me more than taking a college English course in spelling and grammar.

College of William and Mary
February 19, 1944
Dear Folks:

Today I can remember quite distinctly the attitude that suddenly took over Dartmouth when passage by the House Military Affairs Committee of the bill to draft eighteen- and nineteen-year-olds was announced over the speaker system at Soldiers' Field, Harvard, on October 17, 1942.

Yesterday's announcement of the abandonment of the ASTP brought forth a similar—but at the same time very different— attitude here. Basically they were both the same: eat, drink, and be merry, for tomorrow we die, and just plain, I don't give a damn. But when the Draft Act was passed, each of us had hopes and aspirations. We were going to college by choice and studying the courses of our own personal choice. We were resigned to the inevitable. Still, there was some brightness in the future.

In the ASTP most of this is not true. We no longer make up our own minds. We study not by choice but take orders instead. And this is just another one. It was followed by another order that forces us to study and maintain decorum at which the soldiers sneer. In our future there is very little that is bright and very little room for aspirations and ambitions, except the privilege of doing something humble—very humble—for the war. Most of the poor fools here will probably go to activated infantry divisions, where the classification officer will totally ignore their seven or eight months of ASTP engineering training.

This morning after I spoke to you on the phone I had an hour-long argument with Capt. Joseph Shubow, the Jewish chaplain at Fort Eustis, who conducted our service. He was one of the most

*arrogant, outspoken, dogmatic preachers I have ever come in con-
tact with. Instead of giving a sermon, he introduced himself by
telling us what a great guy he was: He graduated from Harvard,
has a congregation with more than a thousand members, takes
hikes with the men at Eustis, and so on.*

*Then, after the service, while we were all talking and eating, he
happened to say that it was impossible for a man to be a Jew
without being a Zionist. As soon as he said that, I was the center
of an argument. I told him I believe I am a good Jew and am not a
Zionist; I'm a member of a religion and not of a "people," race, or
ethnic entity. Without actually using the words "blasphemy,"
"heresy," or "infidelity," he accused me of all of these things.
When I told him that I had been bar mitzvahed and confirmed in
Rabbi Louis Woolsey's congregation, Rodeph Shalom in Philadelphia, he called him "the most wicked man in American Judaism,
a fake and the farthest thing from a scholar." [**Dr. Louis Woolsey
(1877–1953) was a former president of the Central Conference of American Rabbis and a leading spokesman for the
American Council for Judaism, the country's most important
Jewish, anti-Zionist organization.**]*

*He also told me that the rich old Jewish families (like us, I
guess) were Judaism's worst enemies. We are backing away from
our religion, refusing to support and help the people who really
believe, and denying some of the basic tenets. Worst of all, we are
opening our religion to gentiles. Mad as I was, I was hardly a
match for a rabbi, whose profession and military rank forced me
to be always on the defensive. As a result, I left thoroughly exas-
perated but hardly convinced. Next week's sermon will be on
Zionism—in my honor.*

College of William and Mary
March 6, 1944
Dear Folks:

*This afternoon when we returned to the barracks before lunch
there was a notice on the bulletin board of a special meeting of the
entire unit with the major in Phi Beta Kappa Hall at 12:45. We
all went there cracking jokes and trying to make wise remarks in*

order to hide our anxiety. "I'm sorry men, but I don't have the news you are waiting for," Major Schaubel said. He then promised to keep us informed. This meeting was to tell us what he knew today.

This unit will definitely be inactivated between March 15 and 31. After that everything rests in the lap of the gods. He then added that we ought to continue to work and not goof off because grades will be important when they decide to make us into corporals or sergeants. Of course, that is just so much bull—but it's easy to excuse because it is part of an Army officer's duty to keep up morale.

I attended Sabbath services Sunday morning. Although I was at first disappointed because my Zionist chaplain "friend" was not there, I was later very pleased with the sermon his substitute delivered. The substitute was a LTJG [lieutenant junior grade] at the Navy chaplains' school. In his sermon he compared the Jew to Desdemona in Shakespeare's Othello and Germany to the character Othello, who was corrupted by a scheming, conniving Iago. Then he told how the Jew had in many ways been the real "Christian" of the world. He has always (since Christianity) been persecuted but never fought back or held a grudge. It is the Jew who always "turned the other cheek."

College of William and Mary
March 9, 1944
Dear Folks:

For two consecutive nights I have done nothing in study hall but read Disraeli by André Maurois. It is one of the most wonderful studies of one of the most wonderful men I have ever read. Disraeli, as a Jew, particularly interests me. He believed with all sincerity and supported with perfect logic a belief directly opposite Rabbi Woolsey's—that the Jews are a race and not a religion. He was always proud of his Jewish heritage and wrote several books on the "Asiatic mystery." He believed the purpose of the Church (Episcopalian), to which he belonged, was to defend in a materialistic society certain Semitic principles of the Old and New Testaments. People at times called him "a damned Jew" but *always later excused it, saying, "Oh well, he's an Oriental." The fact that he was an Occidentalized Oriental seemed to excuse his supposedly curious actions. I wonder if that could ever happen in twentieth-century America.*

Each day I stay in the Army I am becoming more and more interested in my Jewish background and more and more confused about how I should approach it. I have just taken out of the library Israel Zangwill's Children of the Ghetto, *about which I will report to you in due time. I hope these letters in which I tell you about sermons and books do not bore you. After I have heard or read them, I feel I must write someone about them. My most appreciative audience is still home. Someday I will find a girl to whom I can write something more than sweet little nothings.*

College of William and Mary
March 15, 1944
Dear Folks:

Beware the Ides of March—yesterday the major told us that within forty-eight hours he would have definite information about the date of departure. We anxiously watch every notice on the bulletin board, but we have not yet seen the all-important one.

Rumors are heard every time you go to chow or the latrine. The purpose of the major's meeting yesterday was to deny them all and tell us to take it easy. However, they are still making plans to move us out on very short notice. We cannot send out any laundry this week. We must turn in all reference books to the library. Men are working in the supply room, packing boxes and so on. It seems that we are just spending a life of waiting, waiting, and waiting.

Yesterday Dr. Freud gave us a calculus test. Not a single person in the class got within ten points of the passing grade. He means very well. I try to show him the respect his scholarship and personality deserve, but when I am forced to suffer under him, it is very difficult. Although he can speak the English language rather well and is a good mathematician, he is still European in his thinking and his general approach to life. He cannot understand why we are not earnest about our work.

CHAPTER 3

BASIC TRAINING

BASIC TRAINING, the process by which light-hearted college boys are made into battle-ready warriors, is a rigorous regimen for molding psyche and body. It is tough and demanding. It is not skill training. I did not enjoy it, but it worked. Between the spring and autumn of 1944 I became a soldier.

A few weeks after my assignment to the 95th Infantry Division, I was sent to Camp Pickett, a hastily constructed, bare-bones training site for seventy-five thousand soldiers in southern Virginia. How small cities like Camp Pickett were quickly constructed with no fanfare and minimal disruption of the local economy is an important and little-known aspect of the way World War II was waged on the home front. The encampment was built by prisoners of war, twenty-seven hundred of whom were incarcerated in an adjacent compound. POWs performed a vital role in the war. They constructed large military facilities and acted as the municipal-services departments for many Army camps. They swept the streets, collected trash, maintained roads and fencing, painted and repaired buildings, and operated sewer plants and garbage dumps. They required little supervision. Germans and Italians could not escape to their homelands—and they had little incentive to do so. The food in their camps was adequate, the barracks were warm, and the Red Cross arranged small mail exchanges with their families. Most importantly, they were safe. Some day they would return home unmaimed.

At Camp Pickett I was assigned for no apparent reason to a glider company in the 659th Airborne Engineer Battalion. Airborne engineers are single-purpose soldiers. They are trained to do a few specific things. Chiefly, they demolish bridges and other vital installations behind enemy lines. Glider training was considered a terrible assignment. Glider troops had one of the Army's highest mortality rates, but they did not receive premium pay as jump-school-qualified paratroopers did. My training had two objectives: to strengthen and toughen me physically and to make me so familiar with guns, explosives, mortars, and grenades that I would be unafraid and even casual when handling them. It was exhausting, repetitious, tedious, and unpleasant. But I never saw a glider.

After three months of glider training I volunteered to become a paratrooper. The notion of landing behind enemy lines in a clunky airplane without a motor and with only limited steering capabilities seemed a ticket to certain disaster. Although parachuting into enemy territory was also a dangerous business, a paratrooper's job was better paid and more glamorous. (Even before they were battle tested, girls treated jump-school graduates as daring heroes.)

As a paratrooper volunteer I began basic training once again. It was virtually the same as for glider training, right down to the fact that I never packed a parachute or saw the inside of a plane. Then, on one day's notice, all of the airborne units at Camp Pickett were disbanded.

The reason was the same as that for closing down the ASTP: replacements were desperately needed—and quickly—in combat zones. The next day all of the qualified paratroopers and experienced glider soldiers in the 659th Airborne Engineer Battalion were flown to England. Most of them died the following month in a top-secret mission. With its trained cadre overseas, the airborne units could no longer function. Overnight we became combat engineers—and I began basic training all over again.

Basic training was devoid of military pizzazz. It did not glamorize soldiering. It was supposed to toughen young men—not inspire them. While at Camp Pickett I never attended a flag ceremony—save for a few occasions when we were trucked to Richmond to participate in patriotic events or war-bond rallies. I was surprised and even a little disappointed by the

The 1291st Combat Engineer Battalion during full field inspection at Camp Pickett, Virginia.

absence of flag ceremonies. They had been a summer-camp staple. As a twelve-year-old, I had stood at attention in front of my tent each morning while a bugler blew reveille and the flag was raised. At Camp Pickett the day began when a sergeant blew a whistle and hollered, "Drop your cocks and grab your socks!"

Repeated experience taught me to crawl on my belly through barbed wire, land mines, and other obstacles while machine guns blazed 35 to 40 inches above my head. Several times a week I participated in an exercise designed to dim my anxiety about explosives. A squadron of 20 to 25 men would line up thirty feet from an empty quarry. In his right hand each soldier held a two-pound TNT block with a 20-inch fuse. Fuses were lighted when a whistle blew. Then a sergeant would call off each second until the fuse had burned close to the detonation point. When the sergeant said "throw," we tossed the TNT into the quarry. If one soldier threw too early, the process was repeated until no one anticipated the call. Soldiers who threw early put their buddies at risk. An officer in our battalion had an arm amputated following an accident in a similar grenade exercise.

Bayonet drill was particularly distasteful and exhausting. It involved attacking a dummy after running across a field with your bayonet held above your head. After knocking over the dummy by piercing its torso, you put your shoe in its face while you pulled out your weapon to deliver the final blow. The attack exercises were timed by a stopwatch. I questioned why bayonet drill was required for modern soldiers in a mechanized Army. The answer was convincing: "Japs spend three times as much time on bayonet drill."

Training was directed by Camp Pickett's street-smart, tough, permanent cadre. It included several men who had enlisted before the war, mostly Depression-era flotsam. They held all draftees in disdain—particularly former college boys. They were excellent garrison soldiers. They understood military-training basics: drilling, rifles, explosives, and respect for authority, as well as the backbreaking labor involved in quickly building bridges without power-driven equipment. They enjoyed barking orders and being superior. They controlled weekend passes, which were often awarded or denied on the basis of Saturday-morning inspections. Bedrolls, mess kits, rifles, and canteens had to be displayed in a specific arrangement. A speck of dust in a private's rifle bore could result in his digging a six-by-six-by-six-foot hole all weekend. When it came to enforcing discipline among the enlisted men, our officers, none of whom were peacetime soldiers, deferred to the permanent, noncommissioned cadre.

Combat engineers, regardless of whether they are borne into combat by land, sea, or air, have the same basic assignment: to construct the infrastructure necessary for the efficient operation of a modern Army and to destroy enemy facilities if they are impeding the forward movement of U.S. troops. Combat engineers landed on the Normandy beaches with the first assault troops. Their initial assignment was to use explosives to destroy the tank traps and personnel obstacles the Nazis had planted along the coastline. As part of the second wave, they built temporary storage facilities for food, fuel, ammunition, and medical supplies. In all theaters of operations, the advance units of the Corps of Engineers built roads, harbors, railroads, runways, and bridges. Engineer privates are trained to be manual laborers who can operate under extremely hazardous conditions. It is hard, dirty, unpleasant work—as is the training.

Shortly after I started combat-engineer basic training, I became a medic attached to a combat-engineer battalion. All combat units (infantry, artillery, armor, and engineers) have medical detachments. Although separate, they are an integral part of the unit. Medics participate in all of the training exercises. Their task is to service unit personnel at times of maximum peril. While wearing Red Cross brassards, medics are in theory protected from enemy fire. Under the terms of the Geneva Convention, they are barred from carrying firearms or explosives themselves. If captured, they are supposed to get special treatment in prisoner-of-war camps. Barracks gossip tended to confirm that the Nazis, and to a far lesser extent the Japanese, honored the Geneva Convention.

While in the ASTP, I had been required to take a medical aptitude test. The exam form asked whether I would be interested in attending a medical school if the Army paid for it. I categorically stated my lack of interest. However, after several weeks of back-breaking manual labor as an engineer private, I had become less fussy. I jumped at the chance to be a medic. Their work was easier and cleaner. It was several notches above that of a day laborer in a bridges-and-roads crew.

Two days into my medical training, I found myself giving hundreds of typhoid and tetanus shots. Our unit had been expanded, and several hundred new soldiers had arrived in camp. To keep the unit's medical records orderly, all of the new arrivals were given typhoid and tetanus shots on the same day, even if they had been inoculated the week before. I had received zero instruction in giving inoculations. But by the end of the day, I had given more than four hundred. In one day I became an expert. The new members of my engineer battalion were marched through an infirmary door with their shirts off. As they went through the door, one medic private gave them a tetanus shot in the left arm, and I gave them a typhoid shot in the right arm.

Medics also participated in a monthly ritual known throughout the Army as "short-arm inspection." Regulations required that every enlisted man's penis be examined regularly for venereal disease. At an appointed hour, all of the men in a company would be lined up and told to drop their trousers. Then a medic sergeant would announce, "When the doc comes along, milk it down and pull it back." As the medical officer walked along the line, I or another medic followed with a flashlight and clipboard. Any soldier with a discharge would be told to report for further examination.

Penicillin and other sophisticated drugs have made venereal disease a minimal threat to the efficiency of armies in the last half of the twentieth century, but during World War II, it was a scourge. According to the Surgeon General's official report, 1 in 20 soldiers (49 per 1,000) contracted syphilis, gonorrhea, or some other sexually transmitted disease while in the service. At least once every two weeks during basic training, soldiers were required to attend a venereal disease (VD) movie. Although the actors and scenery were usually different, the central theme was always the same: how one casual contact could lead to a lifetime of misery and the likelihood of deformed and mentally handicapped children. The use of protection and/or prompt prophylaxis could prevent that fate. In most barracks, washrooms, and PXs were posters cautioning against exposure to VD. Four of the most memorable said, "You Can't Beat the Jap with the Clap" (slang for gonorrhea), "Fool the Axis—Use Prophylasix," "Rum and Women Just Don't Mix," and, below the picture of a beautiful Doris Day lookalike, "She May Look Clean, But . . ."

While I was at Camp Pickett, Allied armies assaulted and

invaded fortress Europe. The successful landing at Normandy on June 6, 1944, and the liberation of Paris on August 25, 1944, were followed by quick—but costly—victories in eastern France. Then, in the same week that the 1291st Combat Engineer Battalion arrived at a pre-embarkation staging camp near New York harbor, the Nazis broke through the American lines in the Ardennes forest and began their last successful counterattack—the Battle of the Bulge. The Americans did not prevail in that battle until late January, 1945, after I landed in France.

Medics assigned to combat units received only superficial instruction in medical skills. Two medical officers (a captain and a lieutenant) headed our detachment. The captain was a dentist, and the doctor was less than a year out of medical school. During the last weeks before we went overseas, battalion medical officers instructed us in matters such as morphine injection, tourniquets, splints, wound dressing, VD-exposure prophylaxis, and burn treatment. The semiorganized training was limited to a few days at the camp hospital. There were no formal classes.

We left for overseas staging with our bodies strengthened and our psyches partially dulled to danger. We had doubts about how well trained we were, but we knew that in every battle zone men were serving gallantly with the same meager training we had received.

Indiantown Gap, Pa.
March 18, 1944
Dear Folks:
When we first went to Williamsburg, we were not sure how much we were wanted or accepted. But when we left, there was no question in anybody's mind. Not only had the College of William and Mary made a contribution to us as individuals, but we as a group had made a contribution to the college.

The packing and breaking up of the unit on Thursday were the most efficient things I have seen the Army do. Within three or four hours everything was done with a minimum of difficulty and hardship. In civilian life it would have been impossible for me to move with the ease and speed that I did on Thursday. That morning before going to chow we marched by all of the girls' dorms and sang songs and blew reveille for them. That night after taps the civilian men came over to our barracks and serenaded us with "Auld Lange Syne" and the William and Mary alma mater.

When we left Friday morning we paraded before Dr. Pomfret [John E. Pomfret, president of the College of William and Mary] and Major Schaubel. The whole student body and town came out to see us. Five hundred girls followed us to the station and cheered and cried and "kissed the boys good-bye." It was spontaneous. In many ways it was really thrilling.

The ride up to Indiantown Gap [a distance of approximately 250 miles] took fourteen hours. It was probably a typical ride in a troop train. I tried to read a book but couldn't concentrate: I tried to sleep, but the fellows gave me a hotfoot, so I had to amuse myself playing cards. First I would play bridge and then poker and then bridge again. The boys smuggled the dogs that Major McGinn saved from the pound aboard the train in the women's room. We later smuggled them aboard the trucks that drove us to Indiantown. After drawing bedding we finally went to bed at about two o'clock.

Indiantown Gap, Pa.
March 23, 1944
Dear Folks:

Our life up here has been very easy due to the bad weather. This morning we were scheduled to have drill, but that has been called off because of the rain. I've been at Indiantown for five days, and it has snowed for two and rained for two, and ice has melted for one.

Last night, having nothing to do, I went to Harrisburg for two hours just to look the town over. This post seems to have an unusually lax pass policy. You can walk on or off the post as you please without being bothered by an MP or showing a pass. At the same time, they grant passes to only 50 percent of the men over a weekend. Those are restricted to a fifty-mile radius of Indiantown

Gap. Unless a man lives within that radius or can get an address where he will stay, he cannot get an overnight pass because they do not want the men loitering around the streets late at night.

Indiantown Gap, Pa.
March 30, 1944
Dear Folks:

At this point I would like to murder my friend Rufus L. Because of his ignorance or laziness or obstinacy, or possibly all three, I was forced to stay up almost all night last night. He and I were on fire guard together with one other man. We had to keep ten fires in good shape, including the stoves in the kitchen. When he left at nine o'clock and I followed him, the fires in the kitchen were just about out, and, not being very experienced at fire tending, I wrecked two of the dying fires instead of saving them. (If you let the kitchen fires go out, you are supposed to be on KP the remainder of your stay in Indiantown.) The result was that all three fire guards had to stay up until after four o'clock to save and rebuild the fires. The many difficulties and complications cannot be explained here, but 90 percent can be attributed to that damned fool Rufus. **[Army barracks were heated with coal furnaces, which had to be stoked, banked, and tended during the night. Kitchen stoves were also coal fired.]**

Today we had the first definite information about men shipping out of Indiantown from this company. A group is leaving Monday for a Signal Corps outfit at Camp Pickett, Va. Early next week another group is definitely being sent to Camp Butner, N.C. I am sure I'm not in the first group but do not know about the second.

Camp Pickett, Va.
April 8, 1944
Dear Folks:

It seems that the officers and cadre of this outfit know only three words—"double-time march." Everywhere we travel, we run. We do a tremendous amount of running just for the sake of running and practicing. If nothing else, by the time I leave the airborne troops I'll be in damned good physical shape.

Everybody I talk to around here seems to agree that I'm in the toughest outfit in the Army. One of the men in the battalion next to us asked his CO if he could transfer to the paratroops because of the increase in pay. The CO answered, "Don't even think about it unless you can do forty pushups with one hand." Our officers and cadre never stop talking about our physical condition.

Camp Pickett, Va.
April 12, 1944
Dear Folks:

In all of life you must pay for ease with hardship. My life at Williamsburg and Hanover was certainly a life of ease. After doing only what physical exercise was absolutely necessary for the past two years, I was very soft and in lousy physical shape. Now I'm paying for it with sweat and tears and sore legs. Today we ran between four and five miles (at two different times, about two once, and three the other time), and I'm so sore I can barely walk without a limp and just about keep my eyes open to write this letter. If you had told me a week ago that I would run two to three miles, I would never have believed you, but the Army does wonders for a man—ha ha!

The more I see and hear about this group, the more I think I'm assigned to the Army equivalent of the Seabees. The Seabees land before the Marines, so we land before the Army's ground forces. The chief things that we've learned so far, aside from double-time, are tying knots, removing mines, and using a compass. Without a little more explanation that would sound exactly like the Navy, but in reality it is a hell of a lot different.

As yet, we have gotten no new men in this company. I am not sure whether I'm glad or sorry. At present, there are about thirty men in the company, and they are great guys, mostly ASTP men. They come from the upper crust of the ASTP. However, if we got some new men directly from a reception center, life around here would be a lot easier. [**The basic troop unit for Army ground forces and airborne units was the company. It had a commanding officer and usually its own mess, supply, and support personnel. Although the authorized size of individual companies** *varied slightly according to function (infantry, headquarters, signal, glider, paratroop), companies usually comprised two hundred men divided into two or three platoons.]*

Camp Pickett, Va.
April 16, 1944
Dear Folks:

Last night's trip to Blackstone was my first, and I believe it will be my last unless I'm stationed at Camp Pickett a lot longer than I expect. It is a typical "camp town" with about a dozen greasy restaurants with tremendous neon signs outside, about the same number of crusty, dirty beer joints in the side alleys with neon lights not quite as bright, about ten "military stores" that cheat the servicemen on shoe shines. There is an overabundance of "camp followers," who seem to have no trouble finding soldiers for company.

Tomorrow we start basic training. Although it's probably foolish to speculate about things in the Army, I believe that, for the first few weeks of basic, life will be a little less strenuous than it has been until now. We now have about 160 new men. I'm quite sure they couldn't take the training we've taken during the past week without a little preparatory exercise.

Friday afternoon I took my first Army speed march, and I'm still not sure whether I'd rather march against a watch or run. However, I'm sure as hell I don't like either. My feet and legs are still very, very sore.

During the past week, aside from running, we have learned something about the usual things you expect the Army engineer to be proficient at—laying and removing minefields, building and demolishing bridges and booby traps, using a compass, and rigging.

Camp Pickett, Va.
April 29, 1944
Dear Folks:

Mother wrote me last week telling me that Arthur became a first-class scout. Now the field of merit badge scouting is open for him. I only hope he enjoys it as much as I did.

I was very pleased to hear that Daddy contributed to the
Dartmouth Alumni Fund. In many ways Dartmouth College to
me symbolizes the world that I hope to return to after the war. Of
course, I am glad when you feel the same way and help to preserve
it. I was also glad to read the '46 Tomahawk *[class of 1946
newsletter]*, which almost read like an ASTP obituary. As I read
over some of the ASTP tales of woe, I don't really think I fared too
badly.

Your letter from Dr. deSola Poole was the kind that can't help
but make me mad. He is a rabbi and quite naturally defended another. He probably takes his word in preference to that of some
spoiled brat private. All of the things that Chaplain Shubow says
about the incident have an element of truth in them, but the thing
that is most annoying is the way he tries to make me look like a
sort of stool pigeon—by mixing up the sequence of my questions
and the sequence of his answers. The first question I asked him
was about Zionism. As soon as I heard his answer, I told him I
was a member of Dr. Woolsey's congregation and one of his great
admirers. However, the whole incident has by this time become a
little exaggerated and foolish. Still, being a private in the Army, I
would like to see the whole affair die a quiet and natural death.
**[My parents showed Dr. Louis Woolsey, our family's rabbi,
my letter telling about my discussion of Zionism with Chaplain Joseph Shubow, a Naval officer assigned to a nearby
Navy base. Chaplain Shubow conducted a service at William
and Mary on a Sunday morning for all Jewish military personnel in the area. Dr. Woolsey was offended at Chaplain
Shubow's attack on him. He retaliated by filing a complaint
about Chaplain Shubow with Dr. David deSola Poole (1885–
1970), a prominent New York rabbi who headed a War
Department board that reviewed qualifications and disputes
within the Jewish chaplaincy. Woolsey considered Shubow's remarks a breach of Jewish chaplainry rules. Jewish chaplains
were frobidden to discuss controversial issues from the pulpit,
and Zionism was considered controversial. A copy of Chaplain
Shubow's letter response to Dr. deSola Poole was eventually
turned over to my parents, who in turn sent it on to me.]**

Camp Pickett, Va.
May 8, 1944
Dear Folks:

As I told you on the phone, I am now a qualified rifleman with the M-1 30-caliber rifle. Although the days I spent on the range were long and hard and tedious in many ways, I found it interesting. Most of the things the Army fools with, they bungle, but they've been running rifle ranges for a long time. I don't believe you'll find better ones anywhere. Something that could be both complicated and dangerous is remarkably simple and safe.

Every other morning we now run 9.6 miles without stopping, and each time I make it I realize what good physical shape the Airborne Engineers are beating me into. If anyone had told me I could run nine miles six weeks ago, I would have laughed in their face, but the Army either makes you or breaks you.

Camp Pickett, Va.
May 16, 1944
Dear Folks:

A pretty, quiet backyard, a pleasant, peaceful time with the family followed in less than twelve hours by double-time, TNT, dynamite, rifles, picks, shovels, etc., just doesn't make much sense. I seem to live in wonderful happiness during those thirty-six hours of weekend. Today a whole generation is living a Dr. Jekyll and Mr. Hyde existence. It's remarkable that an Army where 90 percent of the men hate their existence—and just live for the weekends—wins battles.

We spent all yesterday learning something about demolition, which is one of the chief jobs of the Corps of Engineers, particularly the Airborne Corps. TNT, dynamite, and nitro-starch were always words that spelled danger for me. At the same time they were things I had never seen and knew nothing about. Yesterday, for the benefit of men like me, we exploded more than one hundred pounds of TNT, about five pounds of nitro-starch, and miscellaneous amounts of other explosives. It was almost like a Fourth of July with stumps flying and holes being dug. Although most of the men throw TNT around like loaves of bread, I must admit

MY RIFLE

This is my rifle. It is my best friend—without it, I am helpless. Without me, it is useless.

I will master my rifle as I will master life—I will know it as I know myself. I will know its strength and its weakness, its balance, its sights, its "feel".

My rifle will be cleaned before I am cleaned, before I eat, before I rest. It will be ready always. I will be true to my rifle and guard it from weather and dirt, from all harm or damage—as I guard my rifle, so it will guard me in time of danger, shoot straight and destroy the enemy that would destroy us both.

If I am true to My God, true to my country and true to my rifle, we will conquer.

"My Rifle" creed. Each time I took basic training, these somber words were distributed and read aloud.

that I'm still a little scared. Someday soon, when I have the time—and I'm pretty sure I won't—I'll reread For Whom the Bell Tolls *[Ernest Hemingway's novel about the Spanish Civil War, in which one of the most important episodes involves demolishing a bridge]. Soon I'll be somewhat expert at blowing up bridges. Someday maybe I'll be watching a bridge and waiting for it to blow up minus Maria [Hemingway's heroine, played by Ingrid Bergman in the movie].*

Today, in a sweltering sun with packs on our backs, we dug foxholes and machine-gun emplacements. Tomorrow it's a study of gas warfare, etc., including a session in a gas chamber.

In the evenings, we have been having classes also. Our training here is really getting tough.

Camp Pickett, Va.
May 24, 1944
Dear Folks:

These past few weeks have been so full and active that it is just impossible to find time to write letters. You work like hell all day and then return at night with just barely enough time and energy to clean your equipment and prepare for the next day's work before the lights go out.

I have been very lucky in being sent to messenger school. That means that I do not have to work with the rest of the company in the afternoons for two weeks. Although the school is nothing to get really excited about, it may lead to something better somewhere. It never hurts to go to school anywhere, and in the Army it may be particularly useful. Our chief training is in the field so that we can read maps and compass bearings by ourselves when we are carrying messages. After I leave this school, I will be designated as company messenger. As such almost immediately after basic training, I will become a Pfc. That isn't much of a promotion, but these days even the little ones count.

Yesterday I stared one of war's horrors in the face for the first time. One of the finest officers I have come in close contact with, Lt. Paul R. Lyons, was out on bivouac with some of the men from A Company. He was leading an attack party. They were supposed to attack the main part of the company during the course of the night with grenades, tear gas, etc. He was explaining to his men how to use grenades. They were grouped closely around him joking and laughing when he pulled the pin. Instantaneously there was an explosion. When the smoke had cleared, the lieutenant still stood in the center of his men with nothing but shreds left of his forearm and hand. They quickly took him to a jeep and then to a hospital. His arm was amputated just below the elbow. The horrible thing was not that he lost his hand but the way the men seemed to take it. He was without a doubt the most popular officer in the battalion, and everyone liked him. He was a fun-loving, hell-raising MIT graduate who still had a certain amount of dignity and culture. After the men heard that he was hurt, nobody gave a damn. Their only remarks were "He can still make a living." It's hard to see how men can get sublime inspiration from the ruin of a church or a building, but from the ruin of a man, nothing.

I have finally come in contact with a sergeant who is typical of the "regimental sergeant" who is so regularly the hero of movies and the butt of Army jokes. One of our squad leaders was a peace-time enlisted man. In every way he is typical of the old tradition. He joined the Army three days after he graduated from high school, although I'll never understand how he graduated. He has been all the way up and down the scale of noncoms several times. He was court-martialed several times for drunkenness, disorderly conduct, AWOL, and so on. At the same time, he is the noncom who is the most sincere about our training and the only one who has his heart and soul in the work. He is responsible for most of our night and weekend duty and is usually around himself to see that it is done properly. He's tough and hardly the type of character I'd like for a good friend, but with all his roughness and crudeness I'm forced to respect him.

Camp Pickett, Va.
Memorial Day, 1944
Dear Folks:

A year in the Army and the fact that discharge papers are a long, long way away is hardly a pleasant fact, but the bitter is made a lot sweeter by wonderful weekends at home. I can't tell you how much I enjoyed the past weekend. It almost seemed like the good old days, going to synagogue with the family and talking to lots of old friends around the Philmont pool. It's a tough ride and a lot of work to come home, but it won't be long until I come home again. [Philmont was the oldest of Philadelphia's four Jewish country clubs. Membership in each club represented an ethnic subset. Philmont's members were mostly of German descent.]

Last night our battalion had its first real fight. This time it was a free-for-all. To subdue it required the entire Camp Pickett MP force, as well as our own officers. Over the weekend, two large units of mechanized cavalry moved into Camp Pickett. They had the custom of wearing paratroopers' bloused boots after duty hours in town. Of course, our paratroopers objected. They said the right to wear bloused boots was reserved to them. They had taken a great risk to earn the right. Our major sent a note to their commander requesting that they stop wearing the bloused boots. Instead of doing good, the note only made them mad and belligerent.

*Last night a couple of rough fights followed. In one of them, stones were thrown and rifle butts swung. Still, nobody was seriously hurt. Our entire outfit was called out to take part in the fight, but being greatly outnumbered, we still lost. Today the major spoke to all of us. Although he defended the paratroopers to a certain degree, he told us that we had acted like a bunch of babies. He's right, but I don't think the fight is over. [**Paratroopers were respected as brave men who were trained to fight behind enemy lines, and their bloused boots were a status symbol. (Trousers are "bloused" on polished boots when they are turned under at midcalf and secured with a rubber band.) They earned the right to wear bloused boots only after making several parachute jumps. In previous wars, cavalrymen were the soldiers of status, and their riding boots were different from those worn by infantrymen and artillerymen. The mechanized cavalry soldiers of World War II saw themselves as the horse cavalry's successors. Therefore, they felt entitled to a special dress code, including bloused boots. Paratroopers, however, said that learning to drive a tank was no more dangerous than learning to drive a truck.**]*

Camp Pickett, Va.
June 5, 1944

Dear Daddy:

In the course of my life I have usually decided what I should do, where I should go, and how I should do things. Some of these decisions have been important; others have been unimportant; some you have praised, while others you have damned, but today I made one of the most important decisions of my life, and I have no idea how you will feel about it.

Today I signed on the dotted line and volunteered for the paratroops. I feel confident that the invasion will prove them to be the outstanding unit of the U.S. Army, as well as all modern armies. I hope that my association with the paratroops will be one of which both of us can be proud. I do not believe I have been seduced by the false glamour that surrounds any dangerous outfit, nor do I think I have been won over by GI propaganda. Membership in the paratroops has many short-run advantages, but these really did not lead me to the decision. Daddy, please try to understand. I am young and healthy and strong, and certainly I want to come home that way as much as you want me to, but I'd also like to be able to throw out my chest and believe that I had done more than my part.

I am writing to you at the office because I thought this might disturb Mother a little. I would rather have you tell her. Daddy, please believe that I am not trying to cause my parents extra worry and be inconsiderate. I am only doing what I think is right.

Camp Pickett, Va.
June 6, 1944
Dear Folks:

Last night I wrote to Daddy to tell him of my decision to join the paratroops, not realizing that while writing the Allied invasion of France was beginning. This morning I was awakened at 5:00 A.M. when somebody returning from pass turned on the radio to announce the good news to everybody. It's hard to explain how the two things happened together. Certainly the spirit around here is of electric excitement. I don't believe you will see demonstrations and parades in Army camps today, but certainly nowhere is there a deeper sigh of relief and thanks being breathed. With a successful invasion I'm sure it won't be long until I will be coming home for good.

Camp Pickett, Va.
June 11, 1944
Dear Folks:

Thursday I took my physical examination for the paratroops. Although I passed it, I was thoroughly annoyed. Ever since the day I was inducted into the Army last May I have been annoyed at the Army's sloppy physical exams. I don't give a damn whether the standards are high or low, but the examinations ought to be thorough, complete, and honest. On the basis of such examinations a fair judgment can be made, but I've never seen a good physical yet.

*While at Indiantown Gap I took a POR [**preparation for***

Venereal disease poster displayed in enlisted men's clubs, barracks, and PXs (post exchanges) in Pennsylvania, Maryland, and Virginia. It was distributed through official channels by the Third Service Command, which included those states.

overseas replacement] exam, and it was haphazard. Thursday I took the exam for the most rugged outfit in the Army—the group that is supposed to represent the best physical specimens in the land. The one that should have been the best was the worst. They need paratroopers in the Army, and they need them badly. As a result they seem perfectly happy to overlook minor defects as long as you go into parachute service. Since I have been ten years old, I have worn glasses. Although my eyes were never bad, they were never perfect 20/20. However, that is what the dumb boy who examined me wrote down. Because of my color blindness, the Navy and Marines turned me down twice, but Thursday's record shows my color perception as perfect. When I took the color test, the WAC who was examining me noticed that I really was color-blind. She then asked, did I want to pass the exam? When I answered in the affirmative, she said, "OK, you will."

Camp Pickett, Va.
June 13, 1944

Dear Mother:

Letters are getting scarcer these days because we're working like hell. Yesterday we paraded in Richmond at five o'clock and returned by truck. Today we are going on a twenty-five-mile tactical hike and then will stay up all night on a night maneuver. It's on days like this that the Army is really rough.

Camp Pickett, Va.
June 15, 1944

Dear Folks:

Yesterday I think the morale in this outfit was the lowest I have seen it in any outfit in the Army. Our CO must have gotten out of bed on the wrong side, for he gave the whole company hell for their poor morale, dirty barracks, etc., and then proceeded to blame it on the corporals because they didn't drive us enough. Then he reduced four corporals to privates for "inefficiency."

If I ever heard of anything unfair, I believe that was one of the most. There is no question that they were the four most popular corporals (three of them certainly). But they treated us like men.

When they gave an order to us, they gave it in a civil tone. The lieutenant had no definite grounds on which he could either court-martial them or break them, only the vague term "inefficient." I believe what actually happened was that our company commander caught hell because the company was in bad shape. In typical style he passed the blame on to the platoon sergeants, who passed it on to the corporals. Then they took the beating.

To add insult to injury the regular peacetime sergeant, who supervises much of our training, decided we also had a few sins to atone for, so we spent the evening washing the barracks on our hands and knees. Then we did close-order drill. When he saw that we were not taking it seriously and were laughing up our sleeve at him, he made us wash the floor all over again and then roll packs until eleven o'clock. That is the sort of misplaced and misdirected authority that sometimes makes the Army hell. He also said there would be no passes this weekend.

Camp Pickett, Va.
June 26, 1944
Dear Folks:

It's too bad that we have a company commander who, because of his own ignorance and crudeness, resents and punishes the men with education rather than using them to their fullest advantage. Lt. Broadhurst is the first commanding officer I have ever had whom I sincerely dislike. Even in my most broad-minded and tolerant moments, I cannot respect him. When a man isn't blessed with brains or common sense, you don't hold it against him. But when men are arrogant in their ignorance, like Broadhurst and the first sergeant, it's hell.

Last Wednesday everybody in camp got half the morning off to hear a trio from the Conference of Jews and Christians speak. Although I guess the spirit behind those things is always good, I doubt they accomplish very much. All the speeches were clever and nice. But not one of the speakers had the guts to say anything about current events, just "platitudes in stained glass." Rabbi Levy of Philadelphia spoke for Jews. Although his speech might read rather well, it was a very poor one to deliver to a bunch of soldiers. He used lengthy words that 90 percent of the men couldn't understand and talked in pretty little circles in heavy language. The Catholic priest was just the opposite. He told good jokes and had a big smile but said absolutely nothing. The Protestant was the best, but he was not very good. You could certainly feel and hear very definite anti-Semitic feelings all through the audience. Every time Rabbi Levy mentioned God or our Lord, I heard a man behind me say, "Who are they to talk about God when they drove the spikes?" When you can't give a good lecture to a small audience, you probably only create bad feeling.

Camp Pickett, Va.
July 9, 1944
Dear Folks:

This week, like all the others recently, has been rough and one in which I've become less and less impressed with my CO. Although I don't know much about Lt. Liberty yet, he has already made his boss look like a fool. I believe it is only a matter of time until he will take his place. Thursday night we had a night problem, in which we hiked twelve miles after nine o'clock and then tried to lay one-and-a-half miles of minefields before dawn. That is a tough assignment. We didn't get it done—not because the men fell down but because there was no leadership or planning.

In the ASTP the men didn't need real officers to take care of them. The primary job was academic, rather than military. Still, all were men I would have gladly followed into battle. I hope that when I finally go into battle it will be with real soldiers of the kind they produce at VMI and West Point. Not the kind we have now. Friday we built a bridge. When we got it half done, we found the two ends didn't match because the people who were directing us couldn't understand the orders.

Camp Pickett, Va.
July 16, 1944
Dear Folks:

Basic training is finally over, and on paper I am now a fully qualified soldier and an Army engineer. All my training from *now on will be classified as either "advanced" or "special." It was a good experience. I'm glad I did it. Friday we celebrated the completion of basic by going swimming at Buchin Lake, the local swimming hole. It was the second time I'd been swimming this week, so the whole week was not too bad. Wednesday we spent the whole day launching infantry assault boats, which are manned and controlled by engineers, and building rafts and floats for jeeps, trucks, artillery equipment, and so on. As you should have guessed, I made sure that I fell in the water quite regularly. I made a whole day of swimming out of something that was sup-posed to be hard work.*

*I am interested in CWS **[chemical warfare service]** and OCS, but only as a last way out. If by the grace of God I should gradu-ate from OCS, my position would be very much like it is today. I am one of a large group of privates who have no special talents. As a result, we get kicked from pillar to post. If I graduated from OCS I'd be just another dumb shavetail in the same position. The thing I would like most of all is to be sent to an enlisted men's school where I might learn something about topography or radio or any other real specialty. Then you are a specialist and can thumb your nose at the people who bother you or order you around unnecessarily. Understand, I would like to go to OCS but only as a second choice.*

Each time I write a letter of this type I try to think of some-thing new and different to say, but try as I may, I invariably re-turn to the theme of our family. It means no more to one of us than it does to another. When I wish you happiness I am selfishly wishing myself the same thing.

Camp Pickett, Va.
July 19, 1944
Dear Folks:

For the second time in six months my organization in the Army has died while I was a member. It's a funny feeling and a rather unusual one. For some unexplainable reason I've already seen it twice. There has been no explanation about why the Army sud-denly decided to liquidate the 659th Airborne Engineer Battalion.

The present setup seems to be that the qualified paratroopers will remain on jump status. They will go to either Camp Mackall or a port of embarkation [POE], probably the latter. The rest of us will stay here and form the nucleus for the 1291st Engr. Combat Battalion.

Camp Pickett, Va.
August 2, 1944
Dear Folks:

Yesterday I turned in my OCS application. Although it was accepted at the company level, I don't know how long they will fool around with it before it is accepted by the post board. I also put in my bid for the radio operator's job. I don't know what will come of it, as one other man is also trying for the job.

This week one of those typical Private Snafu episodes happened in this battalion. **["Snafu" was an Army acronym to describe military confusion and disorder. The letters stand for "situation normal, all fucked up."]** *Two enlisted men in Blackstone were in a jeep when they saw two rather attractive young women on the street whom they honked their horn at. The two women, being wives of two of our officers, recognized the jeep and the men by their airborne shoulder patches. They let out a hearty "hello" followed by a broad smile. The soldiers didn't know the two women. They thought they had found two good-looking pickups. The result was a short talk, an offer of a lift—and recognition—and embarrassment for all. The husband-officers were good sports about it. The only thing they did was to make a passing remark about soldiers and gentlemen.* **[In the hierarchical, stratified Army of 1943, an enlisted soldier would expect to be disciplined for trying to establish a social contact with an officer's wife. Typical punishment would include no weekend passes for several weeks, digging a six-by-six-by-six-foot hole over a weekend, restriction to quarters for a long period, or extra KP duty.]**

Camp Pickett, Va.
August 8, 1944
Dear Folks:

Tomorrow morning the 659th Airborne Engineer Battalion's parachute company leaves for Fort Meade, where they will be reassigned to overseas combat units. If you don't think they've been raising hell around here the past few weeks, you just don't know. There were more than twenty court-martials this week of men from that company, all of whom had gone over the hill. All the sentences were stiff and I don't think entirely fair. They want to set an example for us. As a result, they say "six months" for almost every AWOL case that comes before them. Our outfit has a reputation for being poorly disciplined. This new major has told the officers that he is going to change it. I'm sure there are better ways than court-martials.

Camp Pickett, Va.
August 12, 1944
Dear Folks:

Usually when you see men leaving Camp Pickett armed and with steel helmets, you expect that they are heading for a boat. You don't envy them. This week the outfit just down the street from us left camp in trucks dressed in full battle regalia. I wished I was with them. They went to Philadelphia to help with a strike. We're not doing a damned thing these days but wasting time. I thought there was a chance that we might also go to Philadelphia. [President Roosevelt ordered the Army to take over operation of the Philadelphia Transportation Company in August, 1944, after an unlawful strike shut down all of the city's subways, buses, streetcars, and elevated railways. More than six thousand workers walked off their jobs after the War Labor Board ordered the company to start training six black streetcar conductors as war replacements. Three days after the Army assumed control of the transportation system and the workers were threatened with the permanent loss of their jobs, the strike was terminated—and the six black conductor trainees began working on the streetcars.]

Now Mother is going to have a laugh. I'm going to be a member of the Army medical corps attached to the engineers. When our outfit was changed from airborne to combat engineers, the Table of Organization (T/O) called for seven new men in the medical detachment. A good friend of mine who is in the detachment suggested my name as an intelligent, interested person. After a short interview, I was accepted and am pleased as punch. It's a good deal. It's a small detachment of fifteen men, almost all of whom are intelligent and good company. Our classes will be mostly conducted by an MD who can probably talk English. The work of the medics is interesting, and I will acquire the type of practical knowledge that will always be useful.

Camp Pickett, Va.
August 21, 1944
Dear Folks:

I have now completed my first ten days in the medical corps. I'm still enthusiastic. As a result of a flat tire and motor difficulty on the bus, I did not get any sleep when I arrived in camp yesterday morning. Then came my first physically difficult assignment in the medics. I was sent out as an "aid man" with one of the line companies on a nine-mile hike. Many of the new men had not done any real hiking or walking in several years. As a result they fell out all along the way like flies. Then is when the medic really has a tough time. He is forced to run up and down the marching column trying to give aid to the men who are griping. At the same time he must push one of his dead feet in front of the other. Tomorrow I will go out as an aid man again on a fifteen-mile hike. This time I expect to prepare for it with a little sleep the night before.

Camp Pickett, Va.
August 24, 1944
Dear Folks:

Today I had another very important reason to be thankful for being a member of the medical detachment. The 22nd Corps Headquarters sent for all the records of the men in our outfit who

The 1291st Combat Engineer Battalion's medical detachment.

completed engineer basic training in order to reassign them to various trained organizations. Although I have completed engineering basic training, it seems that the medics were not included in this order. Our records are still at battalion headquarters. Today almost fifty men were notified that they will leave on Monday for the 100th Division at Fort Bragg. They are "unassigned," which means they will probably end up in the infantry.

Camp Pickett, Va.
September 7, 1944
Dear Folks:

Yesterday I heard one of the first decent lectures I have heard in a long time. Most of the lectures you hear in the Army are delivered by men who don't know anything about their subject, except what they read just before delivering it. They don't care to know any more than what is barely necessary to stumble through a talk. Yesterday's lecture was delivered by a Major Herman, who

was formerly in charge of training medics in mountain evacua-
tion at the West Virginia Maneuver Area, where he discovered
several new methods of lashing litters together. He told us that the
Germans had respected the Geneva Cross (the symbol displayed
by medics of all countries on their persons, jeeps, trucks, tents,
ambulances) in Normandy.

Major Herman told us that very few medics have died from
small-arms fire in the war with Germany. The chief injuries have
been due to land mines and artillery fire. Formerly the medics
tried to work undercover, but they found that very often they were
ambushed by mistake. Now they work only in open fields where
their Red Crosses are prominently displayed and can be seen eas-
ily from both the air and surface. It's really a shame that there
are not more officers who are enthusiastic about their work and
have some talent for teaching.

Camp Pickett, Va.
September 12, 1944
Dear Folks:

For once I really have something to tell you. This morning
*when we came into the dispensary, Captain Evans [**head of the***
***medical detachment**] grinned his smiling face at us and said in*
one of his typical tones of fear, "In case you boys don't know it,
yesterday this outfit was alerted for overseas shipment." Dark-
ness fell on the face of the deep. There had been rumors about this,
but they seemed so unreasonable I didn't believe them—until we
were officially told. Captain Evans warned us to make out a will
and power of attorney. He thinks we will leave in ninety days.

After speaking to the intelligence sergeant at headquarters I
am thoroughly convinced that what has happened is this. We
have been alerted for overseas shipment and have a shipping
number, but it probably will not be possible for us to go overseas
before sometime in either January or February. Actually what
this does is to cut a great deal of time out of our training period.
It gives us a very high priority to requisition equipment. It puts
a hell of a lot of restrictions on me (like making AWOL into
desertion and punishable by death because I would be leaving

*my organization in time of danger). It also means we have a mil-
lion inspections of every conceivable variety. You can easily see
that there is no cause for alarm. I am only telling you this because
you may receive a power of attorney or excess clothing from me
sometime in the near future and might become somewhat
alarmed. There is only one thing about the whole affair that
makes me mad. Evans will not give me either a furlough or three-
day pass until November. He says that, now that our training is
being intensified, I could not recover from missing a day of classes.*

Camp Pickett, Va.
September 22, 1944
Dear Folks:

*Life in the medical detachment continues along its normal
course. Every morning we work for an hour on sick call attending
to the daily ailments and gripes of the men in the 1291st Engineer Combat Battalion. Then we are supposed to attend classes
the rest of the day. They are taught by Captain Evans and the
other men in the outfit with some medical knowledge. In general,
the classes are like most other classes in the Army. The officers
teaching them totally lack enthusiasm for their subject, are poorly
prepared, and mumble to a rather uninterested audience. While
at William and Mary with the ASTP I used to gripe about the
disinterest of the soldiers and the poor teaching methods of some
of the members of the faculty. Now I realize that I have been
spoiled all along the line by Central High, Dartmouth, William
and Mary, and the ASTP before basic training. When I was
taught by field officers and field noncoms, I didn't expect anything, but when doctors and their trained assistants teach you,
you expect a little more. However, don't think that I am griping. I
am always aware of the many advantages I have in the medical
detachment that I would not have out in the field.*

*There is an old saying in the Army: If you can't make a good
company officer, there is always hope that you may make a toler-
ably good supply officer. After my moronic, egotistical commanding officer was relieved of his command, Lieutenant Broadhurst
was made battalion supply officer. Already, in less than a month,*

he has gotten himself in hot water with the new battalion commander. As supply officer, he had supervision over the funds of the noncoms club. Because his work would be easier with some sort of special comptroller (similar to an adding machine), which the Army would not issue him, he then bought one for $150 with the money from the noncoms club. [In 1944, high-speed electric calculators had not yet been developed. Electronic models did not come into popular use for another twenty years.] The major is mad as hell about it. I don't think it will be long before he leaves. However, he was first made to explain to all the noncoms at an opening meeting why he bought the machine for them. After hearing Lieutenant Broadhurst's reasons, they voted almost unanimously not to accept it. You usually hate to see a man get in hot water, particularly in the Army, but in his case, I must admit, I'm glad. Any reduction in grade or responsibility for him would be for the benefit of the Army.

Camp Pickett, Va.
October 4, 1944
Dear Folks:

The destinies of nations and the future of the whole world may be in the balance during the coming week. But this coming week there is also a World Series in St. Louis. In an Army camp all of the news items are subordinated to it. Everybody you pass or see or talk to seems to be talking about nothing but St. Louis, World Series, baseball, hits, runs, errors . . . Nowhere, even on a college campus, have I ever seen a group so completely taken over by interest in a sport.

This afternoon we had a water-purification class, but at three o'clock we left our stream site and went to the service club, where we found half the rest of camp listening to the radio. Later we went back to the dispensary and orderly room, where we found a radio and soldiers excitedly listening to an inning-by-inning description. As a civilian I was interested in but not obsessed with professional baseball. But in the Army I've picked up the all-around enthusiasm. Nowhere else have I seen this sort of all-consuming interest in a sports event. [St. Louis hosted two major league baseball teams in 1944, the Cardinals (National League) and

the Browns (American League). That October was the first
and only time an all–St. Louis World Series was played. The
Cardinals won in six games.]

Camp Pickett, Va.
October 7, 1944
Dear Folks:

*Tomorrow morning bright and early we are leaving for our
week's bivouac at Staunton River State Park. Although the life
will be a little more rugged and difficult than our life in camp, I
am looking forward to it. At least it's something new and different. The last time I slept on the ground for more than a week was
when I went down the Allagash River by canoe [a two-week
canoe trip I took while at summer camp in Maine], and that's
quite different from traveling with an Army that moves in jeeps,
trucks, tractors, etc.*

*Since we have changed our barracks, I have met the problem of
rodents and lice for the first time in my life. When we moved into
the barracks, we found it filled with bedbugs. It was finally fumi-
gated. Now everyone is having trouble with body crabs. The medics
have the rather distasteful job of shaving all the hair off the bodies
of the men affected. This is a hell of a thing to write home about—
sorry, but I'm at the dispensary and just happened to think of it.*

Staunton State Park, Va.
Columbus Day, 1944
Dear Folks:

*Going on maneuvers with an Army in 1944 is sort of like liv-
ing an anachronism. While you sleep on the ground, bathe and
shave out of a helmet, and dig your own latrine, you work with
the most elaborate and modern medical field equipment. Trucks,
jeeps, and ambulances run in and out of side roads with radio an-
tennas waving.*

*I am attached to the battalion aid station, which we operate
from a small tent that looks almost exactly like the one you see in
that famous picture of Lincoln and McClellan at the headquarters of the Army of the Potomac. Inside this small tent we have a*

Marching with fixed bayonets at Camp Pickett.

dentist's chair and drilling equipment, enough surgical equipment to perform a simple operation, and many of the fancy drugs that modern chemistry has just brought into popular use. To date we have not had any serious injuries. In the field even the treatment of simple ones is interesting.

Camp Pickett, Va.
October 19, 1944
Dear Folks:

This week they took from us all our serviceable pants and shirts and put them in a bag so that we cannot damage them before we leave the States. So that you have pants to wear, they reissue you clothing in all sorts of odd sizes that have been previously rejected at a POE. When they start doing things like this, I can almost hear the foghorn blowing.

Monday they conducted a very interesting class for the medical detachment. A dog had his rear end run over by a 2½-ton truck, and the medics were called out to chloroform him. After killing the dog, the doctor gave us an hour class in anatomy. He dissected the dog and showed us the makeup of his heart, lungs, stomach, and so on. Although I expected to be nauseated, I was really very interested and not at all sick.

Camp Pickett, Va.
November 1, 1944
Dear Folks:

By the time you receive this letter you will also have received my telegram telling you that once again our furloughs have been canceled. Any man who makes plans based on the Army's promises is a damned fool. This time our furloughs have been delayed because the inspecting team from the Second Army, which was supposed to have inspected us this week, failed to show up. I don't know the explanation the brass hats have offered for making a whole battalion wait for them while they were probably drinking mint juleps down in Tennessee, but I'm sure it won't be good enough to excuse them for just not showing up. However, I suppose the animals will still put on a good show for them next week.

Not only has my furlough been delayed, but it has also been cut a day because of one of the major's many fiendish ideas. It's an old Army custom that, when a man is given traveling time with a furlough, he is given a minimum of two extra days (one to go and the other to return), but yesterday the major decided that nobody in the Middle Atlantic States would get more than one day. That sort of thing is even more annoying than being stood up by the Second Army. I can conceive of no possible gain for the battalion by giving the enlisted men as little leave as possible. When it's just as easy to give a man a break or not, most people would do it, but not this major of ours. I hate to sound so annoyed at the whole world, but all of the confusion and mess seem so entirely unnecessary. With a little planning, a little foresight, and a little interest in the happiness of the EM [enlisted men], all of this could have been avoided.

We just received a letter from the one medic in the 659th **[the airborne-engineer battalion to which I was previously attached]** *who was a paratrooper. He is now in a hospital in England, having been wounded with the paratroopers on the continent. He tells us that wearing a medic brassard on the arm is almost worthless. Most shots are fired from a distance where the Red Cross armband is hardly discernable.*

Camp Pickett, Va.
November 20, 1944
Dear Folks:

Two weeks at home seemed almost like two weeks in another world. I can't possibly tell you how wonderful my furlough was. Of course I enjoyed the football games, the shows, the date, the boys from camp, but most of all I loved home. Home, I'm sure, is the thing that every man in the Army who has had a real one craves most—that always connotes love and stability, something to come home to, someplace where you are a person and not just another name on a list or another poor bastard in his country's service. All I can really say is "Thank God for those two weeks together." A man can relive these memories for a long time.

Today I moved over to A Company where Martin Cooper and I will act permanently as their company aid men. We sleep with them, eat with them, hike with them, and do almost everything but go to classes with them. I went through a chlorine gas chamber for the first time today without mishap or ill effects. **[The chlorine-gas-chamber exercise was a standard part of overseas preparation. The procedure was simple. As outlined in the World War II "basic field manual," it consisted of pumping chlorine gas—which is not fatal and rarely causes lasting discomfort—into a sealed room. Soldiers spent about five minutes in the chamber, having put on their gas masks as they entered. If a gas mask leaked or had not been put on properly, the chlorine gas caused almost instant choking, coughing, and swelling of the eyes. The objective was to instill in soldiers confidence in the protection that their gas masks afforded.]**

Camp Pickett, Va.
November 29, 1944
Dear Folks:

I don't know whether you find it harder to imagine your son as a good little soldier or as an assistant in the plaster room of an orthopedic clinic. This week I am the latter. On Monday Lieutenany Davidson **[the medical officer assigned to the 1291st Combat Engineers]** *sent six men to the camp hospital to work in the surgical and orthopedic clinic for two weeks, or whatever part of that time we are still in this camp. Although this camp is so empty that we have almost no patients, it is still very interesting work. These days I am almost happy anytime I am learning something. Today I cut a cast from the leg of a man who had a compound fracture of the ankle and practiced putting plaster on some of the other students. Unless you have worked near or with modern orthopedic equipment, I'm sure you can't imagine all the wonderful and unusual tools they have to use. Next week, if all goes well, I will go to the surgical clinic and hope to see a few operations. One of the places I would most like to be assigned in the Army is to a large hospital. There you even have an occasional female face to liven things up.*

Since I have been at the hospital, I have seen some doctors who I pitied more than the patients. The two captains who are assistants to the chief of orthopedics are permanently ill malaria victims who have returned from the South Pacific. Far more horrible than the sight of the boy without the leg is the doctor or surgeon with a brilliant mind, a firm hand, and bright future who now sits around a hospital instead of joining the Salvation Army. Each time I see them I'm glad we're not going to the South Pacific. **[During the early years of World War II, nearly half a million U.S. servicemen contracted malaria, mostly in the South Pacific. The disease, which is often fatal and in advanced stages affects the brain, is transmitted by the anopheles mosquito. Because most of the world's production of quinine, the drug traditionally used to treat the disease, was grown in countries that the Japanese occupied, the disease was particularly devastating for American troops in the battles on Guadalcanal and New Guinea in 1942 and 1943.]**

Camp Pickett, Va.
December 11, 1944
Dear Folks:

Today the 1291st Combat Engineers finally started on their way across the ocean. The advance party of a battalion supply officer, the maintenance officer, and a supply noncom left Camp Pickett today to make arrangements for us at our next stop. The usual policy is for the unit to leave somewhere between five and fifteen days after the advance party.

The approximately three-week break in my letters home in December, 1944, was not due to lack of news, laziness, or exhausting assignments. From the time our unit left Camp Pickett by train until we boarded our troopship in New York, we were forbidden to mail letters. It was feared that some apparently innocent bit of information might be useful to an enemy agent. At Camp Joyce Kilmer, the New York Port of Embarkation troop-staging area, the enlisted men's clubs and PXs did not have the usual row of telephone booths. Notwithstanding these restrictions, I was granted a five-hour pass on December 30, 1944, and used the time to visit with my parents in Philadelphia. Five months later, after censorship was lifted, I wrote a letter explaining what happened after I said my final goodbye to them. It is the first letter in the next chapter.

CHAPTER 4

TROOPSHIP LIFE
IN A U-BOAT ZONE

LIFE ABOARD A TROOPSHIP in January, 1945, was both frightening and unpleasant. U-boats still lurked in the North Atlantic sinking Allied vessels. Most of the troopships had armed naval escorts. The U.S. Army Transport (USAT) *Brazil*, which carried approximately five thousand soldiers, including my own 1291st Engineer Combat Battalion, was the center ship of a convoy in which at least twenty other vessels were always in view. (Official records indicate that there were fifty-seven ships in the convoy.) Depth charges were detonated several times while we were en route. The ship rocked violently, and loudspeakers blared instructions for soldiers to stay clear of exits and to put on full canteens, shoes, life jackets, and warm clothes.

With approximately 360 other soldiers, I slept in one of the ship's smaller dining salons in four-decker "bunks" that consisted of taut canvas suspended from metal poles. The berths were approximately two feet apart—leaving barely enough room to sleep on your side. It was almost impossible to sleep for more than one or two hours consecutively. The lights were never turned off, and the portholes were painted black and sealed shut.

The room stank. One soldier or another was always retching, yelling, or stumbling around. Since there was limited ventilation, the atmosphere was always hazy with clouds of cigarette smoke. Soldiers were forbidden to go on deck at night to get a breath of sea air, and military police enforced this restriction by guarding all of the doors. This was a necessary precaution. There was too much danger of a GI lighting a cigarette, throwing a gum wrapper overboard, or possibly flinging himself over the rail in the black of night. During daylight hours, each unit was allowed a limited time on deck for a little exercise, relaxed conversation, and fresh air. All of the troops on board also participated in an 11-A.M. lifeboat drill. Even then, soldiers were not allowed to go near the railings.

In order to speed the enlisted men through chow lines, mess-hall tables were arranged at stand-up height. With no place to sit, you left promptly after getting food in your mess kit. Shipboard evacuation precautions required that you sleep in your winter clothes. You were encouraged, although not required, to wear your life jacket at all times. If the man in the bunk above you got seasick, you could do little about it except help him clean up the mess. Men waited in long lines to enter the mess hall and to use the toilets. Urinals were improvised in dead-end corridors with a drain along the bottom of a slate-covered wall. Choppy seas made these corridors into slippery "slop alleys."

Dubbed the "Chaplain's Night Club," the mess hall was used for some kind of entertainment every evening when the sea was not too rough. Even though it operated on two shifts, only those who got in line early were able to attend performances, as it took four shifts to feed the ship's white enlisted men in one mess hall. The Chaplain's Night Club rotated performance schedules among movies (only on calm nights), sing-alongs, and variety shows with soldier vocal and instrumental groups, pantomimists, and magicians. On clear afternoons there were supervised boxing matches on deck. Each card was organized so there would be a USAT *Brazil* champion in each weight classification before we reached Europe.

Although organized entertainment undoubtedly contributed to shipboard morale, gambling was the most important form of recreation. You could get into high- or low-stakes poker or crap games anytime you wanted—24/7. Self-appointed croupiers presided over the high-stakes games. They announced the odds on crap points, matched bets, changed big bills, and kept kibitzers and amateurs away from the big-time poker games. Nobody objected to their taking their cut; they maintained essential order.

Officers and enlisted men lived totally segregated lives. Officers were quartered on the deck above us. During the eighteen days at sea, our officers had virtually no contact with us. Instead, the sergeants handled the roll calls, boat drills, mess-hall shift assignments, and minor scratches and bruises. Controlling the fights that inevitably erupt among emotionally stressed men in tight quarters was also noncoms' work. Although MPs guarded every stairway between the floors, I once contrived to deliver a message to the officers' deck. I was enraged when I saw that they ate at tables with linen cloths and waiter service and had a lounge where they could smoke and relax.

The USAT *Brazil* was the first troopship to go directly from the United States to France. Until January, 1945, virtually all U.S. troops destined for combat in France were prepared and staged in England, so we initially assumed that we were headed there. Fear naturally ratcheted up several notches when our destination was announced. Immediate replacements were needed at the front. For many of us that meant that our rendezvous with death was near-at-hand.

When we landed in Le Havre, American troops had not yet achieved victory in the Battle of the Bulge, the largest battle fought on the western front. The battle received its name because several German armies broke through our lines in eastern France and Belgium and created a large "bulge." The encounter began on December 16, 1944, and ended in late January, 1945. Of the 600,000 GIs involved, almost 20,000 were killed, another 20,000 were captured, and 40,000 were wounded.

When we landed, Le Havre, one of Europe's most important prewar commercial ports, had been reduced to a pile of rubble. The Allies had bombed it from the air and shelled it from the sea. Its seaport infrastructure, including piers, railroads, cranes, warehouses, revetments, and sea walls had been demolished by the Germans before they retreated. Underwater mines were planted throughout the harbor. One ship in our convoy sank after hitting a mine. While homeward bound fifteen months later, I took a photo of a broken ship in Le Havre harbor (see page 282). It was identified as part of the first New York-to-Le-Havre convoy, which included me.

Since there were no docking facilities for large ships, the USAT *Brazil* anchored several hundred yards from shore. Troops carrying barracks bags and full field equipment climbed down ladders to landing craft infantry (LCIs), like those that had been used in the Normandy landings. The LCIs took us to within one hundred yards of a beach, and we waded the rest of the way to the shore in subfreezing weather.

The dateline on the following letter indicates that it is out of chronological order. Because of the strict European Theater censorship, I was unable to describe the events preceding my embarkation until five months later. The prohibition on writing about troop movements—even in the United States—lasted until approximately May 15, 1945, a week after V-E Day.

Near Verdun, France
June 4, 1945
Dear Folks:

For a long time I've wanted to tell you what happened to me from the time I kissed you good-bye in the wee hours of the morning at the North Philadelphia station on December 30, until the 1291st Engineers broke up.

Saturday, December 30, was one of those days during which we did absolutely nothing as troops were leaving Camp Kilmer all day for various ships in our convoy. Although we were told that we wouldn't leave until Sunday night or Monday, there was too much nervous tension for the boys to do much but play poker and shoot crap. Everybody in the battalion but me had another one of those Army physical examinations, which is a waste of both the doctor's and patient's time. I was on KP when the medics took their physicals. I did not take it later because, when Sergeant

May [the top enlisted man in the medical detachment] realized it was one of those examinations that it is impossible to fail, he just added my name to the list of people examined. He told me not to waste my time.

Sunday everybody got up bright and early and rolled their packs so that they could leave on a few moments' notice. But we didn't go. Sunday was a typical Army day: We waited and waited and waited.

Monday we did some more waiting until 7:00 P.M., when we finally left. The walk from our barracks to the railhead was without a doubt the most difficult march of my Army career. The walk was not long, but I was weighted down with two medical kits and seven pounds of cheese, salami, etc. My pack contained a shelter half, raincoat, two blankets, a change of clothes, writing paper, prayer book, and miscellaneous other things that I was not ordered to take, a steel helmet, and the warmest clothes I could find (overcoat, field jacket, sweater, and woolen underwear). When we finally arrived at the railhead, we stood in line for almost an hour while jerky second lieutenants checked lists and called roll. The rest of us listened to our backs strain to the breaking point. We had assigned seats on the train, where we found our duffel bags with all the rest of our earthly goods waiting for us. During the ride to the Jersey Central Station on the New Jersey side of the Hudson River there was to be no talking. It was much more difficult for an enlisted man to get permission to go to the latrine than for a Missourian to see the president. From the train we ran between columns of MPs to the ferry, which took us to a Cunard-White Star dock at 48th Street and the North River. We were now also carrying our duffel bags, and mine to my regret contained three loaves of bread to go with my salami and cheese, two extra sweaters, and a half dozen books, etc., to make it exceed several times the five pounds of extra equipment to which you are officially limited. On the ferry I was so tired that I sat on my duffel bag and squashed the bread so thoroughly that I was still finding bread crumbs in unexpected places a few weeks ago.

When we finally got to the Cunard dock, we found a horrible five-piece band and some Red Cross girls waiting for us. The band

*added nothing but noise to the occasion, but the coffee and dough-
nuts were the best I'd ever tasted. Here we stood in line only about
twenty minutes. Finally at about 12:30, through some miracle, I
was able to drag my dead ass and equipment up four flights of
stairs to the promenade deck and so to bed—if you can call that
taunt piece of canvas a bed.*

On board boat
January 2, 1945
Dear Folks:
    *Finally off to fight a war. That sounds dramatic. It sounds as
if my heart ought to be pounding and my breast swelling with
pride. It sounds as if I ought to be proud of patriotic service to my
country in time of war. Not a damned bit.*
    *I don't think 1 percent of the men on board feel as if they are
going off on a great mission, as men have done in other wars.
They're not fighting for the holy grail or to make the world safe
for democracy. They're just a lot of poor bastards who got caught
in the draft and must take the bitter along with the sweet in life.
So it's "good-bye, USA. We're off to fight for the newest thing—
pax Americanum."*
    *New Year's eve has passed and gone. I can say without hesita-
tion that it was very different from all others I've known. In the
past some have been more exciting than others, but none was anything like this one. The shipboard barracks were too noisy to sleep.
The weather was too rought to wait in the line at the movies, so I
played poker. Nothing was mentioned about New Year's eve until
about 11:45, when some wise guy yelled out "Happy New Year."
About the only response that anyone could rise to was a snicker, a
mutter, a sardonic smile. We dealt hand after hand right through
midnight with no stop for celebration—just an occasional one for
some bitter remark. For once I was with a lot of young people on
New Year's eve, and the spirit was not ribald and drunken, but
rather "So what? Another year in the Army."*
    *Although censorship forbids me from telling you the details of
our trip from port of embarkation to the boat, I will tell you that
it was remarkably well done. Although it was very tiring on the*

*men who had all of their worldly possessions on their backs (at
least 150 lbs., including your pack, duffel bag, blanket roll,
gasmask, etc.), it could have been much worse. On the dock there
was an eight-piece band playing and a great many Red Cross
girls milling in and out passing out doughnuts and hot coffee.
P.S.1. Send my dearest love to **Aunt Eva***

*2. I hope **S**ue tries hard **t**o help the **i**nvestigation about her loss
in the **L**iberty Street holdup. **A**t the rate **t**hings seem to **p**resent
them selves **o**n that street **e**verybody who must ride that trolley
must be scared to death. I can't understand why the government
can't do something about this situation. These cheap hoodlums
seem to have the police, the FBI, and everybody baffled. Before
long the Army will be there and put them in their proper place
— the jug.*

STILL AT POE

[Port of Embarcation]

Somewhere off the East Coast
January __, 1945

Dear Folks:

*Last week I said good-bye to my home and family for probably
the longest stretch I will be away from home and love and friendship in my life. Farewells are hard on all of us.*

*Now I am leaving to help fight a war, after spending twenty
months in the States being trained. As I look both forward and
backward, I feel a little like Gulliver [**Lemuel Gulliver, the main
character in** Gulliver's Travels, **Jonathan Swift's eighteenth-
century satiric novel**] and the sequence of experiences he went
through in his travels. First, he went to the Land of Lilliput and
felt large and important, as the people around him were small
and insignificant; so it was with my selfish feelings when I first
entered the Army. Next, I think he went to Brobdingnag, where he
was a midget in a land of giants; so I felt when I first really came
in contact with noisy, bigoted, intolerant sergeants and moronic
lieutenants. Eventually Gulliver went to a country where he
looked at everything through opaque glass. After a time I became
callused and began to look at some things through the rather*

shortsighted eyes of a soldier. Lastly, he decided that all human beings were Yahoos. He then found more interesting company with his horse than with his wife.

Thank God, I haven't become that cynical, but certainly very few men have had their faith in the mind and dignity of man increased by their American military experience. So much for that. Lord knows how it just happened to come to my mind. Now there are new horizons, misty dark ones, but still new ones.

The U.S. Army Transport (USAT) *Brazil* carried approximately five thousand soldiers. Issue number four of the ship's newsletter, *Trip Over News,* tells of a successful Nazi offensive. This was dire news for soldiers en route to combat.

Last night's ride back on the train was uncomfortable, as could only be expected. I was forced to stand up all the way. After sleeping an hour or so this morning, I reported for KP. Since they had nothing for me to do, I did nothing. All day has been spent doing nothing. Always when there is really nothing to do and someone thinks you ought to work, you find yourself working hard avoiding work.

At sea
January __, 1945
Dear Folks:

Trying to write a letter aboard a troop ship is one of the hardest jobs I have tackled since I've been in the Army. This ship is literally packed to the gunwales. There couldn't be more than an inch or two that enlisted men can use where you will not find at least one or two other soldiers. You cannot possibly imagine how crowded we are and how difficult that makes life on a rather rough sea. I am living in a room on the promenade deck, which was probably once a lounge or bar. There are 360 of us living together. The room certainly isn't any bigger than 60 x 60 x 15.

I will tell you more about our accommodations later, but I don't want you to think that I'm griping because our ship is crowded. I realize that is necessary. The thing that really aggravates me, as well as all the other enlisted men on board, is the good accommodations the officers and nurses get in comparison with us. While we live like so many sardines in a can, they live in relative luxury. I don't believe that is necessary.

The enlisted men eat in a mess hall, where they are forced to stand to eat their meals so that they will hurry and not delay the chow line. The officers eat in the ship's dining salon with white tablecloths on the tables. They have a choice of a few table d'hôte meals and service from civilian waiters and mess boys. They generally eat like gentlemen. They have one whole deck reserved for their use. They generally use a lot more room than I believe their numerical count should allow. This is probably the first time I have envied officers or resented their privileges. While I was still in the States, my military life was superficial on weekends. I lived *in a world very far removed from Army camps. When in that world I didn't give a damn about officers, but at sea my entire life is confined by the steel sides and gunwales of the ship. I don't resent their social privileges in any way; it's just that I believe our condition could be considerably alleviated if they were inconvenienced a little.*

With the boat rocking and swaying the way it has been for the last few days, I have had very little time for reading. I did squeeze in enough time to read Will Durant's Caesar and Christ *(don't get the wrong idea. I read a summary in Omnibook). When I reread the story of the decay and fall of Rome, I couldn't help but draw a rather pessimistic analogy between that and the States. When Rome had the vitality to conquer and individuals tried to gain things for themselves and did not depend on the state for the support of their charities, their art, and themselves, Rome was strong and vital and creative. I hate to say it, but I can almost picture the same thing in the United States with the near death of laissez-faire capitalism and the ascendancy of the New Deal. I sincerely hope that my generation will be able to salvage America when this is all over.*

When telling you about my various gripes, I forgot to tell you about one that is a little more objective than the rest. Maybe it's the Navy's idea of democracy. Maybe it was just an accident. My guess is that the blame can be placed with the Army. The officers and white troops are all quartered on the upper decks, while the colored troops are quartered way down in the bowels of the ship where the drone of the motors would drive most men half-crazy. That's the same way their ancestors came to America—the whites on top, and the Negroes in the hold. The Negro has made a real contribution to the war. He deserves equal treatment from the Army, just as he has a right to fair and equal treatment before the law.

I am sure you realize how difficult censorship makes the writing of letters. We are not allowed to date them, tell the date we left, how long we have been at sea, where we are going, where we think we are going, or anything else of any real interest about our trip.

At sea
January __, 1945
Dear Folks:

*The sea has been very rough for several days. The merchant seamen say that this has been one of the roughest trips they have taken. On the roughest day you could feel the whole ship vibrate as the prow lurched forward and the propeller came out of the water, but through it all I have felt fine and have not missed a meal or a possible hour on deck. Thank you once again for the "Seoxyl" [seasickness pills], which I feel sure have had something to do with my good health. [**The naval escort ships in our convoy dropped depth bombs several times. Soldiers, of course, could not tell about this in their letters. I do not know whether the escort ships sighted a German U-boat, or sank one, or both.**]*

Yesterday they started French classes for those interested aboard. I attended and must admit it was quite a new experience in language study. All who attended had phrase books in which the words and phrases were shown in French, then English, and then transliterated French. The lesson consisted chiefly of reciting the words after they were spoken on Victrola records. The most unusual thing was that the officer in charge began by telling us not to pay any attention to the French spelling as the only thing of any importance was speaking French. How different that is from high school, where I learned to conjugate verbs in six tenses and four moods and can't speak a single word.

At sea
January __, 1945
Dear Folks:

We get our news aboard ship from a mimeographed sheet called The Trip Over News. *It is somewhat distorted by clumsy GI hands, but at least we have some vague idea of what is happening in the world around us. I would send you a copy, but for some unexplainable reason, we are not allowed to send it home. It is hard to say that the news content boosts the morale of men crossing the Atlantic Ocean at this time. All that I can decipher*

from the news about the European battle is that the Ameri-
cans—with all their brains and all their supplies and all their
ingenious implements of war—are taking one hell of a licking
from Von Runstedt **[General Gert von Runstedt, the German**
commander during the Battle of the Bulge]*. I believe this*
breakthrough and the American defeat, like Pearl Harbor, ought
to be investigated. The investigations should be followed by court-
martials and honest press releases to the public.

I think I've played more cards during this voyage than I played
during the first eighteen years of my life. When the sea is rough,
there is very little to do but play cards. For the past few days it
was too rough to read or write or even just relax on our bunks.
Most of the time I have played a crazy wild poker game called
"Baseball" with the rest of the medics.

For the first few days we did very well with supplies from the
PX, which were not rationed (with the exception of cigarettes—
1½ cartons per soldier at fifty cents per carton). Everything is
very cheap, but since it is not rationed, it gets used rapidly. PX
supplies rarely last more than a day or two.

I don't think I ever saw as many MPs in a small area as I have
seen on this ship. In every aisle, corridor, and hall and on every
stairway, deck, and rail there are a few. There are both officers
and enlisted men. They are posted to make sure that nobody loi-
ters in the halls or stands too close to the rails or walks around
without his life jacket and canteen or breaks any one of the thou-
sand and one ship's rules.

At sea
January __, 1945
Dear Folks:

Although I have written four other letters from aboard ship, I
have a few spare moments now, and realizing how much my let-
ters mean to you, I am writing this short note. There are only two
things, which I really want to tell you:

*1. Say "hello" to **Aunt Eva** for me. I have thought of her often*
and hope she feels better.

2. Mary wrote that **L**ee Clemson was **a**ccepted for some **n**ew and unusual **d**estroyer escort school. **I**t is something **n**ew when he **g**ets into either **l**arge or rather **e**xclusive schools. He **h**as less scholastic **a**ptitude than a **r**eal moron. A **v**ery narrow margin **e**very time is between him and failure, and it looks like he's even got the Navy giving him his margin.

LANDING LE HARVE

[I probably did not know the correct spelling of Le Havre.]

CHAPTER 5

Awaiting Combat
In Europe

Shortly after wading ashore, the 1291st Combat Engineer Battalion was trucked from Le Havre harbor to Camp Lucky Strike, a partially built tent city near Dieppe. Hastily constructed by German prisoners of war, it was a sea of mud without amenities. The medical tent, like all of the others, lacked a floor and had limited heating and light and no electricity. Water was rendered potable by putting tablets in a lister bag.

Reinforcement depots, such as Camp Lucky Strike, were an essential part of the Army's European Theater strategy. Once committed to battle, divisions were kept in combat zones for long periods. As soldiers were killed or maimed or simply became exhausted, they were replaced by men from reinforcement depots. After the Allies broke through the German lines at the Normandy beaches, at no time was the need for replacements greater than following America's setbacks in the Battle of the Bulge.

Camp Lucky Strike was the largest of the nine "cigarette camps" built in late 1944 and early 1945 between Le Havre and Rouen, Normandy's railroad and inland waterway center. At the time I was there, Camp Lucky Strike housed approximately fifty thousand soldiers. Later its capacity was doubled. Some of the other, larger cigarette camps that played essential roles in the Army's reinforcement-redeployment-staging strategy were Camp Old Gold, Camp Chesterfield, Camp Twenty Grand, Camp Pall Mall, and Camp Philip Morris. Security was the chief reason that camps were named for cigarette brands. Spies and eavesdroppers who intercepted phone and radio communications might be misled about troop unit locations, if they could not tell whether a soldier who was mentioning a cigarette brand was discussing his favorite smoke or the reinforcement depot where he was housed.

Camp Lucky Strike's site was ideal for the rapid construction of a large encampment. In the summer of 1939, just before their war began, the French constructed a small reconnaissance airfield there. A year later, when the area was part of the Third Reich, the Germans expanded the small airdrome into a major facility with a five-thousand-foot runway, adjacent concrete taxiways, and an elaborate electrical system. In September, 1944, when the British captured Le Havre and Rouen, the retreating Nazis destroyed the runways, hangars, and electrical system. A few months later, when the American Army began looking for a site for a large staging area and reinforcement depot in Normandy, the former Luftwaffe airfield met all the requirements; it was a large area where no farmers or small shopkeepers had to be displaced and where nearby highways, railroads, electric power, and water utilities were in place. When I visited the site in 2002, it had come full circle. A portion of the original runway had been rehabilitated, and a flying club specializing in small, single-engine airplanes occupied a modest adjacent hangar.

Although the requirement for troops at the front was immediate and pressing, soldiers at reinforcement depots did nothing—except await reassignment. The harsh weather at Camp Lucky Strike precluded all but essential outdoor activities. This meant that GIs lay idly on their bunks, made short trips to surrounding towns, played cards or dice—and drank. Although U.S. enlisted men did not get a liquor ration (British soldiers did), something alcoholic was nearly always available.

The day after the 1291st Engineers arrived at the camp, I witnessed triage for the first—and only—time in my life. Another unit in our convoy was sent by train from Le Havre to St. Valéry-en-Caux, a small resort town near our tent city. Undoubtedly as the result of an act of sabotage, the train was

Camp Lucky Strike, the largest troop-staging camp in Normandy, was built on cliffs above St. Valéry-en-Caux, a seaside resort town of forty-five hundred. Seven months after D-Day, tank obstacles still littered its beach.

unable to stop at the station and rammed through the terminal, killing an estimated two hundred GIs. The dead and injured were rushed to Camp Lucky Strike, which had not yet established a central hospital facility. All of the unit medics, including me, were summoned to the location where the camp hospital was to be set up. As the trucks delivered men with ghastly wounds, including boards through their torsos, a medical officer would examine them and then point to either the left or the right. On the right were tents with equipment and personnel to treat those with minor injuries. On the left was a morgue tent and several others, where men were given morphine while they waited to die or to be evacuated to a base section hospital. All of the medical personnel at Lucky Strike were called into service to help with the initial heavy work. After a few hours, unskilled medics like me were dismissed.

Censorship kept the news of this dramatic event out of the U.S. press. However, the details are described in a small brochure produced by the tourist office of St. Valéry-en-Caux and available at its modest World War II museum. After visiting the museum in 2002, I sent a copy of the pamphlet to Gene J. Bokor, a college classmate who had been stationed at Camp Lucky Strike at the same time I was. He responded that he was particularly grateful to have the pamphlet. It confirmed for the first time his story about the French sabotage at the St. Valéry railroad station. He had told his family that this deliberate mass killing and maiming of unsuspecting American troops was one of the most terrifying experiences (including frontline combat) of his military life.

A small coal stove in our fifteen-man tent kept the mud from freezing, but it never gave off enough heat to encourage us to take off our outer two or three layers of clothing. As soon as I came into the tent, I took off my shoes and socks and tried to dry them on a hook above the stove. However, the minute I stepped outside to go to the mess tent, medical tent, or latrine, I was ankle deep in mud—and my feet were once again wet and cold.

Meals at Lucky Strike, although calorically sufficient, were not designed to be enjoyable. In addition to powdered eggs or potatoes, a few stewed vegetables, and coffee, most meals consisted of C rations. C rations were small cans whose contents could be served either cold or heated. Although soldiers ate whatever C ration was handed out in the chow line, ten selections were available, including chicken and vegetables, frankfurters and beans, ham, eggs and potatoes, meat and noodles, and pork and beans.

The cold, wet weather made even simple chores difficult and unpleasant. A tent's daily coal ration was measured by the helmet. Each morning two or three soldiers walked a half mile in the mud to get a helmet full of coal from a quartermaster facility. There was no dining tent. Your hot meal C ration and a cup of coffee was put in your mess kit, and you carried it to your tent so you could eat sitting on your cot, which was surrounded by mud. After eating, you returned to the cook tent, often in freezing rain or snow, to wash your mess kit in an

The top image shows the devastated railroad station at St. Valéry after a sabotaged troop train, which was taking GIs from Le Havre to Camp Lucky Strike, plowed through the building and killed more than two hundred American soldiers. The bottom image shows the station in a 1930s postcard.

ashcan of hot water. As unpleasant as life was at Camp Lucky Strike, there were few complaints. After all, we were not getting killed or wounded.

Weeks without a bath added to Lucky Strike's unpleasantness. All personal washing was done outside in the cold. You washed your face and hands—and shaved if you wished—from your helmet, which you filled with hot water in the mess tent. At one point the amount of water available for personal use was rationed. Wooden stands outside the latrine allowed you to steady your helmet at basin height. The cold and mud made it impossible to consider washing other body parts.

On two occasions, the men in our medical detachment made arrangements to take real baths, and both times our plans went awry. While at Lucky Strike, a group of medics discovered a small bar in a nearby village. We asked the barkeep whether the house had a bathtub. When she said "oui," we proposed that she prepare hot water for us to take baths the next night in exchange for cigarettes and coffee. She eagerly agreed. The next night both parties performed on their part of the bargain. In the meantime, however, other soldiers had discovered the bar. Four of us were scheduled to bathe. After the first two completed their baths and beckoned to the third to go upstairs, the drunks at the bar assumed we were taking turns with a French girl, not a warm tub. Our explanation fell on deaf ears. Several drunks ascended the stairs, turned over beds, and ransacked the closets. We ran toward camp—and never returned.

A month later, after we had inexplicably been transferred to another reinforcement depot in the historic city of Chartres, my medic buddies came upon a public bathhouse where the local citizens, who were too poor to have indoor plumbing at home, took baths. The following night all of the members of the medical detachment bathed. The next day we told other soldiers about the relatively clean public facility where one could take a warm bath. To our consternation, they reported back later that a new sign had appeared at the bath house. It said, "U.S. Officers Only." A week later a reinforcement depot staple was welcomed to the scene: a quartermaster shower unit. These units consisted of several tents plus a truck with pumps, heaters, motors, and plumber's tools. After leaving his clothes in the first tent, a soldier walked slowly through a tented corridor with multiple shower heads, somewhat like driving a car through a car wash.

While awaiting orders at Camp Lucky Strike, I secured a one-day pass to Rouen. The extent of the devastation wreaked there by Allied bombings shocked me. In some neighborhoods not a single substantial building was left standing. Many important thoroughfares were still blocked by fallen buildings four months after the Nazis had retreated. I visited the site of the famed—but now ruined—Rouen Cathedral, a world-famous example of French Gothic architecture that had survived for five centuries until the day the Royal Air Force focused on Rouen. Nobody at my level knew or even cared what had happened to the thousands of people who had been made homeless. A review of the Normandy campaign's history indicates that no top-level Allied official cared much, either. Many of today's anti-American, anti-Bush demonstrators in Paris are the grandchildren of the thousands of French civilians who were randomly maimed or killed by Allied bombers. Their understanding—then and now—of how America and Britain treated its allies is vastly different from our own. During the German occupation, freedoms were lost and democratic elections curtailed, but killings of non-Jews were few and unreported.

The Red Cross arranged for GIs on pass to tour Rouen with English-speaking French guides. The tours began and ended with views of Allied bombing damage, and soldiers were encouraged to take pictures of the city's famous cathedral, which had been destroyed by aerial bombings. The Nazi municipal overlords were civil-service bureaucrats who moved into Rouen with their wives and families, while ours were battle-weary fighters who lived in bachelor officers' billets and reinforcement depots. Most American troops, like my GI comrades, saw the French as cowardly people who surrendered to the Germans without a fight. (The World War II Museum in Caen,

Normandy, points out that, in the history of modern warfare, no major nation has capitulated to an enemy army as rapidly as the French did to the Germans in 1940.) Notwithstanding this, the French were solicitous and pleasant to us because we had candy, cigarettes, and money. And most importantly, we appeared to be winning the war.

Since Chartres was the home of one of France's most famous cathedrals and strategically unimportant, it was relatively undamaged by U.S. aerial bombings. Most of the buildings in the city center were unharmed. The two largest and best hotels—the Grand Monarch and the de France—became officers' clubs. A small nearby hotel became an enlisted men's club. The opera house became a GI movie theater, while the public baths became a sanitary facility reserved for U.S. officers. The German military bureaucrats, who occupied Chartres before the Americans took over, functioned as the town's municipal government, but they did not expropriate most of its quality-of-life amenities.

The reinforcement depot in Chartres was housed in a former French-Army garrison used by the Nazi occupation army until 1944. Although we slept on the floor in a building without heat, electric lights, or indoor plumbing, after Camp Lucky Strike it was luxury living. Since a cobblestone courtyard replaced the sea of mud, we were able to spend part of each day drilling, marching, and doing calisthenics. Most of the time, however, we did nothing but await orders.

At Chartres the 1291st Combat Engineer Battalion finally broke up. Individual soldiers were assigned to more than a dozen different units. I was sent to a pumping station on the gasoline pipeline that crossed France from the Atlantic Ocean port of Cherbourg to a point near the easternmost advance of Allied troops and finally to Mainz, on the German side of the Rhine River.

The day I reported to a pumping station near Verdun, I technically became a combat soldier. Everyone stationed east of the fourth meridian and north of forty-seven degrees latitude before March 21, 1945, was awarded the Rhineland Campaign

Sections of Rouen, one of Normandy's largest cities, were almost completely destroyed by the Allies in 1944. Thousands of French civilians were killed by Royal Air Force bombing raids and Allied artillery barrages. When France capitulated to the Nazis in 1940, Rouen had been virtually unscathed. GIs were sensitive to the fact that Allied bombing of nonmilitary targets made them unpopular.

Battle Star—and Verdun was several miles east of the boundary line. Battle stars were both coveted and ridiculed. Having a star attached to your European Theater ribbon confirmed that you had not spent your time overseas as a garrison soldier. But it also did not indicate that you had been a front-line warrior. Campaign star demarcation lines were drawn to include quartermaster warehouses, trucking hubs, hospitals, ammunition dumps, and pipeline terminals.

Somewhere in France
January 18, 1945
Dear Folks:

My first impressions of France were rather mixed as I looked around the harbor from the fore deck of our troopship. My thoughts were about the ruins. Everything within sight seemed to be reduced to rubble. Great steel girders could be seen sticking out from wrecked buildings at rakish angles, twisted into unbelievable shapes. In between all of this, thoughts came back to me of the old France and Paris. Everything is in ruins. The newsreels are mild and unreal. They may be a common denominator, but the ruins we saw you cannot picture, even with a good imagination. We saw almost no people in a town, which formerly had a population of_____ thousand [deleted by censor]. I don't think this destruction was done by the Germans. I am sure 90 percent of it was done by the U.S. Army Air Corps and the RAF. Why have the French welcomed us in the way the U.S. newspapers describe? I think they laughed and danced in the same spirit in which a child smiles when you stop beating him.

While waiting to leave the port, I saw something that may give you some idea of our relationship with the French. Everybody being nervous, most of the men lit up cigarettes while waiting for our transportation. Almost as soon as we were done, a Frenchman came up behind us and picked up the butts out of the snow. As soon as the fellows saw him, they all offered him a smoke. One fellow gave him a full pack, which has tremendous value over here. American-caused inflation is easy to understand. Almost

This picture of the site where I landed in January, 1945, was taken from the ship on which I returned home in April, 1946. We landed by going down rope ladders to an LCI (landing craft infantry), which in turn took us to the beach shown in the picture, where we waded ashore in freezing cold water.

everybody has a Robinson Crusoe attitude toward money's value. Today we changed our American dollars into francs. That is the only type of money we will be able to spend over here. Everybody was required to declare or send home all cash (traveler's checks not included) over one hundred dollars, which they had in their possession. This is an effort to curb and control the black market, which has caused so much trouble over here recently.

While we traveled here, we passed through several small towns including _____ [deleted by censor], which had stores and shops in working order. Although I couldn't recognize any of the French products, I noticed advertisements for five U.S. products (Esso, Mobil Oil, Dunlop tires, Kodak, and Ford), as well as a movie theater that advertised a picture with a French title starring Deanna Durbin. [Deanna Durbin was one of Hollywood's best-known vocalists and female stars during the 1930s and 1940s. She won an Academy Award in 1938, and she played leading lady opposite Barry Fitzgerald, Charles Laughton, Franchot Tone, Walter Pidgeon, and Adolph Menjou.]

There is very little doubt that at the present moment I am dirtier than I have ever been before. The only water we had for washing on the boat was salt water, and as you probably know it is practically impossible to get clean with that. Here it is very cold, so we don't do much washing. (The real reason is that there isn't much water. In one of the companies the men are rationed to a half helmet of water a day for washing.) I believe I will take my first shower to celebrate Easter—maybe.

Now something about the details of our present living quarters. I sleep on a cot in a large tent with fourteen other men from A Company. There are small stoves in the tents. Although they give some warmth, everything is still very cold, damp, and muddy. For meals we usually eat hot C rations, plus fresh bread and some extra vegetable. Although hardly enchanting, the meals are wholesome and palatable. I have no kicks. The worst part of the whole setup is the latrine. If I used the word "repulsive," it would be too mild. There are no pornographic pictures or lewd poems on the walls, but there's snow, ice, mud, a cold wind, and a hell of a stink.

The most difficult thing of all is the fact that the end is nowhere in sight. It's not bad when you're cold at night because you know morning will come. But it's hard when you think that every other night is going to be cold for a long, long time. When no real relief is in sight, it becomes a lot harder. It was easy enough to say, "If winter comes, can spring be far behind?" But after reading newspapers and looking around some of France, it's a lot harder.

Yesterday there was nothing but mud outside. Today we are having a French blizzard (no different from those in Philadelphia). The result of all this is that your feet are always wet, and one of the things you desire most is a room with a wooden floor.

While on the boat I did a lot of griping about the officers' accommodations as compared with those of the enlisted men. But all of those privileges abruptly came to an end when they disembarked. Here their life is no better than ours. They sleep on the same kind of cots. Hold their noses in the same latrines. Freeze in the same chow lines and assume the responsibilities that most EM avoid. I also want to retract all of the disparaging remarks

I've previously made about nurses. They are living here with us. This is one hell of a life for a woman. I am not at all convinced that the Army is wise in assigning them overseas duty, but it does. These girls knew what they were doing when they volunteered. They deserve a great deal of credit.

Somewhere in France
January 22, 1945
Dear Folks:

After almost a week in France I have finally seen something of France and the French people. From first observations I would say that the people and towns are very much like those described in the storybooks. The entire life of the community seems to center about the café.

It is impossible to order whiskey or anything like a mixed drink. There seems to be plenty of beer, wine, cider, and usually cognac, but the most surprising thing is that you can order a beef sandwich without any trouble. American soldiers are willing to pay almost any sort of exorbitant price. Here, as everywhere else, if you've got the money, almost nothing is unobtainable.

We have converted all our cash into francs. It is the only standard of currency that can be used—in or out of camp. It will be used at the PX and telegraph office—when we get them.

Somewhere in France
Helen's birthday
January 24, 1945
Dear Folks:

Although our news coverage was rather poor and incomplete until yesterday, when distribution of the Stars and Stripes *began, we have heard regularly on the radio of the great Russian offensive in the east. It is certainly good news. I don't think any group of men could have received this news more eagerly and enthusiastically than the men in this French hellhole. Any place where people know that a troop movement is forthcoming in the not-too-distant future, rumors fly thick and fast. This place is the same as*

Here I am with Jo Saxe *(middle)* and Joe Rosenbluth *(right)*, members of Congregation Rodeph Shalom's 1940 confirmation class, who were also at Camp Lucky Strike.

all others. With rumors traveling the way they do here, it's hard to believe anything you do not see in print. I'll certainly be thankful when my Time *starts coming.*

*We are finally getting some of the services that people back in the States think you get in camps overseas. Two days ago cable service was made available [***"cables" were overseas telegraph messages; "telegrams" were domestic messages***], and yesterday we received our weekly PX ration of four candy bars and five packages of cigarettes. (All for 17 francs or 35¢ in U.S. money.) They say it won't be too long until we will have showers, a Red Cross, and mail. Then life will become almost tolerable.*

They have finally established a pass policy here. I do not believe it will be too long until I will have a day off on a pass. It is almost impossible to go to Paris and return in one day. I'll probably pick out some other city. You can be assured that I will not choose mud or cobblestone streets if there is an opportunity to do otherwise. It seems that the only kind of transportation available to American soldiers in France is the GI truck. I have seen only one civilian car on the street since I have been in France—and many thousands of GI vehicles. Government vehicles pass you every moment or so, day or night, on all the roads in this vicinity. They say that civilian rail transportation is so irregular as to be unworthy of consideration. Almost all government vehicles will pick you up immediately when they are not traveling in a convoy. On our way here we passed a large freight yard. Almost 50 percent of the railcars there were marked "U.S. Army, Transportation Corps." Most of the French railcars were ancient-looking, four-wheeled wooden affairs, while the U.S. Army ones were eight-wheeled and usually metal. You can always see several civilians traveling on bicycles.

To give you some idea of the cold, I'll tell you what I wear every day. I wear a cotton undershirt, a wool undershirt, a cotton sweater, a flannel shirt, a heavy wool sweater, a scarf, and a combat jacket, cotton and wool drawers, two pairs of heavy socks, plus two pairs of pants, and believe it or not I'm usually cold. It was almost impossible to keep warm at night until yesterday, when we were issued sleeping bags, which made the situation almost tolerable.

As you have probably guessed from my letters, there is very little to do here at nights but talk and eat. Each night when I lie in bed and listen to the other fellows talk, I realize how easy it is for a lawyer to be a shyster or ambulance chaser. I don't think 10 percent of these men know anything about their insurance, yet they pay for it every month and curse the damned lawyers and brass hats who force them to pay for it. They see it as a sort of tribute. Last night I heard one fellow discussing how he was involved in an automobile accident and a lawyer visited him and so on. It was just like the pulp magazines describe it. He did not think there was anything wrong with it. As a matter of fact, he was thankful.

Much of the commercial area of St. Valéry-en-Caux was destroyed by Allied bombing.

Somewhere in France
January 26, 1945
Dear Folks:

The good news of the Russian advance certainly lets everybody here and elsewhere in the Allied world breathe a little easier.

Yesterday while on pass, I heard about the Red advance in an interesting way. We went into a bookstore in a little French town, not too far from here. Before we had a chance to ask for anything, the young female proprietor took us to the back of the store, where there was a map. Then with many gesticulations she said, "Breslau boom! boom! boom! Oou la la!"

The French shortage of fuel, clothing, and cigarettes seems to be just as acute as the newspapers have intimated. American soldiers are forbidden to purchase any food from civilians in France. To do so is a court-martial offense. There are several signs in Rouen reminding GIs about this, but we tried anyway. We couldn't find a single café that was willing to serve us for love or money. All soldiers are required to go to the GI mess halls in these towns or eat Red Cross coffee and doughnuts all day, as we did. The Red Cross was the only heated building we entered all day. In all of the others, people were wearing several heavy sweaters, and the women wore heavy woolen stockings.

After one day in Rouen I can easily understand how a large-scale cigarette black market came into being here. Before leaving the States, I heard lots of stories about how girls were seduced with a pack of American cigarettes, and you could have the key to most towns for a pound of tea. It is damned near true.

Every tenth person you pass on the street, young or old, will ask you for a cigarette. Being a typical American who doesn't use his ration, I always give them one. Several very young children approached us outside of a school and offered us 50 francs, the equivalent of a dollar, for a pack. I'm sure that they wanted them only for their resale value. We went into a lingerie store that had a sign in the window—"English spoken." Gordon bought an article for his girl costing 240 francs, or about 5 dollars. He reached for his wallet to pay, and the salesgirl said she would rather settle for a pound of tea or coffee or six packs of cigarettes.

Perhaps the most worthwhile thing of the whole trip was that I was finally able to take a hot shower at the Red Cross and get a shampoo and a barbershop shave at a local barbershop. After trying to wash with salt water and later out of a helmet, I feel wonderful to be reasonably clean once again.

There were so many men waiting to take a shower that at no time during the day was there less than an hour's wait to get into the shower room. (You have to bring along your own towel and soap— the latter also being very scarce here.) The barbershop, like all the other shops in Rouen, was not heated. I almost froze while I had my hair shampooed, as the barber allowed himself only one pitcher of warm water for my head, and he used that very sparingly.

Of course, no trip to Rouen is complete during war or peace without a visit to its famous old cathedral. What a wreck! I'm sure they'll never again collect money in the States to rebuild the cathedral of Rouen, as they did after the last war. The cathedral,

Allied bombings almost totally destroyed the cathedral of Rouen, the site of Joan of Arc's trial. It has since been completely restored to its pre–World War II condition.

*although never directly hit by bombs, has been badly wrecked by the concussion, etc., from nearby hits. No windows are left. Many of the spires and much of the masonry work is lying on the ground. You are not allowed to enter, as the whole thing is standing only with the aid of scaffolds. Don't damn the Germans for this! It is all the work of our Army Air Corps, which I don't think makes us very popular in France. [**Britain's Royal Air Force was responsible for most of the destruction in Rouen, but I had no way of knowing that.**]*

*This second page of letter #14 should arrive home several days after the first since it left France three days later. The first time I wrote this page I criticized one of the generals in the ETO [**European Theater of Operations**], and I was forced to rewrite it because censorship rules forbid disparaging remarks about any high-ranking Allied officer. I thought one of the few privileges we have not relinquished to the government was the right to criticize our leaders.*

Somewhere in France
February 4, 1945
Dear Folks:

It looks like the Russians are still moving. Each time I pick up Stars and Stripes *and see that they have moved farther, my heart takes a little jump. Little as I am impressed with the Russian political and economic setup, the might of their military machine almost makes you forget about their past record and the records of the men in the Kremlin. [In February, 1945, notwithstanding the heavy aerial bombardment of cities and the intense ground combat along the western front, the Allies were unable to cross the Rhine River. At the same time, the Russians were meeting only limited resistance in their race to Berlin. Most of Poland's major cities fell to Soviet troops in January. By February they had also occupied Budapest.]*

Through "Snuffy" ["Snuffy" Rothman was a fellow member of the 1291st Medical Detachment], who has plenty of nerve and a talent for arranging deals, I am now getting laundry service. A French woman in a small nearby village washes and irons my clothes for a reasonable fee—providing I supply the soap. For a man as clumsy as myself, washing a suit of clothes in a helmet is much too difficult a job, at least while I still have "Snuffy" around.

Last night I saw my first movie in the ETO. Although I had to bring my own seat (my helmet) and keep my feet in an inch of mud, it was a pleasant change. The movie was an old one: "Ziegfield Follies," with Jimmy Stewart, Hedy Lamar, Lana Turner, and Judy Garland, but what Ziegfield, Lamar, and Turner have to offer the boys is ageless.

Although I haven't seen a new American movie since I left Camp Pickett, I still regularly hear the newest American songs. Every time you go into a French café with electric facilities, you hear a BBC broadcast on the radio. For our benefit they are usually playing the AEF [American Expeditionary Force] program, which always has the newest songs, news, sports reports, etc., from the States. On Sunday afternoons you can hear a transcription of last week's New York Philharmonic concert, just as if

While at Camp Lucky Strike, I was rarely, if ever, both dry and warm. Holding fifteen soldiers, the tents had a small coal stove in the middle.

you were back home. I am sure the French are listening to better radio programs than they ever heard before.

Recently I visited one of the most magnificent medieval Catholic churches I have ever seen. It was almost 500 feet long and 80 feet high and had remarkable sculptures and masonry work. It

*was in a rather poor state of repair, as are most other things I
have seen in northern France, but this was in much better shape
than anything else in town. Never have I seen so many beautiful
churches in such miserable, poor-looking hamlets. In the western
part of the States you see ghost towns built around empty mine
shafts. In France they are built around empty cathedrals.*

France
February 6, 1945
Dear Folks:

*Monday I received my first overseas pay of 1,709 francs, which
were exchanged at the rate of 49.5663 francs to the dollar. Of
course I was very glad to get paid but very much annoyed about
the way the whole thing was handled. We were not paid any frac-
tional part of francs. Each man was paid to the nearest whole
franc. Did you ever hear of a business that rounded salaries to the
nearest even cent, times five million, times twelve? However you
figure it, that is poor business. The racetracks pay to the nearest
dime. Army pay isn't as good as a pari-mutuel machine.*

France
February 11, 1945
Dear Folks:

*Another day, another day, another day, and each one is like the
preceding one. The only difference is that on Monday it rained all
morning and in the early evening. On Tuesday it rained in the
afternoon and late at night. On Wednesday it rained every alter-
nate hour morning, noon, and night. The result is always the
same—mud.*

*The drinking situation here is really a sad one. Postprohibition
Americans have been brought up on hard whiskey and powerful
beer. The only drinkable stuff that the Wehrmacht has left in
France cannot satisfy those tastes. The only things you can buy in
most cafés are almost nonalcoholic beer and cider, which tastes
like vinegar. In some of the cafés in larger towns you can buy
poor-grade cognac and calvados, which is similar to our apple-
jack but tastes like a combination of Listerine and ether. However,*

it seems that the GIs finally invented something that satisfies their tastes in the form of "beer avec cognac," which consists of a cordial glass of cognac in a glass of beer. There is so little to do that the drinking problem is a real one over here. More than one soldier has wrecked his guts with some foul French concoction of methyl alcohol and fermented apples.

Somewhere in France
February 17, 1945
Dear Folks:

Since my last letter, I have moved for the first time since my arrival. Security regulations forbid my speculating about the desirability of our new assignment, but I can say that the living conditions are vastly superior. We are now living in a stone barrack in a sizeable town that was built in medieval times. The barracks have served a variety of uses including the housing of French cavalry units before the war and, more recently, the German army of occupation. Although we sleep on the floor and have very few conveniences, we are not bothered by mud, moisture, and erratic fire. My stock is going up.

Today I received three very interesting letters from old William and Mary friends in the 95th Infantry Division. None of them contained much good news. I heard from Hicks, who is still alive and in good shape as a Pfc. in an antitank company, Fletcher Cox (he typed the "Flat Hat" and was one of my good friends), who is a private driving a truck, and George May (Huntington School, Amherst, etc.), who is a corporal in the field artillery. Their letters contained the following interesting information: Barry (he was at the house in July) was awarded the Silver Star for individually knocking out a German machine gun. Dick Fowler, Bob Holland, and Lou Besenzie were good friends of mine who were killed in the course of the 95th's action this fall. One of our old crowd is now a first sergeant in an infantry company, and several others have received promotions. Although I'm glad I didn't have to do the fighting the 95th did, in many ways I wish I had been able to see service with those men I liked so much.

We considered the reinforcement depot at Chartres, France, luxury living even though we slept on the floor and the facility had no indoor plumbing. The building had been constructed in the early nineteenth century for French soldiers and housed German occupation troops until 1944.

France
February 19, 1945
Dear Folks:

My last letter was quite complete so there is very little of interest to tell you in this letter except that I am thinking of you, and:

*1. Tell **Aunt Eva** that I am thinking of her in her days of illness. If I have time, I will write to her.*

*2. Daddy's letter **m**entioned my friend **O**scar and his **v**ery good grades, **e**tc. It was **d**ecided by our **c**rowd that regardless **h**ow little he **a**pplies himself to **r**esearch or tries **t**o play the **r**egular guy he **e**nds up the **s**tar student.*
MOVED CHARTRES

Somewhere in France
February 21, 1945
Dear Folks:

Since we moved last week, life has improved in every way. Not only are our living quarters superior, but the town in which we are stationed is very pleasant, complete with an enlisted men's club, showers operated by the quartermaster corps, and a theater. It is wonderful the pleasure I get these days out of simple things like a cup of coffee, a shower, and a theater.

The QM showers were the first things we visited after we came here. They were great. Do you remember when you had to practically force me to wash and take a shower? Now a shower has become a great pleasure, not only because of its physical value, but probably more so because of its psychological value. Filth has plagued armies since biblical times. Although today we have new cures for the diseases of filth, one cannot help but keep thinking about them. In town they also have a public bathtub house for use by U.S. Forces. I expect to use it before we leave. What an indulgence!

The EM club is really quite nice and attractive. It is the first place for soldiers I have seen in France that is open to "U.S. forces only," not all Allied soldiers. It is run by the U.S. government and a French welcome committee. They serve beer (the poor French variety), coffee, and sandwiches. These are sold for very nominal prices and occasionally are given away when they have profits to divide. They have several French hostesses who come each night and help to make the place a little more attractive. Although most of them talk very little English, it is really quite pleasant to talk to some girls who do not fall into the category of the females who hang around cafés and talk to soldiers.

France
February 23, 1945
Dear Folks:

There is very little to tell you as I wrote you earlier in the morning, but I just received Daddy's letter and want to acknowledge it while I have the time and inclination. Several things interested me:

1. The news that __Aunt Eva__ is improving was of course very welcome.

2. The paragraph __D__addy wrote about __i__nvestigating yellow dog __c__ontracts, etc., at __K__enyon was of __p__articular interest today __a__s I just __r__eceived another letter __i__nforming that all __s__tockholders and capital in general were all wrong. Laissez-faire capitalism and democracy must always go hand in hand. They are interdependent.

P.S. Went to the hospital today and found that Dick L. is not far from here. With good luck we may be able to get together.
<u>DICK PARIS</u>
[My chum Dick Levy was stationed in Paris.]

Somewhere in France
February 25, 1945
Dear Folks:
*   You know how much I enjoy a tub bath and how happy I was when I found they had baths in town for the use of U.S. forces*

Public baths, where my friends and I bathed, were available to all U.S. soldiers when we arrived in Chartres. Within a few days, this sign was changed to "For U.S. Officers Only."

only. Two days ago I went to the bathhouse and soaked for a half hour in a hot tub and spent one of the most pleasant afternoons I've spent in France.

Yesterday I went to the "bains" to do the same thing again and found a big sign on the door "U.S. Officers Only." There was no explanation except that there was an hour's wait the last time I was there. Of course, officers are the only persons allowed to go out with nurses and _____ [deleted by censor]. You'll never convince me that this sort of thing is right. You'll never get a moment of my time or a cent of my money for any club or service for "officers only."

France
March 1, 1945
Dear Folks:

The colored situation, which I have come in contact with over here, is in many ways much more acute than most people at home realize. Twice I have been stationed near towns where there were almost no black women and lots of colored American soldiers. With a pocketful of money and the French attitude toward colored soldiers, they have no trouble making it with the white women. I need not tell you about the resentment that follows. For a while we worked with the colored troops, and the resentment was real and bitter. **[Domestic Army camps and overseas reinforcement depots were de facto segregated. The white soldiers with whom I was segregated had few meaningful contacts with black soldiers. However, racial tensions were real on the streets and in the barrooms of France. Black soldiers' successes with French women—real or imagined—caused the resentment. For most of the soldiers, the notion of interracial socializing was new, shocking, and disturbing. Such mixing was unknown in their hometowns. Even though Northern states did not have Jim Crow statutes in 1945, many still had miscegenation laws. Ratcheting up the level of resentment were the constantly repeated canards about the sexual propensities of black men and the profligacy of French women.]**

CHAPTER 6

WAGING WAR
AGAINST THE FRENCH

PETROLEUM PRODUCTS represented roughly half of the tonnage carried to Europe to supply American troops in World War II. Shortly after D-Day, military engineers began constructing an above-ground gasoline pipeline to guarantee a reliable, steady flow to Allied armies. Tankers offloaded at a floating dock at the Atlantic Ocean port of Cherbourg. The pipeline's final decanting terminal constantly moved eastward as American and British forces advanced toward Hitler's Third Reich. It crossed the Rhine River on the first pontoon bridge shortly after the Corps of Engineers completed its construction. The U.S. Army's gasoline pipeline was one of its most vital war facilities—and it was regularly sabotaged by the French.

As a member of a pipeline pumping-station crew, I observed firsthand how effectively French saboteurs, both amateur and professional, slowed the forward progress of America's armies. My comrades and I watched the Meuse-Argonne region's peasant farmers hamper the operations of one of the mightiest fighting machines ever assembled. From our perspective, they were "the enemy."

The pipeline's above-ground construction made it a tempting target for both Nazi agents and petty crooks. Stealing gasoline was easy. The only tools required were a small monkey wrench and a butter knife. Breaks happened almost daily, sometimes several times a day. Almost all of the major ruptures occurred after a Frenchman failed to properly close a coupling he had loosened to steal "a little essence." ("Essence" is the French word for "gasoline.") Crooks and saboteurs had the same ruse; they needed a few gallons for an essential tractor. Still, virtually all of the soldiers who were assigned to pipeline duty believed most of the French peasants were Nazi sympathizers or, at best, black marketers who did not care that their stealing hurt America's war effort. We despised them. And the dislike was mutual. Most of the pipeline's neighbors appeared to prefer the Germans to us.

Pipeline breaks were a serious problem. Several times in the course of the war gasoline shortages halted major troop movements. A total rupture often meant a loss of ten thousand gallons and the shutdown of pumping operations for at least an hour. Many of the breaks created gasoline geysers. A lighted cigarette near a geyser could (and did) set homes ablaze and kill innocent people. Medics, like me, were assigned to pipeline companies because of the fire danger. There were many serious fires along the pipeline's route, but to my knowledge, none of them was ever reported in the American press.

The importance of petroleum distribution in World War II is discussed in more than a dozen official Department of Defense documents available at the Library of Congress, National Archives, and the Center for Military History in Washington. However, gasoline is usually treated as just another commodity—albeit a very important one—in a vast, complex, worldwide military supply system. While military historians agree that pipelines laid on top of the ground are vulnerable to sabotage, there is almost no literature on control procedures other than surveillance.

Extensive research over several years confirms that this is probably the first published commentary on how French sabotage curtailed the U.S. Army's efforts to get gasoline to its combat troops in a timely manner. The fact that this important story has remained untold for six decades is partially attributable to World War II military censorship and partially to the dynamics of journalism. Pipeline soldiers were not allowed to reveal in letters home their location, their work routines, or the names of their comrades. Since dismantling began a few days after V-E Day, the details of pipeline operations were "ancient history" by the time censorship restrictions were lifted.

War correspondents considered supply services stories dull. At best, coverage was superficial and irregular. The only European Theater pipeline story that received extensive newspaper coverage was the disclosure shortly after V-E Day that the United States had placed a flexible pipeline under the English Channel. Although we did not know it, some of the gasoline we moved across central France was off-loaded from tankers in England. Oil-industry trade journals, particularly the weekly *National Petroleum News,* assigned reporters to cover petroleum's role in winning the war. However, they covered the entire industry from domestic finance, drilling, and refining to the availability of ship dockage, tanker airplanes, rail depots, decanting centers, storage facilities, and construction operations in Europe. The Cherbourg-to-the-Rhine pipeline was only a part of the oil-industry story.

When it was running at full capacity, more than a half million gallons a day moved through the pipeline. Pumping stations were set up ten to thirty miles apart, depending on the terrain and the proximity of population centers. I worked at a pumping station in the Meuse-Argonne region near Verdun, France, a city of twenty thousand, made famous as the site of World War I's costliest battle, in which seven hundred thousand soldiers were killed or wounded. Most of the pipeline was laid a few feet from the Red Ball Highway, the main supply route connecting France's Atlantic ports to General Patton's Third Army. This made most of the pipeline's route easy to construct and patrol.

Almost all of the sabotage occurred along detours away from the Red Ball Highway. The line was rerouted in the Meuse-Argonne region to avoid both the city of Verdun and the major ammunition depot located nearby. Pipelines do not rupture naturally. Only human hands can loosen steel couplings and move rubber gaskets. Often when we patrolled the pipeline we would notice a local peasant tinkering with a coupling.

Station 53 on the U.S. Army's pipeline from Cherbourg harbor on the Atlantic Coast to the Rhine River consisted of four tents, an operations shack (which also served as a parts warehouse), and two lines of pumps. Soldiers slept in three of the tents. The fourth was a mess tent with a table at which we wrote letters and played cards between meals. German prisoners of war built the operations shack and fencing.

When our patrol came along, he usually fled but almost always left behind a partially closed coupling, which our station crew promptly closed. If he fled before we saw where he was working, sometime within the next few hours or days an "unexplained" break would occur.

Sixteen men were assigned to our station: twelve laborer-roustabouts who patrolled the pipeline and kept the pumps and engines running, a clerk, boss (sergeant), cook, and medic (me). The nearest hard-surfaced road was seven miles distant, and the nearest commissioned officer, a lieutenant (an oil-field construction foreman in civilian life), was thirty miles away in Chalons-sur-Marne. Prisoners of war relieved us of distasteful chores such as periodically cleaning the latrine, moving heavy equipment, and building the pipeline infrastructure. The roustabouts' chief job was to keep the French peasantry from hampering our operation.

The pipeline crew's frustration extended beyond anger with our French neighbors who were helping the Nazis. We also resented the fact that we could do nothing about their subversion. We knew who the regular culprits were. Certain peasants in nearby villages brazenly sold pilfered gasoline. Black markets operated openly. French locals knew that no one was ever arrested or punished for pipeline tampering or trafficking in petroleum products. We thought saboteurs should be arrested and jailed at the very least. However, we had orders to try to get along with the French peasants, regardless of their hostile activities. The headquarters brass wanted it to appear that everything was going smoothly between the liberating U.S. Army and the French citizenry. The public trial of a few big-time pipeline saboteurs who claimed to be simple farmers might have had serious international-relations repercussions. We, of course, did not see the big picture. Allowing saboteurs to operate with impunity made no sense to us.

The soldier-roustabouts at Pumping Station 53 did not know that France's rampant—and unofficially sanctioned—black markets were a big-time problem for Allied commanders. Gasoline was only a small part of a vast problem involving U.S.

military supplies and French ethics. The trouble was rarely, if ever, covered in our only news source, the irregularly delivered *Stars and Stripes*. On the home front, the *New York Times* in March, 1945 (while I was working on the pipeline), ran a major war-zone story headlined "Black Markets Strong in Liberated Countries." The article points out that a democratically elected government had collapsed in nearby Belgium because it tried to crack down on black-market activities. It further reports that in Paris "illegal markets have gained such standing that they flourish under the eyes of bored gendarmes."

The pipeline crew's dislike of their French neighbors was exacerbated by what they viewed as a double standard of justice. If an American GI was caught stealing from a local shop, he was routinely disciplined or even court-martialed if an item of great value was involved (though the latter rarely occurred). At the same time, when the French stole large amounts of vital war matériel of strategic, as well as monetary value, it was "policy" to pretend the stealing did not happen. Although the geography and cultures are different, the problems of controlling theft and looting in Afghanistan and Iraq are similar. The U.S. Army has no difficulty disciplining its own troops, but it has big problems stopping thievery by "liberated" peoples.

The bitter, tense relationship between the local peasants and the American GIs at a small outpost in rural France reflected ambivalence at the apex of political power. France's last elected government fled in June, 1940, and the provisional administration that governed the country was headed by an obscure, lower-echelon general named Charles de Gaulle. That government got its limited legitimacy from the Allied High Command, not from the French electorate. On the other hand, the U.S. Army represented itself as a friendly force sent to France to liberate an enslaved people from tyranny. In reality, our Army conducted itself like a hostile occupying force. We randomly killed thousands of civilians through artillery barrages and aerial bombings. We expropriated for our exclusive use France's railroads, highways, harbors, warehouses, farms, and, very importantly, hospitals.

In middle-sized cities such as Verdun, Metz, and Chalons-sur-Marne, the U.S. Army took over the only local hospital to care for its wounded soldiers. I regularly picked up medical supplies, including substantial quantities of morphine, at the 193rd General Hospital, a fully staffed military hospital that occupied the buildings that had been Verdun's municipal hospital. When Verdun became part of a U.S. combat zone, all of the French patients (except those in extremis) were summarily displaced to make way for battlefield casualties. As long as the war went on, virtually no hospital service was available for the region's civilian population. As an Army medic who had access to drugs and supplies, I was often asked to deal with the Meuse-Argonne peasantry's medical problems. Although I was embarrassed that, after four months of superficial, first aid–type training, truly sick people thought I could help with their health issues—including some that were gynecological—I freely dispensed drugs and bandages, which I could requisition (without limit) at the 193rd General Hospital. I helped the farm families who lived near Pumping Station 53, but for most of the area residents, the loss of their hospital just meant still more pain and suffering attributable to the Americans.

In an environment without service stations, a novel petroleum-distribution system was required to transfer more than half a million gallons of gasoline daily to individual vehicles. All of the automotive gasoline that small trucks and jeeps used in France during the war (actually, 97 percent according to *National Petroleum News*) was poured by hand into the vehicles' gas tanks from five-gallon jerry cans (box-shaped cans with grab handles and a small spout). The ubiquitous jerry cans were filled at decanting stations that the Quartermaster Corps operated at regular intervals along the pipeline. In combat zones, thousands of jerry cans were lined up along the roads or at special dumps. Every jeep had at least one can strapped to its rear end so that it could fill up when it ran low on gas. Trucks and ambulances routinely carried several. We kept several dozen fulls at our pumping station, so vehicles were always ready to travel long distances. In the eleven months between D-Day and V-E Day, more than fifteen million jerry cans arrived in France.

Most farmers' barns contained at least a half dozen jerry cans. Since they were not for sale, they could have been obtained in only one way. GIs routinely accepted petty stealing as part of the war. However, interrupting the flow of vital fuel to our combat troops was different. It was not petty. It was important. And both the American soldiers and the French farmers knew it.

Even though the top-level brass did virtually nothing to discourage or impede the black market in gasoline, its position on ammunition, guns, and explosives was quite different. If Nazi sympathizers in the area—and there were many—had gotten their hands on a cache of ammunition or explosives, the results might have been disastrous. Only well-credentialed American soldiers with proper requisition documents could get inside an ammunition depot. I periodically went with our truck to Verdun's Douamont Depot. (Pumps, valves, welding equipment, and grinding tools were classified as the type of war materiel that should be stored at an ammunition depot.) Douamont Depot operated with several levels of security checks, similar to today's metropolitan airports. Located in a French military cemetery where 130,000 World War I soldiers remain buried, Douamont was one of the largest ammunition depots in Europe. Tightly fenced, it was vast and hilly with lots of statuary and chapels, but no living inhabitants. It was an ideal site for ammunition storage. Modern armies do not store ammunition in urban areas, where a single great explosion can start an uncontrollable fire or destroy other military facilities in a chain reaction. In piles the size of railroad cars, war materiel—shells, grenades, rifles, gas masks, and car parts—were segregated by size and special features. Each item was at a marked location on a cemetery road.

Our peasant neighbors made no secret of the fact that they liked their German "occupiers" better than us. In Jubecourt-en-Argonne, a hamlet of twenty to thirty homes near our pumping station, several farmers enthusiastically explained to

Hanlon Waters pumps drove the gasoline pipeline.

me how the village had benefited from Nazi occupation. On a nearby hillside the German government had built for them prefabricated chicken coops and metal silos. These bare-metal farm buildings were part of the Nazi's plan to make Europe agriculturally self-sufficient.

In World War I, the Kaiser's legions were primarily interested in military objectives, and they ended up having to ship food-stuffs to occupied lands at great cost. Hitler's farm-finance planners did not intend to repeat that mistake. Their agriculture program for occupied lands was designed to keep conquered countries happy, while adding to workers' food baskets in the "Fatherland." In the long run, French farm production was expected to play a major role in the "Thousand Year Reich." In the short run, the program had great propaganda value. Nazi broadcasters explained in French that the Allies were trying to starve the peoples of occupied Europe by harassing ships carrying food supplies from neutral countries. Notwithstanding the "heartless Americans," German largesse and ingenuity were allowing them to eat well. The Germans envisioned France as part of a pan-European Reich. Nazi agricultural advisors in the pipeline's area spoke fluent French and lived with the local people. They fled eastward as the Allied armies advanced toward the Rhine, but they left behind friends and lovers who saw us as hostile occupiers.

The Meuse-Argonne agricultural "dictator" supplied the peasants with seed and fertilizer. He told them when to furrow and plant, how much land to use for each crop, and when to harvest. The peasants thus lost their freedom of choice. However, for Jubecourt's humble villagers, "freedom of choice" was an irrelevant abstraction. They admired the authoritarian system that made them more productive, better farmers. We Americans, on the other hand, ruined their fields with spilled gasoline. We compensated them handsomely for the damage done to their land, but they had little use for money. Their lives were their farms.

In addition to fresh eggs (which we traded for coffee grounds and cigarettes), our isolated location provided us with an additional dietary luxury: fresh fish. Carbine fishing was one of our favorite forms of entertainment. Every member of the station crew (except the medic) kept a loaded carbine and a box of ammunition under his cot. In the afternoons we would often sit by a nearby stream with our rifles and shoot at edible-sized fish swimming just below the surface.

On May 8, 1945, V-E Day, I contrived to pick up supplies at Verdun's Army hospital so that I could see—and participate in—the celebration. It was a frustrating day. V-E Day meant peace for the French, but it signified little to us. Most GIs believed that within a few months we would find ourselves shipped to the Pacific theater, where there had been few important American victories—and enormous casualties. On V-E Day, American forces were struggling against an entrenched Japanese army on Okinawa. In that siege, thirteen thousand U.S. soldiers and marines were killed, and forty thousand were wounded. The war against the Japanese was "our war," not theirs. Even the French seemed unenthusiastic about V-E Day. There were few French battlefield victories to celebrate. The American soldiers I talked with at the Verdun Red Cross resented the fact that the high command ordered them to participate in provincial V-E Day parades. We knew that notwithstanding the heroism of a few Free French Army units, France's military contribution to Hitler's defeat was insignificant. We also knew that our Jubecourt neighbors would be happy to see the U.S. Army leave France. Relations were so strained, they did not care if we went to Germany, Burma, an unknown Pacific island, or home to the United States—just so long as we left.

It is not surprising that hostility still lurks deep in the psyches of both young French citizens and young Americans. The success of the gasoline-pipeline system in Europe, of which General Eisenhower was so proud, was achieved despite constant French sabotage. Every soldier who worked on the pipeline knew why there were regular breaks, and he detested the people who were responsible. On the other hand, the Verdun region's peasants did not like their American "liberators" whom they viewed as insensitive foreign occupiers who befouled their farms with spilled gasoline and forced their sick relatives to leave hospital wards prematurely.

France
March 7, 1945
Dear Folks:
Just returned from the theater, where they put on one of the best USO shows I have seen since I entered the Army. The show consisted of a quintet (a cellist, flutist, pianist, and violinist),

plus a baritone and soprano, and all the music was high-grade, good stuff.

Singer Sewing Machines is one of the American products that you see advertised in every village and hamlet in France. In the town in which I am now stationed, the company has a building of its own.

From your letters I gather that you think I am eating poorly over here. Such is not the case. Although we have only dehydrated eggs, milk, and sometimes potatoes, in general our chow is the best I have had since I entered the Army. Of course, over here I have no choice but to eat GI food.

During the past year I have produced and accomplished absolutely nothing. I can think of nothing that I did for myself or the Army, outside of seeing all the new movies, reading a few books, and writing a few letters. If I had learned to fight or build bridges or drink or play cards, it would have been something. Even if I had been up at the front covered with mud I might feel differently. All I did was train and train and train. For what????

France
March 11, 1945
Dear Folks:

I shall begin by telling you what little I am able to tell you about my change of address. The initials "EPD" stand for "engineer petroleum distribution." What little I know about the meaning of that title I cannot tell you at present. From reading one or two of the articles recently published in some of the popular magazines about the part of EPD companies in the war in bringing gasoline from the sea to the front you can probably learn more than I know at this moment. I can however say that I am still a good safe distance from shell fire.

Once again we have changed our quarters, but so far I cannot register any gripes about that. We are still living on cots in a stone building and near a fair-sized town. Although we haven't been here long enough for me to make any interesting observations, I have seen enough GIs on the street to know that the local populace doesn't welcome us with open arms.

Yesterday I sent you under separate cover some of my pictures, negatives, postcards, etc. A very poor job was done in developing these pictures, and they were printed on inferior paper. I took several more interesting pictures, but censorship regulations prevent my sending them at this time.

Tonight when I went to the EM club, I was rather amazed when I saw a kid who didn't look more than six years old in a complete U.S. uniform with shiny paratrooper's boots. I stared at him for a while and was finally convinced that he was not old enough to be in the Army. Then I asked some questions. He was a Sicilian orphan who had been picked up by the paratroopers as a mascot when the U.S. forces invaded that island. They have taken him on every invasion since then. He now speaks very good English and has probably received the kind of broad education one gets only in a barracks room or barroom filled with paratroopers. Now he is the mascot not only of a few soldiers stationed in this vicinity but also of a whole enlisted men's club.

France
March 15, 1945
Dear Folks:

Today I have very few anxieties and am making no speculations about my future. I have fallen into that great wide rut along with the schoolteacher and bookkeeper who live life knowing that there will always be food on the table and that they will be paid regularly. Maybe something will come along someday to add a little spice to their mundane existence. On these days when men are getting their heads blown off not too far away, maybe that's a lucky break—particularly so if you've learned to be a bureaucrat or a pedagogue.

France
March 18, 1945
Dear Folks:

It looks like I have finally gotten a permanent assignment (subject to immediate change without notice). Although hardly the kind of job I expected to be doing when I left the States, it is

A soldier's helmet was his washbasin, bathtub, and shower. At Station 53 we built a washstand. After filling your helmet with hot water in the mess tent, you placed it on this stand so it did not roll away when in use. A metal mirror was the extension. In the background is a small portion of the station's jerry can inventory.

much more pleasant and safe than the one that I looked forward to a few months ago. I am now living with a dozen men at a lonely gasoline pumping station on our pipeline. Although there is a little village of about one hundred inhabitants near us, we are seven miles from the main road.

Not only does my job call for traveling to two of the nearby pumping stations every day or so and dispensing iodine, cough medicine, aspirin, etc., but I have also been asked to give some of the same services to a few civilians in the nearby village. When some of the civilians first came up to our tents to try to sell us fresh eggs and beg for our garbage and leftovers, the men introduced me as "le docteur."

Immediately I was shown a few cuts and bruises, on which I put iodine. Today a young woman came up and asked my advice about a rash on her thigh, which she showed to about half the personnel of this station. I am glad to help them with a little iodine, etc., but I want them to understand (and with my limited knowledge of French, this is difficult) that I am only a first-aid man and not a doctor before they think I ought to know something about obstetrics and assist the local midwife.

France
March 23, 1945
Dear Folks:

I wrote you a longer letter earlier today, and as a result, I have very little to say at this time. However, the two following items came to my mind, and I wanted to write them down before I forgot them.

1. Please send me **Aunt Eva's** address, as I would like to write her a note during her illness.

2. It's been **v**ery difficult for **E**dward to write **r**eplies to the **d**eluge of very **u**nique cards you **n**icely sent him while he was in the hospital in England. He wrote me and told me to thank you until he has time to write you personally.

VERDUN

[Pipeline station 53 was approximately fifteen miles from Verdun.]

France
March 30, 1945
Dear Folks:

What was originally page #2 of this letter must be left out. My censor and I do not exactly agree on "the spirit of the law."

A few nights past I spoke with some local Frenchmen. Whenever they asked me where I came from in America, I told them that I come from Philadelphia. Not a single one had ever heard of it. (That is almost as bad as the Camp Pickett telephone operator who asked me, "Philadelphia, where?") They seem to know the names of only three cities in America: New York, Hollywood, and Reno. **[Reno was notorious in the 1930s as a quickie divorce center.]**

The last one is the direct result of the very smooth propaganda that the Nazis fed to the populace, which is predominantly Catholic. All of the stories that the OWI **[Office of War Information, America's propaganda and information agency]** *has produced about the sexual depravity of the Germans have been more than matched by Dr. Goebbels and his assistants. In the popular magazines published here during the occupation, articles regularly appeared about the "victory girls" in the States. The Nazis wanted the French to think they are the rule, not the exception.* **["Victory girls" were American teenagers, usually high-school girls, who made a public display of seeking out GIs for sex. They urged others to join them in doing their patriotic duty.]**

France
March 25, 1945
Dear Folks:

In one of Mother's recent letters, she asked what I thought about our present system of her writing via V-mail and Daddy airmail and if I had any suggestions. I do. After watching the way mail is handled in the Army and the number of hands that handle it, I have now come to the conclusion that airmail is superior to V-mail. In the ETO they no longer put envelopes on the

V-letters, but a little paste on the side when they fold them. Of course, it takes just the least little jerk to open them, and I don't like my mail from home made semipublic. **[Correspondence between the United States and servicemen overseas was delivered and written in two different formats. V-mail—a system of microfilming mail at the point of origin and printing in reduced size at the place of delivery—was the format the Army preferred. The other was regular letter paper and envelopes. V-mail stationery was available at no cost at post offices and public facilities in the United States. It was distributed to soldiers along with their tobacco and candy rations. V-mail cut delivery time and reduced the amount of shipping space required for mail. It took thirty-seven mail bags to carry the 150,000 microfilmed letters that filled a single mail sack. The numbers thus tell the importance of V-mail. More than one billion V-mail letters were microfilmed between 1942 and 1945.]**

Since we have moved out to this (deleted by censor), we have fried eggs for breakfast every morning. I can't tell you what a big fuss we made over this rather simple luxury the first morning we had them. We secure them by trading our coffee grounds after we have used them—or an orange or a piece of bread and jam, etc.— with the village children for eggs, which they probably steal from a neighbor's henhouse. I almost had some fresh milk, too, when I went to visit a local home, where they were putting raw milk through a separating machine. However, just before I got ready to ask for a glass, a cat who I had just seen in a manure pile climbed into the milk bucket and put both feet into the milk. I decided to wait a little longer. If I were to describe some of the French sanitary conditions I've seen, I could even outdo Steinbeck's description of latrines.

In one of Daddy's recent letters he suggested that when I get to Paris I stop in and see his friend Colonel Middleton, just as if a pass to Paris was like one from Camp Pickett to Philadelphia. Paris passes are rationed. They are given almost exclusively to combat troops.

Somewhere in France
March 31, 1945
Dear Folks:

The way our officers are interpreting the censorship rules to-day, it is next to impossible for me to tell you anything about myself except that I am healthy and more or less happy.

Recently a very interesting article appeared in the Saturday Evening Post, *which discusses the ways in which Germany tried to make Europe self-supporting in agriculture. The author says that our Army is not the only one that has a battery of economic and agricultural advisors who follow right behind the combat troops; the "Boches"* **[the name the French gave the Nazis]** *did it first. You do not notice these things if you are hurrying or are near a large town where there are plenty of cafés to haunt. But we are living near a very small farm village, and it is very apparent there. You walk down the one street, and all you see is dilapi-dated old homes and barns—not to mention the manure piles next to the front doorstep. However, when you look out on two nearby hills you can see several barns and chicken coops that look very modern and well kept. After a little questioning you always get the same answer—Boches. I have walked up close to these modern barns. They are all made of prefabricated stuff. It's a funny war.*

Economics professors spend hours and hours drawing curves and graphs to explain the laws of supply and demand to their students. If those professors could come out here and watch the ef-fect of the French black market on the value of our PX rations, they could conduct a week of classes here.

When we first came over here, the men had rather full supplies of cigarettes from the States or the boat, where their value was al-most the same as their price on the ship. Men were trading two packs of cigarettes for one bar of candy as candy bars were rare at that time. Then European-Theater rationing started. Now each man gets seven packs of cigarettes, four bars of candy, and one pack of gum. The soldiers buy them for cost (cigarettes are 2.5 francs per pack, or five cents). The French are usually willing to pay 100 francs for a pack of cigarettes and 30 to 40 francs for a bar of candy. The result is that the men now consider cigarettes more valuable. GIs now will pay 40 or 50 francs when they exchange cigarettes among themselves. That is their real value.

Somewhere in France
April 2, 1945
Dear Folks:

Although Passover has come and almost gone without my observing it in any of the formal ways that are traditionally and wonderfully Jewish, I do not want to let it pass without a word to all of you whom I love so much and think of so often.

I felt bad about missing Seder not only because it was Seder and I wanted to attend the ceremony, but also because I missed the opportunity of celebrating an important Jewish holiday with other Jews away from home. The farther away from home most Jewish soldiers get and the more they think about this war, all wars, how ephemeral the lives of nations are, the more their Judaism means to them and the prouder of it they become. Regardless of how obnoxious you may think some of our coreligionists from South Street and Brooklyn are when you are secure at home, your attitude changes when you find yourself somewhat lost and far from home.

Somewhere in France
April 6, 1945
Dear Folks:

Several of the clippings Daddy sent me about France make special mention of the critical food shortage here and the resultant "marché noir." When you talk to Frenchmen in the little farm villages around here, you find that one of the chief things that impresses them about the United States, aside from the laxity of our divorce laws, is the laxity of our rationing system. Every time you tell them about our rationing, their answer is always "No restriction." It's hard for Americans to realize how little the French get under their present rationing system. Maybe this will give you some idea:

Civilian barbershops in France were segregated. They served either officers or enlisted men. This sign was on a street in Reims.

4 packages of cigarettes per month for <u>males</u> over 18

1 bar of soap about the size of a bar of a "P&G" for ten people for a month *["P&G" stood for Proctor and Gamble, a popular soap brand in the 1940s.]*

1 shave stick for six months

Less than half a pound of coffee per month

One-half pound of sugar per month

No chocolate, etc., is available, except for sweet little girls who say "bon-bon" to sentimental American soldiers. The food items of the U.S. Army that they seem to desire most are sugar, coffee, flour, and tobacco. The small quantities of these products that they get through rationing are very inferior to ours. The sugar and flour are much rougher in texture and darker in color than ours. The coffee really tastes like hell. If an American at home gripes about rationing to a person who has seen European rationing, I'm sure he'll laugh in their face.

France
April 5, 1945
Dear Folks:

You'll never guess what I had to drink this evening. Not whiskey, not gin, not calvados, not beer, but good, old-fashioned Coca-Cola in the bottle that's made to fit the hand. Just a few moments before we left our staging area in the States to board the bus to the ship, Nick Placenta and I bought two cokes. We drank them to the next time we'd be drinking bottled cokes, believing that would be back in the USA. But not so. As part of our PX ration this week, each man received two cokes, for which he paid 4 francs *[10 cents]*. Although some people may debate whether rye or bourbon is America's national drink, when I saw the excitement caused by a case of cokes and heard the remarks about "the corner drugstore," I do not think calling it the "national drink" is too strong.

France
April 7, 1945

Dear Folks:

Last night I went into the nearest city for the first time in three weeks. Although the GI Special Service movie unit had moved up into Germany and the only place you could buy anything tolerable to drink was at a bar "for American officers only," I had a rather good time just spending the evening in town. Although I gripe about many things out here, I realize that if I was in Burma or the South Pacific, the bars would still be for "officers only," but the EM wouldn't even have a town to mill about in. Boredom is far superior to bullets, so with only those two alternatives, I'm glad to settle for the former.

*My friend Gerald Clark has gone to Infantry OCS here in France. He was admitted just a little more than a month after he filed his application. Infantry second lieutenants are quite expendable. It looks like they need them quite badly. I am glad Clark went. He always wanted to go to OCS, having a respect for military rank and being ambitious to succeed in the Army. And you know what killed Caesar. [**In Shakespeare's Julius Caesar (3.2), Brutus says, "As he was ambitious I slew him. . . . Joy for his fortune; honour for his valour; and death for his ambition."**]*

France
April 10, 1945

Dear Folks:

Once upon a time it was a real pleasure to write home and to my friends and tell them what I was doing and what I thought, etc., but with the present security regulations in force it is almost a chore. With our present, rather dull life, it is quite difficult to write an interesting letter home and not catch hell from the powers that be. The result to date has been both dull letters and lectures, but . . .

You may have wondered what happened to Yoffy and Perlmutter, who attended our Seder last year. Yoffy is in New Guinea with a field artillery battalion. Perlmutter was killed in

*action with the 95th Division during the winter. [**In the spring
of 1944, when I was part of the 95th Infantry Division at
Indiantown Camp, Pennsylvania, less than one hundred miles
from Philadelphia, I invited two Jewish soldiers in my unit to
share our Passover Seder.]***

*One of the interesting things I've noticed in these little country
villages of France is the popularity of the letter V for "victory"
sign made with the fore and second fingers of the right hand.
While at home, I saw Churchill do it in the movies, but that's
about all. When our truck rides through these little villages, we
wave to people, and a large percentage of them (particularly children) stand in their doorways and give us the V sign. I don't
know what the explanation is. My guess is that it is a holdover
from the days when they raised their right arms and said, "Heil
Hitler" every time an Army vehicle passed.*

**France
April 13, 1945**
Dear Folks:

*Today we along with the rest of the world were shocked by the
news of President Roosevelt's death at Warm Springs. The Paris
edition of the* Stars and Stripes *published an extra, but aside
from that there was very little fuss made about it by our unit or
any of the soldiers I saw during the day.*

*However, for the first time in a month I visited one of the larger
French towns in the vicinity and found several shop windows, etc.,
with FDR's picture surrounded by crepe. There is no doubt that
the French lost a real friend.*

**France
April 14, 1945**
Dear Folks:

*Today I entered a synagogue for the first time since we all went
together in Philadelphia last December. I didn't pray, I didn't
speak to the rabbi, I just looked around, thought, and took a few
pictures. I had inquired at the hospital about the general location
of the synagogue. Then I spent most of the morning looking for it.*

On April 14, 1945, a Verdun shopkeeper publicly expresses his mourning for the death of Franklin D. Roosevelt, who had passed away two days earlier. In the spring of 1945, there were many more American soldiers than civilians on the streets of Verdun—and GIs had money to spend.

Verdun, the site of the most famous battle of World War I, was a GI town. Here, on April 14, 1945, American and French flags are draped with black crepe.

I passed it a few times, as the three front windows all had five pointed stars in them.

It is located in what I believe was once the finest section (within a block of the Palais de Justice and what Clara McLaughlin [author of French guidebooks] calls "the best hotel" of a town with a population of between twenty and thirty thousand people. It is set back from the street about one hundred feet, at the end of a semi-alley, semi-courtyard concrete walk. It is quite an impressive sight from the street. Preserved and undesecrated on the highest point of the roof (at the front) are marble Ten Commandment slabs. They rise above the roof four or five feet. On the side attached to the synagogue is a two-story building that in the pre-Nazi days was probably a home for the rabbi or a Sunday school.

The inside, although quite a wreck, has fared well or at least better than many of the famous churches in France. All the objects that had any religious significance have been removed. The only thing remaining to distinguish it from any other type of meeting place is an empty ark. The skylights have been knocked out, the railing of the balcony has been ruined, and the doors and many of the windows have been taken away. Still, I could describe much worse wreckage if I were to tell you about some of the famous cathedrals I've seen in Rouen, Chartres, Chalons-sur-Marne, etc.

While describing the place, I do not want to forget the backyard, where they had a half dozen chickens. Behind the backyard there are several tents, where the quartermaster corps operates showers for American soldiers in the vicinity. After examining every nook and cranny of the synagogue's main building, I went next door to the little building where I hoped to find the rabbi. I had visions of meeting a long-bearded rabbi. After I rang the bell, a French girl hung her head out of the second-story window. When I asked where the rabbi was, the only answer I could get was "pas de mass." I had no trouble understanding that. Every time you ask for something to drink at a bar or café, your answer is always "pas de cognac, pas de calvados, pas de vin, pas, pas, pas—ad nauseam."

Finally, she did tell me that once a week "mass" was said by "l'officier américain militaire." I hope to go to services next Friday night, but it is difficult to get the use of a truck for the evening. Now that I know where to go, I'll attend services before long.

Just as I was leaving, I noticed that the female janitor was hanging out a tricolor with a black crepe for FDR. All over the town there were French flags with crepes out, and many had both French and American flags with crepes. One civilian even stopped me on the street and pointed to the mourning band on his

Interior of Verdun's synagogue, which was cleaned and repaired by American soldiers. The folding chairs were GI issue.

arm. He asked me why I wasn't wearing one. I told him that General Ike's orders were no salutes fired, no parades of mourning, and no mourning bands.

France
April 17, 1945
Dear Folks:

Yesterday two items in the Stars and Stripes *caused more argument and discussion here than crossing the Rhine or President Roosevelt's death. Probably neither item merited more than a squib or a small picture on a back page. The first item was a picture of an emaciated and starved American soldier in a Nazi prison camp. The second was the story that two U.S. soldiers were being hung for raping two German girls. The lines on which we took sides are obvious.*

The Nazis starve our prisoners, shoot Polish officers, and rape and pillage France and Russia, and then some poor GI Joe is hung for raping a local woman. I tried to say that the two should not be thought of together. If something was a crime in the States, it was also one in Germany. Still, death is a stiff sentence for rape. But I was alone. Members of a "liberating" or "conquering" Army get a lot of new ideas about justice.

France
April 18, 1945
Dear Folks:

Just a short note to say "hello." Although life out here is never really exciting, there is always enough happening to keep a medic busy. If he isn't covering himself with foam trying to load the fire extinguisher, then he's knocking himself out trying to explain to a French female KP that before she can work for the Army she must have a physical. As part of that, the hospital wants a stool specimen for a stool culture. Usually gesticulations help make up for a small vocabulary.

*I heard from Gene Bokor [**Dartmouth '46**], who is now in Germany with the Seventh Army. He has been under Jerry [**a slang term for German**] artillery fire and claims he wrote his letter*

within fifty yards of the 105th Howitzer Battery, which was rais-
ing merry hell. The more I hear about what became of the men
who came over to France on the same boat at the same time I did,
the more I realize what good breaks I've had. **[Gene Bokor was on**
the USAT Brazil with me. He spent several weeks at Camp
Lucky Strike before being assigned to a field artillery unit at
the front.]

A few nights ago while visiting some farm people who live in a
tiny, two-room shanty where I'm sure they don't have any books
other than the Vulgate Bible, I noticed a small stack of newspapers
in the corner. About 70 percent of the pile was made up of daily
French papers, and the other 30 percent was the Paris publication
of the Soviet Library of Information. Although you can't honestly
draw conclusions from one instance, the temptation is strong.

The death of Ernie Pyle this week was a real loss to every sol-
dier everywhere. He understood the soldier and presented his case
to the public as nobody else has done during this war. Politicians
and generals write things for and about the soldiers. But one is
always apt to question the sincerity of such characters and won-
der just how much they personally gain from their actions and
statements. After reading Pyle, you never had that feeling. **[The**
sympathetic accounts of ordinary GIs that newspaper corre-
spondent and author Ernie Pyle (1900–1945) wrote made
him a hero to the Army's enlisted men. His war books, Here's
Your War *and* Brave Men, *were best-sellers. He was killed in*
action on a small island in the Pacific Theater.]

France
April 23, 1945
Dear Folks:
They are beginning to print editions of Time, Newsweek, *and*
the Readers Digest *here in the ETO. That's a good thing. It is a*
very unwholesome situation where 90 percent of the men here re-
ceive their news from only one source. That source, although theo-
retically "free," is still run by the Army and subject to its control.
My magazines come only irregularly, but I suppose in the course
of time that will straighten itself out.

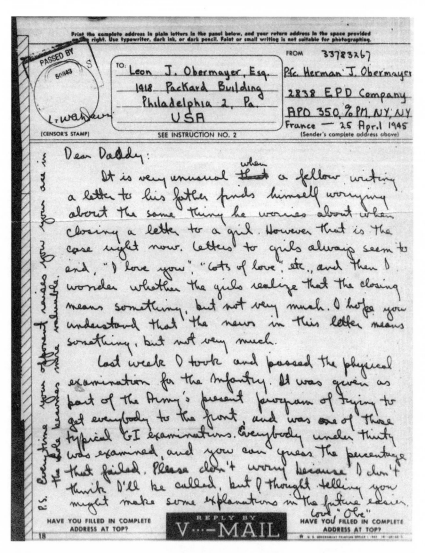

Before e-mail, there was V-mail. In order to show how soldiers carried on correspondence, the above V-mail is reproduced at actual size and in the format in which it was delivered in Philadelphia. Note the censor's signature and stamp in the upper left hand corner. V-mail stationery was approximately 8½" x 10" before photo reduction. By flying the microfilm, instead of carrying letters by air or ship, delivery time was halved.

*Yesterday, however, I received a very interesting letter from Larry
Yoffy [a member of the William and Mary ASTP unit] in the
Philippines. He tells about watching them sizzle Japs alive in their
caves with flamethrowers. He is with an artillery unit. Although
not right at the front with the infantry, they are very close to it.*

France
April 29, 1945
Dear Folks:

*In my letter written earlier today I told you that I had finished
reading all the literature sent me by Rabbi Berger, Judge
Proskauer's "Call of the Hour," and several articles on Zionism
that Daddy sent me. [**Rabbi Elmer Berger (1908–1996) was
executive director of the American Council for Judaism, the
country's most important non-Zionist organization. Joseph M.
Proskauer (1877–1971), a New York lawyer and judge,
served as president of the American Jewish Committee, and he
was also an official consultant on Jewish matters to the found-
ing conference of the United Nations in 1945.**]*

*Of course, the problem of Zionism bothers all of us. At this
point I'm not sure whether I'm trying to rationalize or think the
problem through. One way or another I've decided that the whole
question can really be divided into two almost separate and dis-
tinct questions. The first: the Jew and Judaism in the United
States and Jews' relationship with a local (U.S.) Jewish community, a democracy, a predominantly Christian country, and, last
of all, Palestine. The second: Palestine as a political entity and its
importance in the world, to the Jewish community, and to the
brotherhood of nations.*

*I don't believe that the two are anywhere nearly as closely re-
lated as the leaders of the American Council for Judaism believe.
They always use the broad term "Zionist" and never make Judge
Proskauer's very fair distinction between Zionists and ultra-
Zionists. However, the other way there is plenty of room for subtle,
rabbinical mudslinging.*

*Rabbi Berger's very fine paper titled "Emancipation: A For-
gotten Ideal" is easy to understand. It is hard to take exception*

with his belief about Judaism as a religion and not as a race or nationality. However, when reading this and other papers of the American Council on Judaism you cannot help asking yourself or the author the question, "Must a Zionist believe otherwise?" Although I have read very little of the literature of the Zionist group, a look at the contribution made by some of its leaders to American life would make me believe that the answer is negative.

The second point has me totally confused, due to my ignorance about Jewish, Palestinian, and British politics. The American Council for Judaism is opposed to a Jewish commonwealth and the British white paper of 1939, while they support the word "homeland." None of these has been satisfactorily explained for me. [*The 1939 White Paper set forth Britain's plan for a long-term solution to Jewish-Arab conflicts in Palestine. It envisioned the establishment of an independent Palestine within ten years. The number of Arab and Jewish representatives in the government would be proportionate to their respective populations. Jewish immigration would be capped at 75,000, with 25,000 to be admitted within the year and 10,000 per year for the following five years.*]

The American Council for Judaism opposes a Jewish commonwealth and wishes for a "Jewish homeland" after the war. I assume that, with the exception of the white paper, they wish to return to the status quo ante. What was the political setup of Palestine before the war? Lessing Rosenwald, in one of his papers, discusses the words "state," "commonwealth," and "homeland," but he never mentions the words "mandate" or "pan-Arabic," which you must certainly consider in order to oppose a "commonwealth."

From Professor Bruce's classes at Dartmouth, I remember a mandate as a very complicated piece of governmental machinery created by the League of Nations. But that's about all.

Before opposing a commonwealth, you want to know a few things about antebellum Palestinian internal politics, also. What is the official status of the Jewish agency? What is the official status of Chaim Weizmann, etc.? The ACJ [*American Council for*

Judaism] dope tells me nothing about politics "at home" in Pales-
tine. Judge Proskauer even mentions Palestine's relation to Suez.
There is no doubt that there also ought to be a serious consider-
ation of Jews at the United Nations. Has the ACJ no program to
suggest outside the vague word "homeland"? It would be a hell of
a lot easier to support ACJ if it had a positive, instead of a nega-
tive, program.

As a good democrat, I have one more question to ask. What do
the Jews of Palestine wish for themselves? Their voice is impor-
tant. None of the literature that you sent me ever recognizes that
there is one. Jews of those altruistic, big-hearted nations that have
already successfully interfered in the politics of North Africa,
Italy, and Belgium selfishly show no concern about what is best
for the citizens of Palestine or of the whole Near East.

Out of a sense of personal loyalty, I will support Dr. Woolsey—
whom you know I greatly respect and whose opinion on most
things I will take at face value until he has been definitely proven
wrong. However, it would be a sort of balm to my pride (which
isn't worth a hell of a lot while I'm in the Army) to think my
opinions on Zionism were the result of objective thought. Today
I'm very confused, but being too young to vote, I probably
shouldn't even think about such complex problems.

France
May 4, 1945
Dear Folks:

It looks like the monsoons have really come to France. Today
is the eighth consecutive bad day. Although I am better pre-
pared for it physically and mentally than I was last January
and February, the mud and slop are making rural France look
almost as bleak. While writing this, I am listening to the rain
beat on our tent and debating whether I should get up and
loosen the tent ropes or wait until some more energetic soul
comes along.

In Daddy's letter there was a question about Pi Tau Pi dues. The
Pi Tau Pi card aggravated me. The fact that they are charging me
dues does not annoy me. I can understand that an organization

Although approximately thirty miles behind the line of battle, Verdun, France, was still in a combat zone when this photograph was taken. The pro (prophylactic) station sign points to a facility the Army operated twenty-four hours a day in every French town. After casual sex, soldiers were expected to report to a pro station, where their penises were injected with antiseptic.

whose chief appeal is to men between sixteen and thirty needs money. There isn't any Class of '98 or Class of '11 to help it over this rough spot whose conclusion is certainly not in sight. If the members want Pi Tau Pi when they return, they'll have to contribute now. However, I don't approve of addressing the card to any father. Although it doesn't make any difference in our household, it's none of my father's damn business.

*The news from Germany is certainly good. Still, from all I can see and read, the French, British, and Americans back home are a lot more excited than we, who spend most of our spare time kidding and talking about the move to CBI [**China-Burma-India Theater of Operations**]. It's hard to wax enthusiastic about the conclusion of one war when there is another one to fight.*

France
May 7, 1945
Dear Folks:

In one of your letters you asked about my quarters. I live in a tent with four other men. I am really quite comfortable. Soon after we arrived at our present location we found a pile of Boche lumber that was probably going to be used for barns or silos, but with which we built a floor and a door for our tent. Now neither the wind nor the rain bothers us very much.

The logic of the characters in our headquarters is always questionable. Typical is letter #49, whose receipt you have already acknowledged. As originally sent, the letter was returned with pencil marks that I believe are still discernable on pages two and three. These sections were to be removed from the letter. Why? It made no sense to me, and I blew my top and started asking questions. The reason those sections were cut out was that I was writing home for information that could be captured on my person and be of use to the enemy. Any dumb Nazi agent—and most of them are smart—could go to the New York Public Library and get all of the information, if he didn't already know where every joint, coupling, and station on this pipeline was situated. Of course, in civilian life laws are written by legislators and interpreted by trained judicial minds. In the Army, God knows who writes them, but they're usually interpreted by second lieutenants, whose interpretations differ as their personalities, backgrounds, and courage differ.

France
May 9, 1945
Dear Folks:

V-E Day—the day we've waited for and hoped for for years has come and gone. It brought relief to the GIs who were dodging bullets in foxholes deep in Germany. It brought on drunken celebrations in New York, London, and Chicago. But, for the men like me who are not stationed in Paris but are still a safe distance from the shell fire in the ETO, there was nothing but a few futile attempts to get drunk on "bière." There were lots of bitter remarks about ourselves and the war still to be fought on the other side of the world.

Yesterday I was forced to make a trip to the hospital and stayed in town all day. I watched the French and the GI population try to celebrate. What a hollow celebration! I've seen more enthusiastic crowds celebrating New Year's Eve, a high-school football victory, or a World Series in which they didn't have any personal interest. When the final whistle blows in a football game, it's over. You use New Year's Eve only as an excuse for getting drunk once a year.

*When we heard the announcement over the telephone, the first reaction was not to believe it: "We've heard that sort of stuff too often before." Then, when we finally heard the news, the statements varied, but the sentiment was always the same: "So what? We still have another son of a bitch to sweat out," or "Now that we've won the French and English war, we still have our own war to fight." This has been the sentiment of the soldiers over here for a long time. You can hardly expect it to change with V-E Day. You probably remember the newspaper publicity given to the sign the engineers hung in front of the western end of the first pontoon bridge at Remagen, "The Shortest Route to CBI." [CBI **signifies the China-Burma-India Theater. The U.S. Army first crossed the Rhine River at Remagen.**]*

Now, to tell you what actually happened to me when the news of the victory arrived. When the first news came over the phone, we paid very little attention to it. Most people just weren't willing to believe it until they saw it in print. Ironically, everybody was working very hard. On Monday evening gasoline reached this station on the new line that is being laid to the no-longer-existent western front. There was plenty of brass hanging around (i.e., about three lieutenants). There just wasn't any excitement about the peace. Nobody seemed to give a damn. Finally, I heard church bells ringing and went down to the little village a few hundred yards away hoping to find some excitement or at least a free drink. In the village I found the dozen French soldiers who work in the area firing their rifles into the air while their sergeant was yelling orders and tearing his hair out. Three young girls offered to kiss me. Of course, I didn't kick too much. I let them kiss me three times, once on each cheek and once on the forehead. There were no other American soldiers there, and no other civilians showed up. After a half hour I decided that the nine dispassionate kisses were going to be the gross total of the excitement. Back in the tents I found everybody deeply engrossed in a much more exciting game of stud poker.

On Tuesday I went into town [Verdun] and found the place bedecked with flags and filled with lots of GIs, both black and white, wandering aimlessly and looking for cognac and someone to kiss them Paris-liberation style. At three o'clock they had a formal celebration with a speech by the mayor, a parade by the Boy Scouts and some kids from a church school, a speech from Paris over an amplifying system, and a little music ("La Marseillaise" five times, "God Save the King," and "The Star-Spangled Banner"

V-E Day, May 8, 1945, was a holiday throughout France. The small girl waving an American flag in front of the banner proclaiming "Vive la Paix" was dressed in red, white, and blue. The young people are watching the victory parade at the base of Verdun's World War I memorial. The city was the site of that war's bloodiest battle.

"Vive la Victoire" sign on Verdun's main street, May 8, 1945—V-E Day. Soldiers at Station 53 resented French glee because *our* war was not over. We expected to be on active duty in the Pacific in the near future.

once). It was hardly what you would call impressive. However, there were a few laughs.

The only times the crowd really roared and hooted and hollered was when an ash truck or some MPs would drive by with dejected-looking Jerries [German prisoners of war] in the back of the truck. The crowd loved that. If there had not been some gendarmes and MPs around, they probably would have pelted them with stones. I think the French were more or less insulted about the ignorance of the U.S. soldiers when they played "La Marseillaise" for the first time. The first time they played it, all the gendarmes and Boy Scouts snapped to attention, but the American soldiers, colonels, and privates alike just didn't know what to do. Some stuck their hands in their pockets. Some stood at attention. A few saluted. But most, like me, just stared at a group of officers who in turn stared at each other. Finally, everything was settled when two MPs in a jeep came abruptly to a stop, jumped out, and saluted. As you know, the MPs are supposed to be both the Emily Posts and the Beau Brummels of the Army. Their pants always have a knife-edge crease, and their hats always the correct tilt. It is they who decide when you're too drunk to be on the streets or what areas ought to be off limits to all U.S. military personnel. ["All" refers to the fact that most of the upscale, clean bars in Verdun were off limits only to enlisted men.]

After the parade I went to the Red Cross, where in the spirit of victory the doughnuts and coffee were free, and read the papers. The Red Cross was crowded but dead. Try as you might, you could not instill enthusiasm in that crowd. The fellows just drank their coffee and read their papers as usual. As could be expected on the big day, the radio didn't work. Most of the American soldiers stationed in the area were thoroughly annoyed at V-E Day, as they have been ordered by the commanding general of this section to give a V-E Day parade for the French. Although our unit did not have to parade, I know there is not much fun or spontaneity in parading or standing at attention with your rifle at "right-shoulder-arms" for a lot of people you don't give a damn about.

France
May 10, 1945
Mother's Day
Dear Folks:

In the course of my life I've attended all kinds of dances and hayrides, which had a farm atmosphere, but Thursday night I attended one entirely different from all the others. I've attended barn dances where the only smell of hay was in my straw hat, like some at the Philmont Country Club, or ones where there was farm atmosphere but no hay, like those at the Hanover White Church or the Grafton County Grange [the local lodge of a national agricultural fraternal association in Hanover, New Hampshire, whose dances I sometimes attended during my time at Dartmouth], but all of these affairs began before midnight and had music to which I could dance at least a few steps.

Thursday night's dance was held in a town five kilometers away. It was held in celebration of the return of a man who worked in a German forced-labor gang for more than four years. Here everybody works out in the fields until the last light of day has left the skies. They do not eat supper until between ten and eleven o'clock. Therefore, they could not think of going to a dance much before midnight. Not being a pitcher who needs a little workout in the bull-pen before going to the mound, I did not relish the thought of a three-mile hike before the dance. But here the only type of transportation available is GI, and the penalties are rather severe for driving French civilians. Once at the dance I found several kids whose mothers, had they been Americans, would never have thought they were old enough to go to a shindig beginning at midnight. The only music at the dance was supplied by an accordion. The one dance they danced was absolutely beyond me.

After all my walking I didn't stay more than a half hour, as I couldn't dance without running into a half dozen couples. It didn't take me long to realize that I just "didn't belong." Of course, I must add that the dance was held in a room adjoining a real barn, and there was no doubt about the smell. If a few months over here hadn't immunized me to the smell of manure, I would have said the place stank like hell. Some of these French kids are really rugged. They dance 'til six o'clock, then eat breakfast, and then put in a twelve- or thirteen-hour day behind a moldboard plow.

France
May 12, 1945
Dear Folks:

When yesterday's discharge plan was announced, I am sure that you did a little figuring, just like I did. There is a chance that I may get 5 extra points for the battle star awarded those who took part in the "Battle of Germany" **[It was later officially termed the Rhineland campaign.]** *We were inside the boundary of the Zone de Guerre, as it was defined before the crossing of the Rhine. Although almost nobody here will have the number of points necessary for a discharge, I have heard very little grumbling. Most everyone believes it a fair and just system.* **[The redeployment and discharge formula announced after V-E Day provided that soldiers who earned eighty-five points (credits) would return to the States as soon as transportation was available. There were four types of credits: months served, months served overseas, combat credits (battle stars, decorations for bravery, etc.), and parenthood credits (number of children under eighteen). I had 32 points (22 months of service, 5 months overseas, 1 battle star, no children) on May 15, 1945.]**

France
May 14, 1945
Dear Folks:

Enclosed you will find my expired PX ration card, which I thought might interest you. However, don't think that we get all of the items listed there like beer, fruit juice, and towels. If I were stationed in a large city like Paris or Rouen, I would probably be able to get all the items on the list. Although we do not get a great many of the items listed on the ration card, I believe our company manages the PX quite efficiently. One officer and one enlisted man are in charge of the PX. Although they do not devote all their time to it, they spend several days a week working on it. Our regular

rations of cigarettes, cigars, candy, etc., come every two weeks, and
we get two bottles of Coca-Cola every week. The following are
items and amounts listed on the card that we get every two weeks:
tobacco (1 package); candy (12 packages); candy rolls or gum
(3 packages); cigars (3); cigarettes (12 packages); matches
(4 books); soap (1 cake).

After this, we cut cards for all sorts of items that are left over
because of indivisible numbers. Other items are rationed to indi-
viduals once every four or eight weeks. As a result, only a few of
these items come for the sixteen of us every two weeks. Everybody
takes their ration, regardless of whether they want it. Then we do
all kinds of bartering. The value of the things is determined both
by their real value and their value in the French black market.

The big subject of discussion around here is still the business of
the German atrocities and the two fellows hung for rape in Ger-
many. Of course, all of these discussions end up on some tangent
far away from the central theme, but from them you can see with-
out being a trained observer that damn few soldiers think we are
fighting a war for principles.

Jubecourt
Meuse, France
May 16, 1945
Dear Folks:

*The censorship and press regulations of SHAEF [**Supreme***
***Headquarters Allied Expeditionary Forces**] have been dis-*
cussed all over the world during the past two weeks due to Ed
Kennedy's premature release of the peace story, the suspension of
the correspondents who went to Berlin without permission, and
the Elmer Davis program for the press in Germany. I don't think
*very much of the criticism has been favorable. [**On May 7, 1945,***
in an unprecedented action, the Supreme Headquarters Euro-
pean Theater suspended the Associated Press's news-filing
privileges. Edward Kennedy, chief AP correspondent in Eu-
rope, broke the Army's news embargo on the German surren-
der that day. The news appeared in newspapers before the

Delivering a replacement pipeline engine. We did not have dump trucks, so we used the lift of one truck to tilt the other.

United States had formally notified its Allies and friendly nations through diplomatic channels. After worldwide protests by wire services and editors, the retaliatory suspension was lifted.]

I don't know how you feel about the Kennedy incident, but if I were his boss, I would publicly reprimand him and then give him a pay raise. Recently, in San Francisco Walter Duranty [New York Times *foreign correspondent]made a distinction between the "scoop" group and the erudite group of newspaper reporters. I believe men of the "scoop" group, like Kennedy, are being paid for being a little unethical and pulling a few fast stunts. He was just the sucker who got caught.*

Jubecourt
Meuse, France
May 18, 1945
Dear Folks:

*This is an important letter. It marks the beginning of a new pe-
riod in my letters. From now on I will not be bothered with that
most obnoxious personal element in the rather confusing system
of military censorship. Starting with this letter, I will seal my
own letters, and they will be censored by the base censor. Not only
am I allowed to seal my own mail now, but many of the restrictions on writing about locations, assignments, rumors, morals,
etc., have been removed. It's a happy day when one of those cher-
ished American freedoms, which was stolen away from you, is
partially returned.*

*All of us who have seen Dr. Goebbels's work fear control of the
press and free correspondence. [Josef Goebbels (1897–1945)
was the Nazi minister of propaganda.] Now that the fighting is
over and security violations will not endanger American lives, we
must all guard ourselves so that we do not let the diplomatic fears
of minor politicians lead us back to strict censorship.*

*My exact location is in a field about one-third of a mile from
the very small town of Jubecourt-en-Argonne, which you will
find only on a map whose U.S. equivalent would include Sciota
[a small town in Illinois where my father was born] or North
Belgrade [the location of Camp Kennebec in Maine]. However,
you may be able to find a map that includes Clermont-en-
Argonne, and if you draw a line from there to Verdun, Jubecourt
will be about a quarter of the way along that line.*

Jubecourt
Meuse, France
May 19, 1945
Dear Folks:

*I have been running all over to personnel officers trying to find
out something about a school program that is being started in the
ETO. But nobody seems to know anything about it, except what
they read in the <u>Stars and Stripes</u> (I can now underline the things*

Probably the most effective way to hurt a soldier's morale was to exploit his anxiety about the steadfastness of his wife or girlfriend. I found a pile of these eye-catching propaganda pieces in a *Stars and Stripes* newspaper rack in Verdun's Red Cross center. Since Germans were forbidden to be in the area (Verdun was still part of a combat zone in March, 1945), the leaflets were probably planted in the U.S. facility by a French Nazi sympathizer perhaps working as a cook or janitor.

MIRROR — WISE

A Precarious Story

Joan was in her room and just about to change because she intended to go to the Cinema with Bob. She had done that quite often since John, her husband had left for the front. — Why shouldn't she? Bob is a good friend of John's and he certainly wouldn't object. Everybody understands that Joan cannot always sit at home alone for years, without any companionship. —

Yesterday Bob came a little earlier than usual and entered Joan's room just as she was adding the last tou.. of rouge. She didn't mind his staying for they were really good friends — and so accustomed to each other.

As she rolled on her stockings, Bob told her all that he had done during business hours that day; and then she noticed that the elbow of his jacket had a little grease spot; so she took it and cleaned it. — What could anybody think wrong about that — among friends.

And then — — — Neither knew how it happened, she felt his strong body leaning gently against her — and then — they kissed — for a long — long while.

Joan was in a dream — — — she was feeling that marvellous something that she had missed for so long — it was so wonderful. Then she opened her eyes — and there was that horror before her. Was it a dream — or was it reality?

She looked in the mirror and saw . . . . . . John! John in the arms of another! In the arms of Death!

But no, it was not John embraced by Death — — — it was YOU — and it was not Joan looking in the mirror but YOUR wife.

Joan is still alone.

And so are all the millions of other wives and girls.

But war goes on.

The Nazi propaganda piece's reverse side was more devastating than its front. Any normal male who had been overseas for a long period would likely be disturbed by reading about his wife with his best friend.

that I think ought to be in italics, as I don't think anyone will
continue to enforce the rule about not underlining words).

This week our campaign star was approved. On R Day (the
base date for calculating discharge credits), I had 32 points.

Recently in a special four-page edition of the New York Herald Tribune *(Paris edition), there were six ads (all the same*
size). I can't help listing them as I thought they were well done
and evidence of good advertising. They were for (1) Time, Life,
etc.: Now that U.S. mail service has been reestablished in many
parts of France, their European subscribers should send their ad-
dresses and catch up on the part of their subscriptions they missed
during the German occupation; (2) Hart, Schafner, and Marx,
which said only "Congratulations on a job well done"; (3) the
Waldorf-Astoria hopes to see you when you return; (4) the New
Haven RR, something about when you return; (5) Florsheim
Shoes, very little outside of their name; and (6) Abraham and
Strauss, a department store in Brooklyn.

Jubecourt
Meuse, France
May 20, 1945
Dear Folks:

This is the letter I've wanted to write you ever since I left the
1291st Engineers. "Security" regulations prohibited my writing
it until today.

The 2838th EPD Company operates the pumping stations,
runs pipeline maintenance, and crews tank farms, railheads, and
truck risers on the gasoline pipeline that runs from Cherbourg to
the farthest forward stationary point of our troops. Our section
runs from Chalons-sur-Marne to Etain. Our headquarters are in
Chalons-sur-Marne. Although I have been to our CP **[command**
post] *in Chalons only once since moving out here, we have con-*
stant telephone communication among all of the stations.

One of the explanations for the delay and confusion in deliver-
ing and sending mail is the fact that it must come and go through
Chalons-sur-Marne. It changes hands several times in the course

of its trip here. This is how the mail gets from Chalons to Pumping Station 53: The mail clerk picks it up at the APO [**Army post office**] in Chalons-sur-Marne sometime in the afternoon. Then he sorts it in our headquarters. After that, it is taken to Pumping Station 51 (near St. Menehould) by truck. Then they call 52 (Clermont) on the phone, and their truck (used for rations) comes out and gets it at 51. After this, 52 calls 53 and 54, and they decide whether the maintenance truck from 53 or the lieutenant's jeep from 54 will get the mail at 52. You can easily see how it gets lost. When these vehicles are busy, the mail sits around a tent or operations shack until somebody is able to get it.

As a medic I am charged with the medical problems at stations 52, 53, 54, and 55, which really means that I am the doctor for the men on the pipeline from Clermont to Etain. As our truck at Station 53 regularly patrols the line between 52 and 54, I visit these stations quite regularly, but 55, which is at the end of our section, is sort of an orphan.

Near Verdun, France
May 28, 1945
Dear Folks:

Although I appreciate all the clippings you sent me, I must comment on "Major League Baseball, 1945." It came just in time to be of use in one of those classic arguments: What would have happened to Joe Jackson if he had been able to read and write? or to Ted Williams if there hadn't been a war? These arguments are always carried on with the sincere hope that nobody will produce a record book and add facts that can't be contested. [*Joe Jackson (1882–1951) batted .408 in 1911 but was banned from baseball after he was named a co-conspirator in the plot to throw the 1919 World Series. Ted Williams (1918–2002) batted .406 in 1941, but his career was truncated when he enlisted in the Marines in 1942.*]

Although there are a great many things to tell you today, I do not want to forget about my trip to Reims last Tuesday. There is no doubt that it is the cleanest, most up-to-date, hospitable large city I have visited in France. Of course, being the home of Gen.

Ike's headquarters, there is more brass walking on the streets than GIs. That's one place where it is necessary to salute. All over town there are signs posted telling you to be careful about your uniform and saluting. Not being on a pass, I was damn careful and stayed out of trouble. Before going any farther, I might add it is also a very good town for a soldier. Where there are a lot of generals, you usually find the enlisted men well taken care of. In Reims, they have not only a very nice Red Cross Club, but also one or two other enlisted men's clubs, a place called "GI Joe's," where a transient can get a free sandwich, a GI beer hall, and a GI barbershop.
[There were separate barbershops for officers and enlisted men.]

Soon after arriving in Reims, I visited the cathedral, which until three weeks ago was the city's chief claim to world fame. Although the cathedral was beautiful and massive, I can't say I was very impressed. Of course, this, like most of the other cathedrals I have visited over here, had its stained-glass windows removed. They have been replaced by the smoky glass you find in bathroom windows. While I was there, several workmen were busy taking the sandbags from the front. The cathedral seems to be surrounded by American names, as the name of the street in front of it is Rue Rockefeller and the square next to it is named Myron Herrick, whose most famous action in France, to my knowledge, was riding out to the Paris airport one May morning and meeting a good-looking blond aviator from Minnesota. **[Myron Herrick (1854–1929) was the U.S. Ambassador to France who greeted Charles Lindbergh (1902–1974) when he completed his solo flight from New York to Paris in 1927.]**

Near Verdun, France
May 29, 1945
Dear Folks:

Today is an anniversary for me, hardly a pleasant one, but a memorable one. Two years ago I got a serial number for the first time in my life, took my first slipshod Army physical, and listened to the first of many poor talks on VD and the Articles of War.

Sunday night I saw the first show I've seen since I saw Jacobowsky and the Colonel *with Mother in November.*

[Jacobowsky and the Colonel *deals with anti-Semitism and how it was accepted and embraced by Europe's elite. Written by S. N. Behrman (1893–1973), it is based on a novel by Franz Werfel (1890–1945), one of Europe's leading literary figures between the two world wars.] Although the interior of the theater did not look too different from one of the little theaters on 47th or 48th Street, it was less than twenty feet from the Meuse River, and you had to get in line two hours before the show started to get a seat. The play was* Anything Goes *by P.G. Wodehouse, with songs by Cole Porter and real, live, pretty American girls including Joy Hodges, who starred in* Best Foot Forward. *It was very well done. I had a good time. Many lines were added for this special Army production including lines about the jail in Fayetteville, Section 8* [insanity discharge], *and "no compris," but the thing that really put the play over— and always seems to me the big difference between a play put on strictly for soldiers and a production where the actors are afraid that a sarcastic Walter Winchell or Wollcott Gibbs or George Jean Nathan* [well-known New York theater critics] *are in the audience—was that the actors seemed to be having a good time.*

In one of your recent letters you asked about my washing, mending, etc. I am very happy to tell you that I haven't washed or mended my own clothes once since coming to France. I have always been able to find some lady who was glad to make a little extra money and even happier to get the big bar of soap I would take from the mess tent each time I would bring her my laundry. Although I have never told any of these women anything about mending, every time I would give them a pair of socks with a hole in them or a shirt without a button, it would come back clean and repaired. With the great shortage of soap and the great expense of running water here in France, everywhere you see people beating the dirt out of clothes. Even in fairly large cities like Chartres, Chalons-sur-Marne, and Verdun they have quays, which are similar to the slanted wharves from which you put canoes into the water, where the women go to wash every morning and afternoon. They get down on their knees and dip the wash in the river and then pound it with boards. The same thing happens in the little villages, either along a stream or in a special building where everybody washes. Maybe they do that in some parts of the United States, but I never saw it. As I have told you several times before, I don't think the people here ever take showers or baths. They're always amazed at the amount of trouble an American soldier will go to to take a shower.

Near Verdun, France
June 2, 1945
Dear Folks:

Thursday night I went to the chaplain's Hebrew class, but there was none. The only people there were the chaplain, his assistant, and me. He tried to make a three-man choir out of us, but that was a dismal failure. Instead, we discussed Zionism and Reform Judaism for two hours. I enjoyed talking with the chaplain a great deal. He is a Zionist and very Orthodox. He has a temperament most unusual in preachers. He wants to simply discuss, not convert, and impress.

His attitude on all Jewish problems is based on a very wholesome philosophy of loyalty to Jews. He refuses to consider the economic effects of unrestricted immigration anywhere, particularly on the Arabs in Palestine. He believes that his first interest and loyalty ought to be to Jews today and not tomorrow. With all the rest of the world looking out for its own interests, Jews ought to look after the immediate problems of Jews.

I told him that as long as I was doing almost nothing, I would like to see something of Europe. He has agreed to take me with him on June 11 when he goes up to look after some matters for the families of Jewish soldiers buried in Luxembourg. Going AWOL with the chaplain will be something for the books.

The mail yesterday included a very interesting letter from Dick Levy, who is now somewhere near Munich. He, like almost everybody else I know in Germany, doesn't see how the U.S. policy of "nonfraternization" will ever work successfully. He compared it to prohibition. He said the only difference was that everybody's doing it.

Station 53's mess tent with a large canvas (lister) bag in front. All drinking water at fixed encampments was drawn from such bags to which GI-issued purification tablets had been added. On the right is part of the station's inventory of filled jerry cans (flat, five-gallon containers).

Near Verdun, France
June 9, 1945

Dear Folks:

Censorship has returned. We do not know the details of why or how, but in any form it's odious. I don't think unit censorship can be justified in any but the most critical of military situations. Although I know nothing about why our mail is being censored again, I do know that I hate those eyes peering over my shoulders as I write.

The big news of this letter is that I have finally gotten a Paris pass. Tomorrow evening I plan to go into Chalons to sleep and then will be driven to Reims to meet an early morning train to Paris. It is for forty-eight hours. Although I don't know whether that means Tuesday night or Wednesday morning, it is a good deal. I'm very happy about it. This afternoon I called Colonel Bill Gold [a Westview Street neighbor] at his office and made a date to see him.

Near Verdun, France
June 14, 1945
Dear Folks:

I don't have time for a long letter, but I want to tell you about our unit in an uncensored letter. Our unit was alerted for shipment from the ETO. As a result, censorship was again imposed last week. Of course, nobody is sure which way we are going.

Paris is a great city. I don't know how much it has changed since before the war. Except for the food situation, it doesn't seem any more affected by the war than Washington or New York.

Paris was everything that stories, books, rumors, and hopes said it would be: beautiful, expensive, entertaining, immoral. Now I have seen France. The cold dismal days along the Channel coast; the wreckage of Normandy; the small cities like Chartres,Chalons-sur-Marne, Verdun; the farmers of the Meuse; and finally Paris, which seems to be worlds away from all the rest of France. My pass was a total success from the standpoints of entertainment, sightseeing, and business. The only way to properly tell you about my pass is to tell you about my experiences chronologically.

Monday morning at 6:00 A.M. I left Chalons-sur-Marne by jeep for Reims, where with another soldier on a three-day pass I took a 7:28 A.M. train for Paris. The train was a GI train with French cars that were filled with fellows going to Paris on a pass from Germany. To everybody's surprise, it ran on schedule, arriving in Paris at 10:00 A.M. After standing in line for about three-quarters of an hour and paying forty francs, we were assigned rooms in the Hotel Ecosse (near the Gare St. Lazare). We took a bus to the hotel. When we arrived there, we were assigned to a small annex, the Hotel Grieche, where I had a large, single room with a nice bed with sheets and an innerspring mattress, a washstand, bureau, table, and two easy chairs.

In the course of the day, I visited the Arc de Triomphe. Although it was massive and beautiful, I can't say that it impressed me except as a great big chunk of masonry. While under the Arch, an officer called me down the only time while I was in Paris. Not knowing any better, I walked up to the burning memorial lamp and stood within a few feet of it with my hands in my pockets and my hat cocked on the back of my head. I was admiring some nurses on the other side when a major came up to me. I should salute the light when passing or stand at attention, he told me. Did I know he could have me court-martialed, etc.? He was drunk, but I said, "Yes, sir."

While there, I met one of the Red Cross tours, which cost sixty francs, and joined up with it. We stopped at the Eiffel Tower, Trocadero, Invalides, Notre Dame, and the Louvre.

The tour ended at the AEF *[American Expeditionary Force]* Club, which is in the Grand Hotel *[a Cunard-White Star Line hotel]*, so I went in there to relax. It is a magnificent hotel. If luck had been with me, I might have been assigned there. It has a large dance floor, coke bar, beer parlor, ice-cream bar, barbershop, shoeshine room, and telephone service, etc.

Colonel Bill asked a Sergeant Kleinstein from his office to have supper with us, the three of us returned to his quarters. His room was elaborate and beautifully appointed. If the occupant hadn't been a good friend, I would probably have been as annoyed—as I usually am—at the unfair privileges accorded officers. After washing up, the colonel then asked the sergeant and the private first class whether they thought the three of us could kill a quart of champagne. You know the answer—and the result. In the meantime, a captain came in who was a lawyer, a Princeton man, and a friend of Bill's, and he was also invited for dinner. We ate at the ETO headquarters field officer's mess and had a very pleasant time together discussing the Drew Pearson article about Generals Lee and Lord and General Patton, who everybody thinks is both an SOB and a genius.

Near Verdun, France
June 15, 1945
Dear Folks:

Monday night after the show, I went to a dance at the AEF Club, where they played good American music. I danced with a couple of girls who talked my language (a WAC, a British girl, and a Red Cross girl). Although the place was a little too crowded for comfort, it was a very nice dance. Everybody seemed to be having a good time.

It was at this dance that I met a second friend from Philadelphia, Gordon Taplinger, who was in my class at Central High School. He went across part of France and all of Germany with an armored division. He was promoted to sergeant for bravery. He is now stationed in southern Bavaria. He is one of the many men you meet from Germany who has a sad story to tell you about the U.S. nonfraternization policy. Last week he was reduced from a sergeant to a private for fraternizing.

After supper I went to the Paris Stage Door Canteen, where I again met some friends. This time it was Sergeants Lowe and Malory from the 1291st Engineers, who are now in the 2836th EPD company. After staying there an hour or so, I decided to walk down the Champs Élysées, where I met another very good old friend from the 1291st—Ray Grund. He was in Paris just for the evening and had a truck. He asked if I would like to drive around Paris with him for a few hours. Of course, the answer was "yes." With him I saw more of Paris than I could have seen on any official tour. After going to a dance, getting lost on the subway, walking about five miles, and meeting a guy who wanted to sell me a Zeiss camera that he had taken from a Nazi Lieutenant General, I finished my second day in Paris.

Outside the hotel I was always followed or propositioned by men trying to buy my soap, candy, cigarettes, clothes, etc., men selling useless trinkets and junk perfume, and prostitutes whose profession you can always accept with a smile, but whose boldness and nerve can be damned annoying. These people are waiting outside every building where American soldiers get together. It's a wonder more don't get punched in the nose by GIs or have MPs chase them around the block.

The afternoon I spent with Gordon doing something I never believed I was capable of doing—walking from one perfume bar to another trying to buy some for Mother on the Rue de la Paix. It was really quite interesting. Although you still won't be able to lure me into Blum's or Bonwit's in Philadelphia, it was rather enjoyable in Paris. I have never heard of any places where they have regular perfume bars in the States like they do on the Rue de la Paix. Almost every store is out of the famous-name brands. If they have a little, there is always a long line, about 80 percent of which is made up of American soldiers. After going to a couple of stores, I probably would have decided that there were better ways to spend an afternoon than in perfume shops. But I met a WAC who insisted on dragging me to Coty, Chanel, Houghbigant, Tabu, Guerlain, Arden, Patou, and about a dozen more whose names were longer, but who were also sorry that they had nothing to offer. The thing that amazed me was that we didn't go to a single store where they didn't have salesgirls who talked fine English. Finally, I got twenty cc of Shalimar, which I will send someday soon.

Later I went with a group of soldiers to one of the famous Paris nightclubs for a few hours and afterward went to bed. As for the nightclub, the prices were exorbitant (120 francs for cognac). The rest you can see at any dive on Arch Street.

Near Verdun, France
June 18, 1945
Dear Folks:
There is no doubt that sometime within the next two or three weeks I will be somewhere else. Today we stopped pumping through both of our gasoline lines. Shortly after V-E Day, the last aviation gas entered the pipeline at Cherbourg. It was immediately followed by saltwater. It reached the last aviation gas station at Chalons last week. The last motor-vehicle gasoline left Cherbourg about two weeks ago and reached here today. *[One-third of the pipeline moved aviation gasoline; two-thirds*

The main transportation artery for moving men and materiel to the front was the Red Ball Highway. Along that roadway—near the beginning of the communications zone—was a billboard indicating the fines for violations of highway regulations and other infractions. Enlisted men were fined two dollars—and officers five dollars—for failing to salute.

moved automotive fuel.] So we have a maximum of forty-eight hours of pumping left. After that, wait, guess, and sort out the rumors. The outfit that ran the line from Paris to Chalons-sur-Marne stopped working on Sunday. They have already left for a Pacific-theater staging area. **[Immediately after V-E Day, the Army established redeployment camps near France's Mediterranean ports so that troops could be sent speedily and directly from Europe to the Pacific Theater of Operations.]**

Verdun, France
June 23, 1945
Dear Folks:
Moving day is coming soon. I don't know where or when, but I know that we have finished our job here. It won't be long until we

Soldiers routinely removed rotors and spark plugs from parked jeeps so that they would not be stolen. Still, soldiers were required to post guards when parking in the communications zone. With thousands of jeeps in the European Theater and no central registry to keep track of them, vehicles could be stolen and abandoned with impunity.

*will move somewhere. Last night we pumped our last gallon of
water. Today we start dismantling the station and preparing the
equipment for shipment. There is a new rumor every hour. Their
great abundance only proves that nobody knows anything beyond
the orders of the day.*

*My trip to Luxembourg on Wednesday was certainly a great
success. I found it a clean, progressive city where an amazingly
large number of young people speak English. After asking a few
questions, I found that the Germans were responsible for the wide
usage of English. Before the war, it was a real bilingual city, but
when the Germans came in, they forbade the teaching and general usage of French. English was substituted for French in the
schools. In some of the back streets you can still see signs with both
"Rue de Xxxxx" and "Xxxxx Strasse" on them.*

*The people all seem to take great pride in their duchy and its
independence. Almost every shop window has in it either a picture of the grand duchess or the seal of the royal family. They
proudly show you a great stone bridge across a stream in the
center of the city. It is one of the largest bridges in Europe, which
the Nazis left standing. They have a story about how some patriotic citizens tricked the bridge guards and cut the demolition
wires.*

*Luxembourg is also a very enthusiastic Boy Scout city. On the
wall of a barbershop I found a Boy Scout poster that the barber
had saved from the pre-Hitler days when he attended a world
jamboree. The kid who took me on a tour pointed out the Boy
Scout headquarters proudly. He told me they had already reorga-
nized one troop.*

Chalons-sur-Marne
June 29, 1945
Dear Folks:

*Another day in which there is nothing to do but wait. This life
is the easiest one imaginable—not a damn thing to do but stay
out of the way of the MPs. We live in an old French barracks and
sleep until the German prisoners of war, who clean up the joint,
wake us up by knocking against the cots with their brooms or*

mops. Last night we listened to Article of War 28, which says that it is desertion to go AWOL (punishable by death, etc.). Now we are preparing to move. As far as I know those are the only instructions we have received other than a few concerning the turning in of equipment.

CHAPTER 7

PARIS

Glamour City, GI Town

AMERICAN GIs had a love-hate relationship with Paris. Every GI wanted to go there on leave. Assignment to an Army department garrisoned in the City of Light was the best posting in Europe. Still, many soldiers—perhaps most—were vexed by the fact that while more than fifty thousand American soldiers were killed fighting to liberate France, Parisians in the top social echelons were enjoying most of life's luxuries. They understood why life in the Third Reich's most important capital after Berlin was relatively pleasant (except for Jews). Parisians did not harass or challenge the Nazi bureaucrats who ran their city.

Still, in many ways Paris was a "GI town" in the summer of 1945. Thousands of American soldiers were there at all times. Billboards along the Champs Élysées advertised American stores and products. In areas frequented by GIs there were more MPs than French gendarmes. MPs regularly checked whether officers and enlisted men saluted each other on important thoroughfares. If an enlisted man failed to salute properly, he was issued a summons, similar to a traffic ticket. Saluting summonses were paid off at a traffic-court-type facility in the Paris Opera House's basement.

The official soldiers-on-leave guide to Paris warned that 42 percent of all venereal disease in the European Theater (from North Africa to Ireland) was contracted in Paris. Much of this is attributable to the fact that prostitution was legal (and unofficially sanctioned by the U.S. Army) in Europe's top glamour city. Whores were periodically checked for diseases. Those who carried validated permits and health certificates in their purses could openly solicit vulnerable GIs, some of whom had not talked to a woman in months or even years.

Most GIs were perplexed and astonished at the way Paris's licensed prostitutes blatantly and aggressively promoted their wares. For many it defined the difference between the French and Americans. They had low moral standards; we did not. To many GI Joe's, the fact that U.S. military police benevolently watched over the "whore bazaars" that operated within a block or two of each of Paris's six large enlisted men's clubs seemed inconsistent with the maintenance of military discipline. But the top brass probably had just the opposite view. They unofficially acknowledged that whore bazaars played a useful role in maintaining order among the troops. Satisfying sex-starved soldiers tended to minimize barroom brawls and rapes. The Army's official involvement was limited to low-level military police. This allowed the generals to deny they were involved in Paris's legalized prostitution.

MPs were part of the whore bazaars. While overly rouged women of various sizes and shapes preened and sauntered along the sidewalk, soldiers surveyed their options from the street. MPs constantly patrolled both sides of the street, but they did not interfere with the sex commerce. Whoring is a cash-in-advance business the world over. The money part of the transaction was conducted openly, in plain view of the MPs. Nothing was furtive. The liaison was concluded in a nearby fleabag room that was registered at the local gendarme station to an individual girl and/or her pimp. MPs were charged with maintaining order—and nothing more. They interceded in soldiers' fistfights, helped girls who got beaten up, tried to see that drunken GIs did not get robbed or leave their passes and transport documents behind in brothels, and advised that the nearby enlisted men's club included a pro station that was staffed 24/7.

Soldiers knew that Paris's legalized prostitution was a big business, as well as a well-established part of the city's social fabric. Only after it became unlawful did I realize the magnitude of the operation. A front-page headline in the *Herald-Tribune* of December 18, 1945, tells all: "Paris Shuts Its Brothels, Releasing 6,000 Rooms; Students, the Bombed-Out, and Repatriates to Get Lodging." The story that followed began this way: "Paris clamped down on its official brothels yesterday, an event unprecedented in the capital's history."

I was transferred to Paris because the Theater Provost Marshal's office had a critical need for clerical workers. A routine war-zone story in a Midwestern newspaper, which the wire services redistributed nationally, made a local European-Theater, military-justice problem into a cause célèbre. It reported that hundreds of soldiers were incarcerated for long periods in Army jails without being charged with a crime; Americans were being denied habeas corpus, a basic right. Several congressmen proposed holding hearings. Veterans' organizations demanded the Army take immediate action.

Although imprisoning American soldiers for long periods without arraigning them before a judge advocate appeared sinister, there was little evidence that basic liberties were willfully compromised. Rather, the unfortunate situation was an unintended consequence of the reinforcement system. Reinforcement-depot soldiers, fresh from combat, often got into drunken brawls and committed petty crimes. They were rarely hardened criminals. After arrest, they were locked up in base-section guardhouses. The arresting officer was often another soldier passing through the depot. Before formal court-martial procedures could be initiated, the arresting officer and the witnesses had moved on. Since there was no officer to prefer charges (or even a knowledgeable one to move for dismissal), the culprit languished quietly in a guardhouse. Incarcerated soldiers had little incentive to disturb the status quo. During a shooting war a guardhouse in the reinforcement depot is a desirable place to be. It is safe and dry, and prisoners are usually served hot meals.

Following the furor in Washington, General Eisenhower ordered base-section guardhouses cleared of all but truly dangerous criminals. The Theater Provost Marshal was charged with assembling a task force to investigate the alleged crimes, review imprisoned soldiers' military and criminal histories, and, where appropriate, clean up their service records. A former Philadelphia neighbor of mine was the task force's recruiting officer. He organized a staff that included a psychologist, academic criminologist, military-police officers, and a judge-advocate-general's liaison, plus several lawyers and clerks. I became one of the clerks.

The Red Cross tried to arrange for soldiers on leave to participate in at least one unique Paris experience. That might consist of an opera visit, evening at a cabaret, boat trip along the Seine, symphony concert, first-run U.S. movie, clubhouse seats at the local racetrack, sports event, or perhaps simply a view from the Eiffel Tower. I was issued a ticket to attend the races at the exclusive Auteueil Steeplechase Course, which, like the equally prestigious Longchamps Course, ran a full schedule of meets and operated a clubhouse restaurant throughout the war. My first racetrack experience was enjoyable, but my thoughts extended beyond horseflesh. I was troubled by a nation where, while a deadly war raged on its soil and the general populace was on tight food rations, thoroughbreds were well fed and immaculately groomed.

Although Major League Baseball and the National Football League continued to operate throughout the war, thoroughbred racetracks were shut down by James F. Byrnes, director of the Office of War Mobilization. *[As chair of the War Mobilization Board, James F. Byrnes (1882–1972) directed all homland war activities. He was a Supreme Court justice before taking the position, and he was secretary of state afterward.]* Baseball and football were considered important for national morale. Horse racing, on the other hand, was perceived as a sport dominated by the socially elite. In France only the very rich owned thoroughbred stables. Throughout the Nazi occupation, Parisian aristocrats had no trouble securing permits to hire jockeys, trainers, grooms, and stable hands, and buying rations to feed large animals.

For several nights in August, 1945, immediately after the

atomic bombings and the Japanese surrender, I cruised Paris cafés and public squares, hoping to find some victory parties or celebrations, but it was a frustrating experience. There were no victory festivities. Parisians could not have cared less about the outcome of the Pacific war. That was "our war," not theirs.

After the guardhouse cleanup was completed, the special task force disbanded, and I became chief clerk in a division of the Theater Provost Marshal's office. I processed the paperwork of American soldiers held prisoner in European Theater jails. Most of them were guilty of crimes that, if committed by civilians, would be punished by prison terms or execution in the U.S. civilian criminal-court system. My duties included typing cables that went to the executed soldiers' next of kin. If a court-martial order read "To be hung by the neck until dead," the cable read "Cause of death: judicial asphyxia."

Shortly after V-E Day, the Army commandeered France's premier resort region—the Riviera along the Mediterranean coast—as a recreation area for soldiers. A grandiose project (partially paid for by reverse lend-lease funds), the area offered rest and relaxation to approximately ten thousand military men and women each week. The Riviera Recreation Area Command managed 144 hotels in six cities, plus countless restaurants, cabarets, and theaters.

In October, 1945, I had a Riviera furlough. A week in the Hotel Ruhl, Nice's largest deluxe hotel, was a treat; I enjoyed a bed with an innerspring mattress, sheets, and pillowcases, an en-suite bath and a lobby area where I could purchase the *Herald Tribune* daily. In Nice's premiere prewar casino, the Palais de la Méditerranée, the Red Cross operated a snack bar, library, pool, and ping-pong room, a movie theater and a pro station.

The military caste system was so deeply ingrained that it was that assumed soldiers could not adequately relax if superior officers were billeted in the same city. Nice, the Riviera's largest city (1945 population: 242,000), was reserved for enlisted men. Officers below the rank of major vacationed in Cannes, the next largest municipality. Female soldiers were housed in a smaller resort city, while colonels and generals stayed at a still smaller, but more posh, resort. Billboards around Nice emphasized the fact that, even if an officer was in Nice on official business, GIs were not expected to salute. General Eisenhower was participating in a summit of Allied brass on the French Riviera when he learned that one of the meetings was to take place in Nice. He immediately requested a change of venue. As he saw it, convening general officers and their entourages in Nice would interfere with the no-sa-luting, no-spit-and-polish environment he had promised his troops on leave.

Two areas in Nice were off limits: the beach and a large casino where French civilians gambled. Although German mines were substantially cleared from the harbor, mine debris was a continuing danger along the entire French coastline. Swimming and beach recreation continued to be dangerous for several years. Streets near the casino were cordoned off, and MPs guarded all casino doors. Since dice and cards are integral parts of a soldier's environment, making glamorous casinos off limits appeared incongruous and unfair. GIs did not understand that MPs at casino entrances were part of the solution to a major problem that plagued the Army of Occupation—the robust and growing black market. Tons of excess Army supplies and equipment had become part of Europe's underground commerce. The *Herald Tribune* reported that in October, 1945, European Theater soldiers transmitted more money to the United States as postal money orders than the month's total troop pay. Restricting the amounts that soldiers could send home was a crucial part of black-market control. If soldiers were allowed to gamble at big-time casinos, they could justify having almost any amount of cash.

The Army of Occupation headquarters moved from Paris to Frankfurt shortly after I returned from furlough, and I moved with it.

Paris, France
Independence Day, 1945
Dear Folks:

Once again I am living on a really beautiful campus. This time it is the Citée Universitaire de Paris. The Army has taken over the whole place. The Theater Provost Marshal's personnel are living in part of the U.S. building. Right on campus there is a PX, a coke and beer bar, movie theater, library, etc. Notwithstanding the fact that there are bed checks and inspections, it looks like a good deal.

This letter is being written in a beautiful library. In many ways it resembles some of the rooms in the Dartmouth Library. Although it is not equipped with many books, the quiet, learned atmosphere of a library is quite pleasant. The entire attitude all around the Citée Universitaire is pleasant.

At the Theater Provost Marshal's office I work in the rehabilitation and confinement division. My first impressions of the people in the office are good. The definition of my duties is rather vague. They will probably involve typing, filing, etc.

In many ways our status is similar to that of civilian civil-service workers overseas who receive cigarette rations, live in comfortable barracks, eat in GI restaurants, report for work at 8:30 A.M., and leave at 5:30 P.M. Although I have no particular desire to be a civil-service worker after the war, for the present it is very satisfactory. I live with six other men in a dormitory room that has electric lights, closets, and a washstand.

Paris, France
July 5, 1945
Dear Folks:

Each day I think more and more of the officers with whom I am working. They are so very different from the selfish and ignorant shavetails I met in the engineers. Today I went to the personnel section to see about getting paid for the month of June. The minute Major Wilkinson heard that I wanted to get paid he reached for his wallet and urged me to let him lend me some money. I refused, but the spirit that prompts men to make *gestures like that is the type of spirit which helps to make life pleasant and livable. [Major Roy Wilkinson, Jr. (1916–1995), a combat artillery officer and prewar lawyer, was assigned to the Theater Provost Marshal's office to work on the over- crowded guardhouse problem. In the 1990s, he served as an associate justice of the Supreme Court of Pennsylvania.]*

As you probably know, until about six weeks ago, the only American publication published in Europe was the Paris edition of the New York Herald Tribune. *In the past few weeks several more have made their appearance. Until yesterday, when the* New York Post *put in an appearance, not a single one of the pub- lications was strongly Democratic. As a matter of fact, you could say that one year ago four out of the five publications were strongly anti-Roosevelt. The publications were* Time, Newsweek, *the* Chicago Tribune, *and the* New York Times *(its Sunday re- view with certain special, added features). I do not know who is responsible for choosing the papers that will be published here in Europe or granting permission, but the choice is some sort of a tribute to those beliefs in the freedom of the press, which I like to think we have not kicked overboard for the meaningless term "military expediency."*

St. Cloud, France
July 8, 1945
Dear Folks:

The men who are stationed in Europe as part of the Occupa- tion Army are now receiving a liquor ration by order of General Ike. The liquor rationing is being worked out by allotting each noncom one-half of an officer's ration. For eighty-four francs each, the following is rationed to four noncoms: one bottle (quart) whiskey, one bottle (quart) champagne, one bottle (quart) gin, one bottle (quart) liquor. It's not a great deal. Still, if our plans work out, it ought to be good for two or three parties. [Since we could not agree on who was to get the whiskey and gin, and who the less desirable champagne and cordial, we resolved the dilemma by deciding to consume the entire ration at a monthly party.]

St. Cloud, France
July 11, 1945
Dear Folks:

Life in St. Cloud is much more active and useful than life at
Pumping Station 53. I find myself looking for a few spare minutes to write letters instead of writing them regularly to help keep
idle hands active, as I did a few weeks ago.

It looks like our setup may be much better than the one we formerly had in Paris. St. Cloud seems to be one of the finest suburbs
of Paris. The street on which we have both our billets and our office looks very much like the seven-hundred block on Westview Avenue. [The Obermayers lived at 821 Westview.] Our billet is in
a home that must once have been the home of a lawyer with fine
aesthetic tastes. We found in his closets and cellar many very
beautifully bound leather books on the law. Additionally, we
found many fine books on, and specimens of, French painting and
sculpture, as well as the scores of many of the famous operas of
Verdi, Wagner, and Debussy.

The view of Paris from our window is similar to the one you get
of San Francisco from the observation tower on top of one of the
hills. Although the home in which we make our office is in a very
poor state of repair, the Army has arranged for ten or twenty
POWs to come around every day and cut the grass, prune the
trees, and so on. They have contracted with a French contracting
outfit to have the offices painted. Colonel's demands get only the
best. We are only a block or so away from the St. Cloud railroad
station, which reaches the Gare St. Lazare in Paris in about
twenty minutes. The train, the ride, and the crowd are similar to
those on the Paoli and Chestnut Hill locals in Philadelphia.

Believe it or not, someday soon your soldier son overseas may
be writing home for golf balls. One of the finest golf courses in
France is less than two miles away. We can secure clubs, the use of
the course, and one ball through Special Services, but I will probably have a great deal of difficulty going around the course with
only one ball.

Although I like Paris and the nice billets, the thing that I really
like here is the officers and men that I work with. Sergeant

Murrman is hard working, earnest, and sincere. After the working day, he is still a very good guy. I am sure his boss thought he was pretty good because he promised to get him back to the States to work for him as soon as he gets a permanent assignment. Although I may have given you some of this information about the officers before, I will take my chances and repeat them. Colonel [Frederick S.] Lee was formerly provost marshal of the Eighth Air Force in England. He is really a wonderful guy—the type of man you expect to meet as a successful businessman or a socially prominent character at a swanky country club. Lieutenant Colonel Slingluff is a lawyer by profession, but before coming to the Theater Provost Marshal's office, he was a member of the Twenty-Second Corps' headquarters in the general staff corps. He landed in Normandy on D-Day and followed combat troops all the way across Europe until V-E Day. He has lots of points and hopes to return to the practice of the law sometime within the next year. The other enlisted men in the office are all high-grade office personnel. More than 50 percent of them have been with this office for longer than two years. Of course, WACs are WACs. Try as I may to overlook my old prejudices, certain facts become more and more apparent. The same type of woman joins the WACs as men join the regular Army as enlisted men in peacetime. However, they always call Tommy "savior of his country when the guns begin to shoot." [Rudyard Kipling's (1865–1936) poem "Tommy" ridiculed England's elite, who looked down on the common soldier (Tommy Atkins). "For it's Tommy this, an' Tommy that, an' 'Chuck him out, the brute!' But it's 'savior of 'is country' when the guns begin to shoot."]

Although we are continuing to work as usual, you can already hear bands and rockets and crowds as the French are preparing for the biggest binge in their history. The first Bastille Day since the liberation will be celebrated for three days with continual parades and all-night street dancing every night. If things go right, I hope to get into town tomorrow night and get in on a little of the excitement. A three-day celebration with activities all day and all night is something that no American city would have the courage to try.

St. Cloud, France
July 15, 1945
Dear Folks:

Although we worked all day yesterday, last night I went down to see the big celebration [Paris's first Bastille Day since its liberation]. I thought it was rather disappointing. It was typically French and certainly not worth taking part in. All the buildings were covered with bunting. A few noble bartenders with a wise eye to business had British and American flags hung out next to their tricolors and Crosses of Lorraine. The most beautiful flag display was the tremendous French flag that was suspended by a complicated set of cables in the center of the Arc de Triomphe. The Place de la Concorde was lighted up almost as well as a ball diamond. Thousands of people milled around and tried to dance while a couple of bands made noise and U.S. jeeps tried to drive through the crowd.

I do not particularly like street dancing of the French variety, but they certainly go for it in a big way over here. For every little occasion they hold a street dance. They seem to find plenty of people who like it well enough to dance until six or seven in the morning and then work all day. The thing that seems most remarkable to me is not their love of dancing but the way they are able to keep such large functions under control with their mild-looking and mild-acting gendarmes. I have never seen a gendarme carrying a pistol. With their billy clubs alone, they maintain order and control traffic on boulevards like the Champs Élysées, where they have no stop-and-go lights. A great volume of that traffic—probably 80 percent—runs on black-market gas that came to France through military channels.

St. Cloud, France
July 16, 1945
Dear Folks:

Things are continuing to improve in St. Cloud. Today our own PX opened. This PX really came as a surprise to most of us, as 135 men do not rate their own PX, but the inspector general thought his boys ought to have one. Now we do. [The Inspector General's staff was also assigned to St. Cloud.]

In one of Mother's recent letters, she told me how much she was enjoying Bill Mauldin's book. I'm glad. I've read his cartoons for six months now and almost swear by him. He's the heir to Ernie Pyle in the hearts of the soldiers in Europe. When you are finished with it, please send it on in a package. [The generally disrespectful, unshaven, disheveled soldiers Willie and Joe, creations of **Stars and Stripes** cartoonist Bill Mauldin (1921-2003), were favorites of American troops in Europe. Mauldin was a Pulitzer-Prize winner while still a cartoonist for **Stars and Stripes**. His antiauthoritarian perspective and vast popularity prompted General George S. Patton to threaten to ban distribution of **Stars and Stripes** to the Third Army.]

St. Cloud, France
July 19, 1945
Dear Folks:

It looks like on top of all my other duties before long I may be driving a big limousine with more electrical gadgets than a fancy Packard. Colonel Slingluff was formerly with the V Corps. While V Corps was going through Germany, every time they picked up a good automobile belonging to an important Nazi, they gave it to an American officer. Colonel Slingluff and another colonel jointly own the car of which we have just taken possession. The other colonel is going to use it until he goes home next month. After that it will be ours. All of the enlisted men are going to drive it some of the time. It will give us an excuse to get out of Paris once in a while and see the country. In the evenings in Paris, we will be able to use it whenever it suits our fancy.

St. Cloud, France
July 25, 1945
Dear Folks:

Last night was spent very pleasantly at our new PX drinking real American beer. Our new PX is the nicest one I have seen since I entered the Army. The "wet canteen," where they serve beer and coke, is a heavily carpeted, well-decorated living room of a large St. Cloud home. Both the officers and men use it as a private organization club.

The deal here in St. Cloud seemed just too good to be true or to last. And it was. Sometime within the next week or so, half of the Theater Provost Marshal's office is going to move to Frankfurt. Nobody is very happy about it. They say that Frankfurt is more crowded with GIs than Blackstone, Va., or Fayetteville, N.C. None of the officers below brigadier general will have any of the comforts they enjoy in Paris.

It may interest you to know what the Army's overall plans are for the disposition of troops in Europe. Com. Z [communications zone] during the war meant the supply sections behind the combat troops. Now it means everything in Europe outside the American occupation and supply areas. It is planning to go out of existence next May after a 50-percent personnel cut in September or October.

Com. Z headquarters are in Versailles. Although not actually under the commanding general of Com. Z, we are not part of the occupation Army either. With a lot of jobless brass in the provost marshal's section (like everywhere else in Europe), high-ranking officers keep inventing jobs for themselves to stay away from the China-Burma-India Theater and continue to live in the type of luxury that only a Rockefeller, Mellon, or Morgan knew at home.

St. Cloud, France
July 27, 1945
Dear Folks:

Just returned from my first visit to the "liberal synagogue" of Paris, where I heard one of the most brilliant sermons on Zionism or anything else I have ever heard. The service was conducted by the chief Jewish chaplain in Seine section.

In his sermon, the chaplain tried to show a very pessimistic— but very true—picture of Judaism in Europe. It can never again rise to its former position of prominence and brilliance. Then with logic which would probably not satisfy a lawyer but was

*very convincing in a sermon, he showed how the Jews had to leave
Europe and had no place to go but to Palestine. After recognizing
all of the difficulties in forming a commonwealth in Palestine, he
concluded that the only positive action Jews could take would be
to support political Zionism. We Jews must act positively, he said.
He is leaving on Sunday for the World Zionist Congress in
London and will report back next week. If possible, I will go to
hear him.*

St. Cloud, France
July 29, 1945
Dear Folks:

*By a recent order of General Lee each enlisted man attached to
USFET [**U.S. Forces European Theater**] (rear) works only five
and a half days a week. In our division we worked out a system
whereby all of the enlisted-man staff was off on Sunday. We arranged among ourselves which weekday afternoon we took off. I
have not worked since yesterday afternoon. During the past day
and a half, I have relaxed and enjoyed myself.*

*I took a tour of Versailles this afternoon. The biggest laugh of the
tour came at the very beginning. The guide was pointing out to the
group [**Canadian soldiers and me**] the main palace and the various auxiliary ones for the court. Then he pointed across the street
and said, "There are the stables and coachmen's quarters. Now
they are used as the headquarters of the U.S. Army in France." The
Canadians and British who always think—correctly—that our
government takes much better care of us in the way of amusements,
living quarters, etc., got quite a laugh out of that.*

St. Cloud, France
July 30, 1945
Dear Folks:

*Yesterday we received a mimeographed bulletin from the U.S.
Army Postal System with figures on how long it is taking mail to
go to and come from the States:*

*Mail from the U.S. (average number of days between date of
postmark and date of delivery in the European Theater)*

V-mail	7.4
Airmail	6.7
Parcels and prints	28.2

Mail to the U.S. (days from postmark date to date dispatched from the European Theater)

| V-mail | 3.1 |
| Airmail | 4.4 |

St. Cloud, France
August 4, 1945

Dear Folks:

Back in the States you probably know more about the French political situation than we do over here in France. Still, I'm sure you have no conception of the propaganda war that is being waged in Paris between the various political factions, both domestic and foreign, that want to justify past actions and rise to power.

A major international exhibition opened in Paris. I visited it today. Every important government faction or foreign government has some sort of an exhibit along the Champ Élysées today. The U.S. government has a large and extremely well-done exhibit. It tells about the war against Japan and how we are exerting all of our efforts in that direction. It helps explain our failure to meet our agreements with UNRRA [United Nations Relief and Rehabilitation Agency].

Both Yugoslavian groups have buildings and exhibits. [In the summer of 1945 the form and control of Yugoslavia's future government was unclear. This was a harbinger of the Balkan wars in the 1990s. Marshal Tito's communist partisans asserted a claim based on their military contribution to the Allied victory, but prewar politicians still dominated in Belgrade.] The British have a tremendous war exhibit. The British, French, Canadian, and Americans have a joint war exhibit. Various French political groups have exhibits, but I have not gone to visit them because, with my limited knowledge, I was sure they would definitely feel that I was an intruder. Half of the magazine literature sold at the newsstands is published by the propaganda agencies of foreign governments, including France's most popular magazine, Voir, which is published by the United States Office of War Information (OWI). The biggest and most popular exhibit in Paris is an American one that does not deal directly with politics: the U.S. Army Air Force show under the Eiffel Tower. It is probably a more complete air force show than anyone has seen back in the States. It includes the Norden bombsight, which has never been shown to the public before.

St. Cloud, France
August 5, 1945
Dear Folks:

This morning I attended very beautiful and impressive services at the famous Rothschild Synagogue on the Rue de la Victoire. Although the Rothschild Synagogue shows very definite signs of wear and tear and wanton destruction, it remains one of the most beautiful synagogues I have ever visited. The doors have been removed, and many of the beautiful stained-glass windows are broken, but the pews, the Hebrew inscriptions on the wall, and the tremendous eight-branched menorah before the ark are all in good shape. With a little money and a few supplies—neither of which the Jews of France have—it could again be made into one of the world's most beautiful synagogues. Although 150 people didn't even start to make the place look crowded, easily that many worshipers were there this morning. Twenty-five percent were French civilians.

This afternoon I went to visit the Louvre. Although I probably should say that I was thrilled with the "Venus de Milo," the "Winged Victory," the "Mona Lisa," and "Whistler's Mother," I'm afraid I can't say so. Only a very few paintings are on display. Most of the famous ones are still in Germany. The ones that are being shown have only been on display about three weeks.

Each time I go to an art museum like the Louvre, I become more and more aware of one of the great gaps in my education: Greek and Roman mythology. It seems that there are very few works of art, ancient or modern, written, painted, or chiseled out *of stone that you can enjoy to their fullest without a thorough knowledge of mythology. Although I suppose "Winged Victory" was originally designed with a head, the thing that impressed me most was the idea that the classic statue of victory has no head. In the course of time, a hollow will probably wear into the chest where the heart belongs.*

I can answer your question about U.S. currency now. American soldiers can get three and four times their value for five and ten dollar bills. All the hustlers in Paris seem to hang out around the "Rainbow Corner," the Seine section's PX, and a few Montmartre bars where you can always find GIs. Of course, it is not exactly legal for American soldiers to carry U.S. currency, but they always have a place to sell it. It is illegal for the French to own it, but most of them do not hesitate to buy it.

Our move to Frankfurt seems to be temporarily postponed, chiefly because the officers can't find anything in Germany that compares with their elaborate St. Cloud apartment houses. About a dozen men from the Theater Provost Marshal's office are already in Wiesbaden, but so far nobody from this division has gone up there permanently. Colonel Lee is spending this week in Germany looking over installations and so on. I still have hopes that we will not leave here until after the first of October.

St. Cloud, France
August 12, 1945
Dear Folks:

Each day the news gets better and better. Each day my hopes rise higher and higher. Each day home seems nearer and nearer. I don't think it will be too long until I will live once again as a civilian. The news has been wonderful for the past week. But there has been very little excitement in Paris. When the great word finally comes, I suppose the chief celebrants will be American soldiers. The French won their war three months ago.

[One week plus one day elapsed (August 6 to August 14, 1945) between the dropping of the world's first atom bomb on Hiroshima (there were approximately seventy thousand killed) and Japan's unconditional surrender. During that

Stage Door Canteen on the Champs Élysées.

week a second atom bomb was dropped on Nagasaki (there were approximately forty thousand killed), and the United States firebombed much of downtown Tokyo.]

When I tell you what I have done during the past two days, you will not believe that I am in the same Army where I was forced to call Lt. Broadhurst "sir" and run errands for Sergeant Wilhelm [my company commander and drill sergeant at Camp Pickett].

Friday night after work I played golf at the St. Cloud Country Club with Sergeants Lyle, Lindquist, and Murrman. Although I did not break fifty, I played very well considering my golfing skill and lack of practice. St. Cloud is a beautiful country club. For a greens fee of fifty francs (about one dollar), you receive a set of Special Service clubs, one ball, and the use of all of the club's facilities, which includes a beautiful bar (far more elaborate than anything at Philmont Country Club) where you can order drinks made of scotch and gin, as well as the usual French drinks of vin blanc and cognac. Our Ryder Cup teams used to practice there before going to England.

St. Cloud, France
August 15, 1945
Dear Folks:

This is a great day. All of our prayers and hopes of the last two years have been answered. We won! Soon our lives will return to normal. We'll be able to look back at this war as men who are a little wiser after an unpleasant experience.

Although I suppose there was a great deal of excitement in America last night and today, Paris has been quieter than usual. The only real celebrants were GIs, who are not here in large-enough numbers to swing the city along in their celebrating spirits. The only signs of excitement in downtown Paris were the paperboys hawking extras on the street corners and a feeble, forced celebration at the American Red Cross's "Rainbow Corner" on the Boulevard Madeline.

On Friday morning I expect to fly to Frankfurt with Colonel Lee and Major Wilkinson for about ten days. We are going to

*Germany to set up advanced headquarters for the confinement
and rehabilitation division. At present I have no idea what I will
do there. However, I believe it is a good deal. I enjoy working with
both of those men. When you travel with colonels, you usually eat
from plates instead of mess gear and go by air instead of in the
back of a truck. I probably will not receive any mail during that
time, so do not expect acknowledgments. We originally expected to
go on Thursday, but since that is a holiday we could see very little
excuse for wasting a holiday in travel when we could just as easily waste a workday.*

St. Cloud, France
August 24, 1945
Dear Folks:

*As soon as anybody returns from Germany, the first question
that everybody seems to ask is about fraternization. From all I
could see there isn't very much. I took off one whole evening to
walk around Frankfurt and get orientated. Try as I might I
couldn't get a single person to say "hello" to me. They all seemed
to look at me as though I'd done it all myself. Of course, lots of
the men know fräuleins quite intimately, but those associations
with women can hardly be called fraternizing with the German
public. The word "fraternizing," as the GI uses it today, concerns
nothing but women—"friendships" based on candy bars and
cigarettes.*

*Last Friday evening I went with another soldier to hear a mag-
nificent piano recital at the Palais de Chaillot. It had been advertised as a Chopin concert, but it turned out to be a piano recital
without a single Chopin number. It was one of those tremendously
beautiful things that you cannot help enjoying, but I left it a little
confused and disappointed with myself, as I seem to be every time
I come in contact with real art these days. If art has any real purpose, it is because the appreciation of it is a sensual experience,
not some sort of a passive, intellectual one. But damn it, I always
seem to miss it. Here was something I would really have liked to
take part in, but every time I try, I find I'm not mentally
equipped.*

Paris, France
August, 25, 1945

Dear Folks:

Marty Cooper visited me in Paris and told me all about the group from 1291st Engineers who went with Captain Davidson to Maastricht and what happened to them after that outfit broke up. From all reports Marty Cooper and several friends from the 1291st Engineers had a very good—and very easy—assignment for five months. They did very little work and were stationed near several large cities. They had a racket by which each of them sent home more than a thousand dollars. They were stationed in Holland, where there were relatively few Americans, all of whom were paid in guilders. The Nazis wrecked the Dutch currency system. Nobody has any faith in it. The result is that it is very hard to buy anything with guilders. It is almost impossible for a Dutchman to change his guilders into Belgian francs, which have value, but it is very easy for a GI to do it at an Army finance office. Belgian francs sell for between four and five times their value in Holland, and it is only a short trip from Maastricht to Liege or Antwerp.

*Talking about money, did you hear that all of the soldiers in France are receiving $17.50 per month extra to help make up for the beating they take on the French-franc exchange rate? This is a rather unusual scheme as everybody gets the $17.50 regardless of his rank or pay scale. Instead of equalizing the exchange rate, they give you a consolation prize. [**From my first days in France, when I was required to change all my U.S. currency for French francs, I, as well as every GI I knew, resented the fact that we were paid in overvalued French money. The unfavorable exchange rate seriously hurt U.S. troop morale. Although the top brass was very much aware of the situation, they did little to correct it. An April, 1945, article in the** New York Times *pointed out that "most American soldiers thought they were getting a raw deal in France" and it might have "an adverse effect on Franco-American relations." The article said that the GIs' attitude could be summarized as follows: "We didn't mind fighting to liberate France, but we don't* *like paying for it, too." Representative Paul J. Kilday of Texas introduced a bill in Congress to require that service personnel in France be paid either in American dollars or at the current New York exchange rate if paid in local currency. Kilday said that, in order to please the French government, American soldiers were "getting only half their pay."]*

"Coop" and I got caught in some of the tremendous celebration the French were putting on for "Liberation Day" *[the first anniversary of the Allied entry into Paris]*. The crowd was so dense in the Place de l'Opéra, where they were broadcasting "Rigoletto" while Lily Pons was singing inside, that it was almost impossible to get through. They needed tanks to maintain order. There were also many parades and a very elaborate fireworks display. With experiences like "Liberation Day," you feel justified in snickering at the French assertion that they care about the Japanese war. Celebrations like Bastille Day, Liberation Day, and V-E Day all stem from the people themselves. They show conclusively their lack of interest in "our war."

Yesterday morning I got up early and played eighteen holes of very poor golf before lunch. The more I see the St. Cloud club, the more I wonder how any people who seem as down-at-the-heels as the French can maintain a place like that.

St. Cloud, France
September 18, 1945
Dear Folks:

Even when I don't leave the office all day and come back at night to write letters, I like being near Paris. Tomorrow I have arranged a very special birthday celebration *[September 19, 1945, was my twenty-first birthday]* for myself here in the big city. I arranged to take Cecil Davis, Jacobson, and Murrman (if he returns from the UK) to one of those famous, wild nightclubs in Montparnasse that Somerset Maugham *[Between the world wars, W. Somerset Maugham (1874–1965) was one of Britain's most popular novelists and playwrights. He idealized Paris in his books. His works include* **Of Human Bondage** *and* **The Razor's Edge.***]* seems to love and know so well.

This evening I decided that I had one other good friend here in Paris whom I ought to invite, so I called Hud Stoddard [Central High School friend and a State Department courier passing through Paris] and asked him to go with us. To make it a real party, he invited us to have dinner with him in their rather elaborate mess in the Hotel Wagram. I thought you would like to know that I am really arranging a party for the big day.

St. Cloud, France
September 21, 1945
Dear Folks:

Now I am a man. Christ, that sounds silly. Whenever you say that, it sounds trite and somewhat foolish, but as I say it today, it sounds almost funny enough to laugh at. The day did not go off exactly as we had expected before I became a soldier. Still, I had a very pleasant and happy day, everything considered. A great deal was added to the day by the many kind attentions I received from home. The package with the razor, cookies, knife, golf balls, etc., was great. The letters and cards from each one of you were all just another bit of evidence that I have the most thoughtful family a man could have.

I worked in the office all day as usual and then had supper with Hud Stoddard, Cecil Davis, and Jake as Hud's guests at the U.S. Embassy's employee mess at the Hotel Wagram. After supper, Hud had to go back to work, so the three of us went out to Montparnasse. After visiting a few dives, we sat down to a bottle of champagne.

St. Cloud, France
September 28, 1945
Dear Folks:

Last night I decided that if the rest of the family could make regular trips to the races, I shouldn't let my stay in one of the world's great racing cities pass by without another trip to the races. This time I went to the dog races at Courbevoie. Although I felt the same way about them that I did about the horse races, I had a very good time. Dog racing is an evening sport in Paris.

The races begin at seven and end sometime between nine-thirty and ten. There is no doubt that gambling is fun. I guess I will always enjoy going to races regardless of my opinions of the relative beauty of a perfectly executed double play, an off-tackle play from the T, and a horse or dog race.

I don't think I told you what a great and wonderful book I thought Bill Mauldin's Up Front *is. He is one of the few men who have brought before the public what Hansen Baldwin [*New York Times *military correspondent] and most other people in the know consider the greatest problem in the Army today: the very strained relationship between the officers and the enlisted men. Everybody around here is really worried about it (I spent almost two hours discussing it with Majors Wilkinson and Blake). They all talk about the incident when the Queen Elizabeth landed in NYC. As the officers walked off the ship, the enlisted men stood on the decks and booed. It is very unusual and unnatural when the men on a winning team can do nothing but damn the captain, the manager, and the trainer.*

St. Cloud, France
September 29, 1945
Dear Folks:

People often ask why I prefer to be stationed in Paris. I could just as easily be stationed in Frankfurt and not do a bit of work. Down here I put in a full eight hours and more than six days a week. The answer is that last night I went to a ballet, and the night before I went to a dog race. As long as I can enjoy myself after working hours, I don't mind working hard during the day.

Last night I went to see a Ballet Guild production brought over here by BBA, the British equivalent of our camp shows, Red Cross, and so on. Although it was all very interesting and enjoyable as a medium of expression, ballet is entirely beyond me. It was beautiful, passive enjoyment, like looking at a pretty picture or letting music on the radio put you to sleep, but whatever stories or ideas the ballet was supposed to put across I missed.

Last week saluting was abolished here in Paris, as it is now almost exclusively a leave area. By December 1 they expect to have all but a small, residual force out of Paris. This is very good news. The more GIs that leave, the better Paris will be for those that remain. The order abolishing the saluting was issued by General Larkin, the commanding general during General Lee's absence. It has certainly been well received by everybody. General Lee is probably having a fit. He is a real stickler for discipline, military courtesy, etc., and I believe a failure as a commanding general. His public-relations men have done a good job for him. Nevertheless, history is not written by public-relations officers, promoters, and advertising agents.

St. Cloud, France
September 30, 1945
Dear Folks:

The thing I want to do most is to get out of the Army and get home. Regardless of what the local gossips or the newspapers may tell you, it can be done. Officers and enlisted men from this headquarters are leaving every day for either short periods at home or for discharges, regardless of their point scores.

The rules say that an enlisted man cannot be requested by name, but with the backing of the proper high brass, it can be done around channels instead of through them. The time when the safe and wise thing for a soldier to do was to stay in Europe is rapidly drawing to a close. Men with fewer than forty-five points (I have forty-one) are being placed on occupation Army rosters. It will be nowhere as easy to get off those rosters as it is to get home during these days when redeployment has a priority over everything else.

Colonel Lee likes me. I don't think he will let me go any sooner than he must. (If I would show any interest in staying here a year or more, I could probably get a spot commission, but all I want to do is get home.)

Assuming I will stay here until sometime late next spring, I am planning on the following:

1. As soon as Colonel Lee leaves (Friday) I will try to get a furlough. I believe Major Wilkinson will approve it. If he does, it should come through sometime in November.

2. After my furlough, I expect to apply for admission to one of the two-month courses for GIs over here, either at a civilian college or an Army university. My preference is a civilian college.

3. After that I expect to do nothing but work to get home.

However, I want you to understand that all of these things are indefinite. The most important thing is getting home. In civilian life it is much easier to make plans for the future because you have somewhere to place your faith. In the Army you must take what is best at the moment. By the time you expect to take advantage of certain opportunities, the odds are ten to one that the Army has changed the system or some general with a hangover has issued some asinine order that will put innumerable obstacles in your way, which will probably be rescinded by the time you have changed your plans. I am the beggar. I know it. I know that the wisest thing to do if someone offers me a loaf of bread is to grab it, run, and eat it. Don't ask or worry about tomorrow.

St. Cloud, France
October 2, 1945
Dear Folks:

This morning we received from the War Department a copy of a cable that I assume will get publicity all over the country. Although the point system is being continued in theory, in practice it is being thrown out the window. After November 1, any man with 60 points who is stationed in the States can get discharged, while the ETO shipping schedules call for getting only the men with more than 80 points out by November 1. What I believe this means is that any man who was lucky enough—or had enough political influence to get home or stay home—will be out of the Army by January or February, regardless of points. **[In response to a public demand for quicker redeployment and discharge processing, General George C. Marshall, chief of staff, testified about the Army's demobilization plans before a joint meeting of the House and Senate Military Affairs Committees on September 22, 1945. Quickly demobilizing an eight-million-man Army required complex planning and logistics, he explained. He was proud of the fact that, since the Japanese had surrendered five weeks earlier, eight hundred thousand men** *had been discharged. A planned reduction in the point-score threshold would speed up the process.]*

St. Cloud, France
October 3, 1945
Dear Folks:

On Friday night I ate with Mr. Claster and his group at the Hotel Raphael. Then we went to a party in an elegant room in the hotel. I certainly hope they don't send many groups of prominent citizens, like Claster's group, over here. All of them will leave thinking that the Army is a great and wonderful institution run by a lot of charming colonels and generals who throw wonderful cocktail parties. A man in Claster's party in all seriousness asked me how I felt about electing a "modern" general to the presidency. He felt sure that the soldiers who served overseas and had seen the Army work would support General Ike or any other important general as a bloc. I just said, "Yes, sir," and walked away. It would have been impolite to laugh. If I had tried to explain, I don't think he would have understood. [A family friend, Joel B. Claster, was an executive of a large scrap-metal brokerage. He was a member of a delegation of iron-and-steel-company executives the Army had invited to develop a plan for the disposition of millions of tons of scrap metal in the European Theater of operations.]

Saturday night I had dinner with a rather interesting and very nice French family. Early last week I went to the French welcome committee and told them I would like to be invited to a French family for supper. They arranged that I eat at the home of a fellow who is studying to be an English teacher at one of the Paris colleges. We had a very pleasant meal, which in typical French style took two and a half hours to eat. Then we went to a dance. Although the dance eventually turned into a brawl, I had a good time. I expect to see my new French friend again soon.

One of the things I have longed for most since coming over here has been fresh milk and milk shakes. Now you can get milk shakes, sodas, and sundaes in Paris six days a week at the Seine section's PX fountain shop. It is really the best thing of its type

*here in Paris. I'm sure it does a lot more good than all the Red
Cross clubs run by a lot of thrill-hunting, brass-crazy women.
This is run by the Army for the Army. As much as I don't like to
see things run by the Army, I don't believe the Red Cross is a hell
of a lot better.*

St. Cloud, France
October 13, 1945
Dear Folks:

    *Casey struck out again today. There was less joy in European
Theater headquarters than there ever could have been in*

A kiss from Joel
Claster, a family
friend, who
promised my
mother he would
deliver a kiss for
her. A steel-
industry execu-
tive, Claster was
consulting on
the disposition
of millions of
tons of scrap
metal in Europe.

Mudville. [*Mudville and Casey are references to "Casey at the Bat," a popular poem by Ernest Lawrence Thayer. The poem told how the town of Mudville's sports hero, Casey, struck out in the ninth inning of a baseball game.*] I don't know what your reaction was to the news about the return of the troopships to the British and the resulting lag and snafu in redeployment. Everybody here has a feeling of resentment and an unexplainable feeling that the bottom has dropped out of the world. I can't understand it. The people who run the country write stories and make speeches about their debts and obligations to the men who served in the Army and Navy. Then they knife them in the back.

I feel certain that if our government had been tough about it, we could have kept the Queen Elizabeth *and the* Aquitania. None of the blurbs that public-relations men will distribute to the newspapers in the next few days will convince me otherwise. We've been double-crossed or the nearest thing to it. We put our faith in a group of men who were not willing to fight to take care of us. You can bet it wouldn't have happened in October of an even-numbered year. I can understand—and most of the time approve of—American large-scale charity in Europe, but it's almost impossible to condone forgetting your own men and taking care of somebody else instead. [**On October 11, 1945, the War Department withdrew from troop-redeployment service the 85,000-ton** Queen Elizabeth **and 45,000-ton** Aquitania, **both of which were owned by Britain's Cunard Line. These ships started bringing home Canadian troops instead. It was estimated that, because of their speed and a combined 24,000-man troop capacity, 125,000 fewer U.S. soldiers than originally planned were sent home in the winter of 1945–1946.**]

St. Cloud, France
October 15, 1945
Dear Folks:

Half of the month of October has passed, and it looks like I'm farther from Philadelphia and Dartmouth than I was six weeks ago. Never before have I felt that my government has failed to recognize its duties and responsibilities, but today I feel this way

*very strongly. When they brought us over here, they promised
that, when it was all over, they would bring us back as quickly as
possible. Now it seems that their first interests are British politics
or Dominion trade or English troops. Any soldier who puts faith
in an Army promise is either a moron or a wild gambler.*

*In her letter Mother asked about how much I get paid each
month. My base pay is $78.00, plus 20-percent overseas pay. This
gives me a gross of $93.60 per month.*

*Sunday night I saw a movie with Mickey Rooney and Judy
Garland where the dialogue was in English, and beneath each
scene there was a French caption. At the movies they also had
considerable propaganda about what a wonderful guy General de
Gaulle is. His government has many flaws, but his propaganda
machine is very efficient.*

St. Cloud, France
October 17, 1945
Dear Folks:

*Three years ago today was one of the big days of my life. I took
my first drink of hard liquor, heard that the draft act for eigh-
teen- and nineteen-year-old boys had been passed in committee,
and saw my last Harvard-Dartmouth football game. Today, well,
I'm dreaming.*

*There is a great deal of fuss being made in Army circles these
days about the tight controls on money that are being instituted,
the devaluation of the pound last month, and the coming devaluation of the franc. Now nobody can send money home or purchase
a money order unless he has an official form signed by his commanding officer (this includes all officers below the grade of major). Even then, after November 1 I will not be able to send home
more than my monthly pay minus allotments and deductions. If
things go according to plan, I believe the devaluation of the franc
will help make things approach normal for the GIs in Paris.*

*Tonight I expect to go to see and hear Marlene Dietrich at the
Olympia Theater. I have never seen her. [**Marlene Dietrich
(1901–1992), film star and chanteuse, was famous for her
shapely legs and signature songs, "Lily Marlene" and "Fall-***

ing in Love Again." She always performed for standing-room-only GI audiences. Her last act was unforgettable. After each song the men would chant, "the legs! the legs! the legs!" Finally, after the last number she would slowly raise her slinky, sequined evening dress to show her legs. When she got to midthigh, instead of hose clasps at the end of her girdle garters, soldiers saw the shoulder patches of the units she was entertaining.]

St. Cloud, France
October 22, 1945
Dear Folks:

Today is a big day in France as it marks the birth of the "Fourth Republic." Although I couldn't feel any excitement about the election, only a blind man could have failed to see it. All over the city there are signs that say "Votez-vous" and "Oui-Non." They are painted on the sides of houses, in the middle of streets, on the walls of latrines, on railway-station platforms, and even on the gate to our building. On both Friday and Saturday afternoon several trucks with loudspeakers rode up and down the streets in the Opéra area, and men were handing out literature on the corners. I assume America is pleased with the results.

[In October, 1945, the French elected a new president, Charles de Gaulle, and chose a new form of government, the Fourth Republic. It was considered an incongruous election with lop-sided victories for a conservative military leader and Communist assembly candidates.]

Yesterday I had a very full day that began with nine holes of golf in the morning at the St. Cloud Country Club. The condition of that course still amazes me. Although the fairways were covered with leaves, the greens and tees had been raked and trimmed early Sunday morning. This is just another one of the things that is hard to understand about Paris, a city that has such acute shortages and yet still supports exclusive shops such as Sulkas, Dunhills, Moylneaux, and the St. Cloud County Club in pre-1939 style. (Some of the enlisted men at headquarters have met the Duke of Windsor playing golf at St. Cloud.)

St. Cloud, France
October 25, 1945
Dear Folks:

I was very much interested in Daddy's enclosures and comments about Earl Harrison's report on the situation in Jewish displaced-persons camps. The report has caused very little comment here. Many of the people in this office are quite familiar with the whole DP [displaced persons] situation. At one time the camps were administered by the same group in this office that administers the prisoner-of-war camps. [Earl Harrison, a Philadelphia lawyer and family friend, was the U.S. member of the Intergovernmental Committee on Refugees. He made a special report to President Truman titled "Displaced Jews in the U.S. Occupation Zone, 1945." Harrison's report was harshly critical of the Army of occupation's treatment of Jewish displaced persons in the U.S. zone. In part it said, "We appear to be treating the Jews as the Nazis treated them, except that we do not exterminate them. They are in concentration camps in large numbers under our military guard instead of SS troops." President Truman wrote General Eisenhower a letter of rebuke, which he released to the press.]

People at home have no appreciation of how all the petty, mean, and selfish instincts come out when people live close together and are treated like animals. Displaced persons are hard to handle. They are even harder to make happy. Even realizing how difficult the problem is, I do not think that the United States has the right type of personnel to administer displaced-persons camps in Europe. The Army and most of its leaders are rather intolerant of these problems. Most of the overseas UNRRA [United Nations Relief and Rehabilitation Administration] personnel are ne'er-do-well, adventure-seeking, white-collar workers who can't handle the job. At the head of most of these tremendous camps are very petty men who have been chosen because they know a foreign language or some other equally poor reason.

The conditions in the Jewish DP camps have improved. Still, I can't see how any Jew can think Harrison was wrong to overstate their cause. Those are the kind of Jews, who, when discussing Zionism, always tell you about the interests of the Arabs and the British Foreign Office. Everybody else in the world is looking out for their own interests first, last, and always. I can never understand why the Jews don't.

Nice, France
November 1, 1945
Dear Folks:

It's not Atlantic City. The scenery on the French Riviera is beautiful, but the beaches themselves are rocky and short. They in no way compare with the Jersey beaches.

I am trying very hard to enjoy the sporting place of kings. The Army has done a wonderful job here. It is almost impossible to honestly gripe about the place.

As you probably know, last year the Army set up the USRRA [U.S. Riviera Recreation Area] to facilitate giving combat men a week's rest, recreation, and recuperation. This organization took over almost all of the large hotels in Cannes, Antibes, Grasse, and Nice for soldiers, as well as several theaters, restaurants, and the giant, Jay Gould–financed Casino de la Méditerranée, which is now the American Red Cross headquarters, where I am writing this.

Cannes is off limits for enlisted men. Nice is off limits for officers. These rules are strictly enforced. We are not plagued by the old distinctions that can make life so miserable. At some of the smaller resorts—like Antibes—between Cannes and Nice, they have special areas for women officers, general officers, etc.

The ride down here from Frankfurt, although hardly a joyride, was much better than I expected. The train had about half cushioned seats and about half wooden benches. Still, there was enough room so that you could usually find two seats to curl up or stretch out on. We ate our first meal in Karlsruhe in a restaurant near the railroad station that the Seventh Army had taken over. We ate the other two meals in special GI messing centers along the track. These messing centers were established for the sole purpose of taking care of troop trains en route the French Riviera.

Troop trains did not have dining facilities. At Dijon, France, the Army established the "Merry Messing Center," an eating and rest facility for troops en route Riviera furloughs.

They are a good idea because they allow soldiers to get a good meal with a cup of hot coffee very rapidly.

Yesterday afternoon, notwithstanding the miserable weather, I took one of the three tours that are offered free to GIs in Nice. These tours are sponsored and paid for by the Army but are run by the American Express Company. I went on the trip that went up in the mountains to Grasse, then down to Cannes and along the coast road back to Nice. We left at 11:30 and had lunch in the beautiful Parc-Palace Hotel in Grasse, which has also been taken over by the USRRA. All along the coast you can see pillboxes, etc., that the Nazis built here. They feared southern France would be invaded here. The pillboxes are well camouflaged and placed, but as coastal installations go, they don't compare with the Maginot-type setup of the Nazis in Normandy's chalk cliffs.

Being dead tired, I went to bed early after dancing a few dances at one of the GI nightclubs in town. In about six of the GI hotels they have set up GI nightclubs where they serve beer (you can bring your own cognac, etc.) and have an orchestra and an occasional cabaret. They are very nice. They have the further advantage of being cheap in a country where everything is very expensive, but they also have the disadvantages of being GI.

Every afternoon tea dances are held in one of the hotels. This afternoon I went to one at the Riviera Palace Hotel in Cimiez, where they served tea, doughnuts, candy, etc. You are asked not to bring a date unless she's a WAC (and there aren't any WACs there). The girls are selected for you by a none-too-selective process.

As you probably know, the gambling houses here are off limits. The whole city-state of Monaco (Monte Carlo) is off limits to American troops. British troops, although not allowed to go to the casinos, are allowed to go into Monaco, which is supposed to have some very beautiful shops. The only type of gambling that is allowed is slot machines, which they have in the lobbies and bars of each hotel. The only type of machines they have are French

I was granted a one-week furlough at the Riviera recreation area in October, 1945. My billet was the Hotel Ruhl, Nice's largest hotel.

A leave area was established on the Riviera after V-E Day. Nice was reserved for enlisted men; Cannes, for officers; and smaller resorts, for generals and WACs. Enlisted men's recreation activities were directed from the "Casino Red Cross," which occupied Nice's swank Casino de la Méditerranée.

machines, so that even if you hit the jackpot, you win less than fifty cents. I was quite surprised about the way in which the United States respected the neutrality of Monaco. Upon asking some questions I found out that the Germans did the same thing. Even during the days when they feared an invasion here, they did not occupy Monaco.

*This afternoon I intended to go shopping, etc., but I forgot that this is All Saints' Day and nobody in France works. Tomorrow is All Souls' Day. They don't work then either. This business of church holidays being state holidays certainly makes for plenty of vacations. They must have done some fancy manipulating to find the man-hours to build the Maginot Line. [**During the 1920s and 1930s France constructed an elaborate and expensive defense system along its eastern frontier where it borders Germany. The above-ground fortification had twelve-foot-thick, reinforced concrete walls, and underground it had railroads, hospitals,*** supply depots, and arsenals as well as living quarters for thousands of troops. Named for André Maginot, the French minister of war who conceived and promoted the project, France's frontier-defense system was often described as Europe's single most costly public-works program between World War I and World War II. When the Germans invaded France in the spring of 1940, the fortification proved virtually useless since the Nazis entered France through the Netherlands and Belgium, where only a minimal defense system was in place.]*

This morning I went on the second of the three tours that are offered. The third, the boat trip to Monte Carlo, may be off indefinitely as a storm has loosened several floating mines in the area.

In the evening I visited a few of the bars and cafés that are not run by the Army. They were just as plushy and expensive as I expected. All of the bars over here where you can put your foot on a rail and order a drink are called American bars. It is very difficult to get a good explanation of why. Most people seem to agree that the style did not start in the United States.

German fortifications in the Riviera area were still in evidence five months after V-E Day. Along Nice's Promenade des Anglais, a concrete bunker camouflaged as a bathhouse was being demolished.

Seeing the world is a wonderful thing—if I could only see a date for returning home.

Nice, France
November 4, 1945
Dear Folks:

Down here away from everybody, I have plenty of time to read the papers and brood. The news seems to be 100-percent bad. Everybody seems to be talking and thinking and planning for another war in a few years. It seems to be a foregone conclusion. The powers that be are planning how to win it—not how to avoid it.

Saturday I went to one of the synagogues here, where they have both GI and civilian services. Out of curiosity, I went to the civilian service, where there were only three other American soldiers. Of course, I missed most of the service as it was conducted in Hebrew, except for a prayer for country in French. Although Nice was occupied by both the Italians and the Germans, the synagogue showed no signs of having been desecrated in any way.

German soldiers had mined Nice's harbor. Swimming and all beach activities were prohibited because of continuing mine danger. The salvaged mines were stored behind a seawall.

A German pillbox along the Grand Corniche Road, which connects the
Riviera's major cities.

They seemed to have a regular rabbi conducting the service. The "schamuz" [chief usher] was dressed like the one in the Rothschild synagogue was on Yom Kippur, with a frock coat, a Lord Nelson hat, and a big heavy chain that dangled around his belly. One of the most interesting things about the place is that they had five everlasting lamps hanging before the ark [the usual custom is one]. The really wonderful thing about the synagogue is the big, four-bladed fan that was suspended from the ceiling. What a genius. Think how the crowds loitering on the streets on Yom Kippur would diminish if the coolest place in the neighborhood were the synagogue.

St. Cloud, France
November 10, 1945
Dear Folks:

Tonight I am going to a dance in Versailles given by the Prisoner-of-War Information Bureau, where I have some friends. As long as I am active, I don't have as much time to be annoyed as I might otherwise be from the fact that there is really almost nothing for us to do over here. Several other people and I are busy. But it is all created work, similar to shovel-leaning WPA [Works Progress Administration] jobs.

This afternoon is a holiday as will be Monday in honor of Armistice Day. Although all of us are glad to get time off, I can't see how anyone can help snickering at this big celebration in honor of Armistice Day when they haven't even officially declared this war over. [Although the Germans agreed to unconditional-surrender terms on May 7, 1945, detailed peace treaties were not completed until 1946 and 1947. The official treaties delineated new national borders, set forth areas to be jointly controlled by the victors, and stated the amount of reparations to be paid to small nations such as Greece, Albania, and Ethiopia. The foreign ministers of Britain, France, the United States, and USSR signed final treaty documents in Paris on February 10, 1947.]

The first news about the telephone service from Paris to the States does not look very encouraging for a call during the next

The Nice recreation area was off limits to officers. Enlisted men on leave did not have to salute or deal with "Off Limits to Enlisted Men" signs at bars, restaurants, or public facilities.

Sign in front of Nice's "Casino Red Cross."

few weeks. Not only are there tremendous queues outside the exchange, but mechanically they are also having trouble. The first day only one man made a call to the States. Today three days after the service began, they have a two-day backlog. Stars and Stripes *is raising a lot of hell about the men who made the fifty practice calls. The people who made the practice calls turned out to be about twenty colonels and other officers in the office of the chief signal officer. Yesterday* Stars and Stripes *published a list of the names of the people who made the calls and where they called.*

Today and tomorrow they are having a rather interesting but certainly ghoulish celebration. Twelve bodies are being put on display (men, women, and children who died as part of the French resistance, in various battles in which French units participated, or in a POW camp). In the course of two days they are going to be taken, with processions following, from the Arc de Triomphe to Les Invalides (Napoleon's tomb) and then on to the Tomb of the Unknown Soldier. It is almost bizarre enough for me to want to go and see it.

St. Cloud, France
November 13, 1945
Dear Folks:

After December 1 the U.S. Army in Europe will be entirely administered from Germany. The Theater Provost Marshal's is one of the first staff sections scheduled to move. With special trains, etc., they expect to have the entire headquarters moved by the end of the month.

The closeout of the American installation in France has been accomplished much faster than anyone believed possible last August. The Army has already given up the use of the port of Cherbourg. It expects to be out of both Le Havre and Marseilles by January 15, 1946. After that the U.S. Army will use only Antwerp and Bremen as ports and Antwerp only until May. There is no better indication of the closing down of operations than the closing of ports. [I can personally attest to the fact that the Army had not turned over operation of Le Havre's port facilities to the French in April, 1946, when I headed for New York on the Colby Victory troopship. Until the summer of 1946, Le Havre remained the chief port of embarkation for soldiers redeployed to the States. This required an extensive military involvement in harbor infrastructure, as well as "cigarette camps" for organizing and preparing homebound GIs.]

Yesterday afternoon after writing you, I went to visit the Mosque of Paris with a friend of mine named Zollo. That is one of the many interesting places in Paris that the average tourist never goes to see. It is a large, modern mosque that was built in 1926. You can identify its Oriental minarets several blocks away. They have a regular tour for which they charge five francs to all but Americans. It is conducted by a Muslim who seems to be a moron and who tried to chisel cigarettes, although it is against the rules of his religion. Far more interesting than the building itself was the information we got about the seventy thousand Muslims who live in Paris. Notwithstanding Hitler's many statements about race, and particularly a Semitic race, he went out of his way to be nice to the Arabs in Paris. As I thought about it, I really wasn't too surprised.

St. Cloud, France
November 16, 1945
Dear Folks:

Today the Theater Provost Marshal's operations were officially suspended in Paris when we packed the files in preparation for the move to Germany, which will take place on Monday and Tuesday. I hope this will be the last Army move I will have to make against my wishes. As I think about leaving Paris, I can't help but think of the time I left Williamsburg and then the time I left the United States. Here in Paris I had a chance to get away from the Army and live a life that was almost civilian. Although Frankfurt is probably the best city in Germany for soldiers, except possibly Berlin, my whole life will revolve around the Army and Army people, where an enlisted man is still someone to be talked down to instead of talked to as an equal.

CHAPTER 8

GERMANY

Occupation Army, War Crimes Tribunal

LIKE MOST BUREAUCRACIES, the U.S. Army of Occupation in Germany was overstaffed and slothful. My work was tedious and dull. I was not conscripted to be a government clerk. I wanted to get out in the worst way.

American GIs were taught to hate and fear Germans. On arrival in postwar Germany, soldiers were given an official brochure signed by a lieutenant general. It was titled "Don't Be a Sucker in Germany." Its main points were:

- Don't believe there are any "good" Germans.
- You won't find any German . . . who will admit to having been a Nazi.
- German women have been trained to seduce you.
- All underground operations are hidden under sentiments of respect, morality, charity, and religion.
- Do not hesitate to search the beds of sick people.
- A kid can shoot you just as dead as a grown man.
- Don't believe that it was only the Nazi government that brought on the war. People have the kind of government they want and deserve.
- Would you be friendly to a foreign Army that has occupied your hometown? If some friend of yours shot one of their men, wouldn't he be a hero to the whole community?

The notion that an enlisted soldier in Germany would at least have the fringe benefit of observing and understanding a foreign culture was unrealistic. The Army's nonfraternization policy (which was relaxed in late 1945) forbade meeting German girls, eating with German families, attending German sports events, and even visiting German pubs. Getting caught breaking nonfraternization rules could—and often did—result in a reduction in grade, court-martial, or a delayed return home, depending on the gravity of the specific offense. I was unwilling to take the risk.

History may judge the Nuremberg war-crime trials as the most important event that took place in Europe in the decade following the cessation of hostilities. Never before had the motives and ethics of a great nation's leaders been examined and tested before an impartial tribunal.

In November, 1945, twenty-two officials (one in absentia) were indicted before the international military tribunal that was convened by the victorious allies (United States, Great Britain, France, and the Soviet Union) in Nuremberg. All were indicted on three basic charges: launching an "aggressive war," committing war crimes, and committing crimes against humanity. The trials lasted ten months. Half of those indicted were executed (Hermann Goering committed suicide a few hours before he was scheduled to be hanged). Of the remainder, three were acquitted, and the rest were sentenced to prison terms of varying lengths.

The tribunal's moral and philosophical tone was set by the lead prosecutor, Robert H. Jackson, a U.S. Supreme Court justice on special leave. In his opening statement Justice Jackson said, "The wrongs which we seek to condemn and punish have been so calculated, so malignant, and so devastating that civilization cannot tolerate their being ignored because it cannot survive their being repeated."

I was one of a tiny contingent of Americans who attended the trials. They were held in Nuremberg's municipal courthouse, where there was only enough room to accommodate ten visitors daily from each Allied nation. The ten visitor seats assigned to the United States were usually spoken for months in advance. Most of them went to people with important résumés: prominent judges, legal scholars, lawyers, generals, local politicians, and officials from friendly countries other than the Big Four. Few, if any, went to twenty-one-year-old sergeants whose only credential was having completed his freshman year at college.

The day I attended, December 14, 1945, was historic—and, of course, uniquely memorable for me. It was the day the first documentary evidence was presented to the court—and the world—proving that the Nazis had killed six million Jews. Prior to that date statements about the number of Jews exterminated had been anecdotal. According to the December 15, 1945, *New York Times,* an American major "presented evidence to support the charge that, while they had lost the war, the Germans had succeeded in achieving one of Hitler's major war aims—the almost complete obliteration of the Jews in Europe." The story's headline read as follows:

Trial Data Reveal
6,000,000 Jews Died

The *Philadelphia Inquirer*'s front-page story began with these words: "The world today heard precisely what happened to Europe's Jews. . . . It was another documentary nightmare in Nuremberg's house of horrors. . . . They told how 1,165,000—we repeat, 1,165,000—Jews were exterminated in the abattoirs of Auschwitz and Birkenau alone."

On the letterhead of the "Office of the U.S. Chief of Counsel, International Military Tribunal," I wrote home about how Hitler's designated successor, Luftwaffe Commander Hermann Goering, was the Nazi hierarchy's leader—even in the prisoner's dock. Though stripped of his authority and titles as well as all of his badges of rank, his fellow prisoners looked to him for guidance and directions, as did the defense and prosecution lawyers. A few months later he demonstrated the same intelligence and resourcefulness when Justice Jackson cross-examined him. In response to a question from Justice Jackson about the Nazis' extermination of Europe's Jews, Goering replied by comparing it with the genocidal treatment of the

TRIAL DATA REVEAL 6,000,000 JEWS DIED

Evidence at Nuremberg Cites Brutality Used by Germans in Extermination Campaign

By RAYMOND DANIELL
By Wireless to THE NEW YORK TIMES.

NUREMBERG, Germany, Dec. 14—A story of shame and horror was placed before the International Military Tribunal trying twenty-one of Adolf Hitler's chieftains today when, for the most part, out of official German records, the United States prosecution showed that after the Germans' conquests in the east and west they had sought to create living space for their own people by exterminating all dissident elements of the population and plundering the rest.

Major William J. Walsh of 1175 Park Avenue, New York, presented evidence to support the charge that, while they had lost the war, the Germans had succeeded in achieving one of Hitler's major war aims—the almost complete obliteration of the Jews in Europe.

In support of his case Major Walsh offered an affidavit of Wilhelm Hoe~ ~ajor in the SS, which d   t Adolf Eichmann,   ociated with Heir~   's appointed tas~   ~-Nazi ele~
~   approx~

mind recoils," Capt. Sam Harris, another member of United States Supreme Court Justice Robert H. Jackson's staff, took up the proof of how the Germans had systematically looted the countries they had conquered and had driven unwanted persons into exile or concentration camps, which for the Jews almost invariably meant death.

For his proof, Captain Harris relied upon thirty documents, most of which had been captured by American forces from the German High Command files and other German archives. By Hitler's own order, it was shown, the German conquerors embarked on a considered plan to decimate the population of the countries they had overrun to pave the way for an influx of German settlers and make possible those countries' complete Gemanization.

Abuse in Alsace Cited

That this policy had been in the west as well as the east was shown by a document recording the fact that between July and December, 1940, 105,000 "undesirables"—that is Jews, Gypsies, insane people and intellectuals—nad been expelled or prevented from returning to their homes in that part of Alsace Hitler planned to absorb into his Greater Reich.

The German plotters' av~ aim, i~   ~~~ ~ "the ma~ a~

Here is part of the December 15, 1945, *New York Times* report of the first documentary evidence of the Jewish massacre at the hand of the Nazis (I had attended the trial on the preceding day).

Indians by the United States. When Justice Jackson asked if it were true that the Nazis had abolished democracy, Goering responded, "We no longer found it necessary." Both of these statements made headlines throughout Europe. Most historians believe that, in this one-on-one encounter, Goering had outwitted Justice Jackson, a famed prosecutor before his elevation to the Supreme Court.

Although I was fully aware of the Nuremberg tribunal's historic importance, the week following my attendance at the trial I recorded my doubts about the ethical underpinning of courtrooms in which military victors evaluated the morals and motives of the vanquished. During the past decades genocidal wars have raged in Cambodia and Rwanda with death tolls in the hundreds of thousands, but no war-crimes tribunals have been convened to try the national leaders involved. Slobodan Milosovic, former president of Yugoslavia, has been on trial in the Hague, Netherlands, for more than two years for war crimes, including "ethnic cleansing." Regardless of the outcome, the trial's tedious meandering through legalistic mumbo-jumbo tends to confirm the merit of the questions I raised in December, 1945.

Following the marquee trial of Hitler's top henchmen in 1945 and 1946, Nuremberg's small courthouse was the scene of eleven follow-up trials. The second-tier Nuremberg trials dealt with specific areas of Nazi criminality, like using humans in painful and usually fatal medical experiments, murder, cruel treatment of prisoners of war, and using slave laborers until they died of exhaustion and/or malnutrition. Most of those tried were sentenced to long prison terms, and more than two dozen were condemned to death.

From Nuremberg I also wrote about how the Army's rigid caste system made it difficult for my longtime friend (a lieutenant) to be a gracious host. Although I surreptitiously shared his living quarters, I had to wear one of his sweaters to cover my sergeant's stripes at mealtime. The entire Grand Hotel, headquarters for the U.S. prosecution staff, was off limits to enlisted men. U.S. officers could entertain nonmilitary men and women and military women (WACs) in the hotel's dining salons, but they could not have enlisted men as visitors. On Saturday, when the trials were in recess, we went on a sightseeing trip with two civilian females on the prosecutor's staff. In picturesque Rothenberg-am-Tauber my host and the two women enjoyed an elegant lunch at the famous Eisenhut Hotel, while I was barred from entering the hotel lobby. I was forced to eat alone at a transient enlisted men's mess.

The central figure in the denouement of the Nuremberg trials was the hangman. I got to know him when I was chief clerk in the confinement and rehabilitation division, which processed the paperwork for the execution orders of the Army of Occupation's military court. After he hung ten Nuremberg defendants in the autumn of 1946, I wrote an article for the Dartmouth *Jack-o-Lantern* about Master Sergeant John Woods, the Army's executioner. Woods believed he had a wonderful job. He earned a master sergeant's pay while working fewer than thirty days a year. Before the war he was paid on a piecework basis by whatever state required a hangman's services. (He was one of the Western world's last practitioners of his specialty.) In Woods's view, the most difficult part of his work was not springing the trap but rather examining and measuring a condemned man's neck the day before. This routine was necessary in order to be sure the knot would be firmly placed between the ear and the spine (often with the aid of a suction cup). The placement of the knot determined whether the doomed man died instantly of a severed spine or painfully by strangulation.

Working in Frankfurt's I. G. Farben building, Europe's largest office structure, was like working in the Pentagon. The Supreme Allied Command, which was headquartered there, employed more than ten thousand people. In November, 1945, the Allied armies began permitting Germans to work in the Farben building. It was difficult to reconcile the harsh nonfraternization warnings that had been issued a few months earlier with the fact that the Army's top brass was hiring Germans to be our coworkers within the occupation bureaucracy.

Most of the GIs I worked with resented the presence of hundreds of unguarded German clerical workers in the Farben building. Still, we were ambivalent. We knew they were our replacements. The more the Army hired, the quicker we would go home.

My stay in Germany ended in January, 1946, when I was one of 750 soldiers chosen to study for two months at a Swiss university. I was assigned to the University of Geneva.

Frankfurt, Germany
August 20, 1945
2:30 P.M.
Dear Folks:

Yesterday in the rain I took a sightseeing trip to the only city in the vicinity that has not been bombed to bits: Heidelberg. It has very few essential industrial plants. During the war it had several hospitals. Therefore, it was not subject to strategic bombings. When the infantry entered it, the commanding general gave orders not to fire because he felt that firing on Heidelberg would be like firing on Princeton or Cambridge. It is a beautiful city with mountains surrounding it, tree-lined streets, and a gentle river flowing through the center.

You will never understand the unusual feeling of walking down the streets here in enemy territory. In France, whoever you said "hello" to on the streets returned your greeting. Here many Germans stare right through you and walk on. For a radius of approximately one-half mile around the Farben building, where we have our headquarters, there is a six-foot-high barbwire entanglement. You can enter the area only after passing a guard. No Germans are allowed to live in or enter the headquarters.

Frankfurt, Germany
September 3, 1945
Dear Folks:

Now it's all over. I'm a peacetime soldier in the headquarters of an occupation army. Being in such a position against one's will is something that ought not be forced on an American, but . . .

The railroad bridge over the Main River at Frankfurt am Main. This photo was taken in November, 1945.

We arrived here yesterday morning after a relatively pleasant sixteen-hour train ride from Gare de l'Est in Paris to the South Station in Frankfurt. The train we traveled on was a special "duty train" (as opposed to a "leave train"), which carries mostly headquarters personnel on a nonstop run from Paris to Frankfurt. The train has two sleepers, three coaches, and a diner. The latter is the real luxury, as on most train rides, both here and in the States, you eat either K or C rations in transit. As luck would have it, while we were eating breakfast, the train stopped opposite another train that was carrying freezing displaced persons in boxcars and

*flatcars. The experience of sitting in a clean dining car while a
French waiter pours your coffee and hearing and seeing a lot of
men, women, and children begging and yelling outside your window is not too pleasant. It could happen only in Europe in '45.*

Frankfurt, Germany
September 9, 1945
Dear Folks:

*I just returned from the Mickey Rooney-Bobby Breen show
called "OK, USA," which opened here last week. I enjoyed the
show, even though it was one of the corniest and poorest shows I
have seen since entering the Army. People (including me) stood
in line several hours to get into the theater. If the show had not
been advertised with names like Rooney and Breen, I doubt
whether anybody would have gone. Rooney directed the affair,
and the fact that none of the cast had practiced was obvious.*

*My trip last Friday with the brass was interesting and enjoy-
able. The three of us (General Wessels, Colonel Lee, and Corporal
Obe) left shortly after nine o'clock in a Plymouth sedan with a
driver for Wildflecken, where UNRRA is maintaining one of
Europe's largest displaced-persons camps (eighteen thousand
Poles). They live in beautiful barracks that were formerly used by
two German mountain divisions. The camp is a small city with
regular hospitals, maternity hospitals, jails, cemeteries, etc. Their
conditions are miserable (241 men, women, and children in a
31-room barracks. All their meals are semiliquid and are ladled
from a giant vat into a can or bucket. Still, they do not want to
return to Poland.*

*Friday morning they had arranged for a train to take 1,500 of
them to Pilsen on their way home, but at the last moment they
could get only 567 to go. I suppose eventually they will have to
return whether they want to or not. General Patton is the commanding general of the area where Wildflecken is located. His
comment on the situation, which I believe is typical of the Army,
was "Who the hell asked the Poles where they wanted to go anyway?"* **[SHAEF assumed responsibility for the medical care,
housing, and feeding of several million displaced persons at**

the war's conclusion. The Nazis had shuttled trainloads of people from conquered nations around Europe to work in slave-labor camps. After the Germans' defeat, the DPs had no money, no families, no houses, and no identification papers. Each occupying power managed the DP camps in its zone of occupation. Initially Jews were treated the same as all other DPs (Poles, Czechs, and gypsies, for instance). The problems involved in housing, feeding, and maintaining order among these vast, unhappy, homeless populations unfortunately kept many of them in camps.]

Later in the day we went to Würzburg, which is just a big pile of rocks. Würzburg has no major industries and received no major bombings until April, 1945, when the 42nd Division was across the river and asked the town to surrender. The town refused to surrender, so the commanding general called in the Ninth Air Force, which dropped bombs indiscriminately on the city for an hour.

Now to tell you something about our billets and what reminded me once again that I wanted a flit gun. We live with other headquarters personnel in a large, brick, former SS barracks about seven miles outside of Frankfurt. Physically, they are much better than any of the other living quarters I had before I came to the Theater Provost Marshal's office, but it is the dirtiest place imaginable with several varieties of bugs and vermin in our room. We have almost no transportation facilities, so it is very difficult to travel to and from our billets. However, I am sure things will improve as soon as things get organized in this city of confusion.

Frankfurt, Germany
October 28, 1945
Dear Folks:

I was offered a Riviera furlough beginning Monday. Knowing the Army as I do, I took what was offered to me and ran.

The Army still does not let you forget that this was once an important enemy city. The headquarters area is still surrounded by a triple barbwire fence. Inside the fence no German may live without special permission, and no GI may go without identification. This is not just a small area but a large section of the city,

Destruction in Frankfurt am Main. This photo was taken in September, 1945, at Bahnhof Platz, across from the railroad station.

inside of which is the Farben building, at least a dozen other important government buildings, officers' billets, WACs' billets, officers' and enlisted men's clubs and so on. Our office is in another section of the city, but nobody below the grade of general can enter our building without showing proper identification. You are still allowed to carry guns during your off-duty time. Most of the men who go out at night by themselves carry pistols.

Frankfurt, Germany
October 29, 1945
Dear Folks:

   This morning I spent almost two hours at the Frankfurt Allied Military Government office discussing the various things the Oberndoerfer family [cousins who fled Germany in the mid-1930s] asked me to look into for them.

   When you go to an office as a member of the American military government, you can see one of the reasons why the Americans here like the Germans. They really snap when you enter a room. Although there may be a hundred Germans lined up when you enter an office, they all step aside. You walk to the head of the line. Any GI will tell you that he likes that kind of respect shown the victor, instead of the self-praise and flag waving of the French. I know that this is the wrong way to think, but it's easy and natural.

There's very little else to tell you except that yesterday I saw my first football game of the 1945 season—in Victory Park, Frankfurt, between the 508th Parachute Infantry (Ike's personal guards) and a local signal corps outfit. It wasn't much of a football game, but there was a lot of spirit and good fun. The stadium in which it was played was one of those new, large sports projects the Nazis built. It includes a large swimming pool, several smaller stadiums, tennis courts, theaters, etc. The stadium and the swimming pool are two of the most beautiful I have ever seen.

Frankfurt, Germany
November 23, 1945
Dear Folks:

The past week has been full and active—full of interesting activities and hard work, full of aggravation, and so very full of Frankfurt. After a five-month respite, it's back in the Army, where your after-hours' activities consist of movies, poker, reading, and a few drinks from the mouth of a bottle. Things have improved physically. I suppose they will continue to improve, but the spirit and surroundings are still Army, the Army that I so sincerely hate.

I don't think I told you about the automobile I drove to Frankfurt this week. Its history is rather interesting. It gives you a good idea of how the Army works over here. When V Corps went through combat, every staff officer above major was given a looted sedan. When it came time for the V Corps' officers to go home, these cars were supposed to be turned over to a Third Army motor pool. However, a colonel who is a friend of Colonel Lee's decided to give the car away instead. After a few legal manipulations, the title to the car was transferred to Colonel Lee. The car finally arrived in Paris just before Colonel Lee left for the States in the be-

ginning of October. So that no extra papers about the looted car would pass through official hands, the maintenance and repair of the car were taken care of in an ordnance shop run by a friend of Major Blake. Its drivers were listed as Blake, O'Brien, Heine, and me. We are accountable to nobody but ourselves. If some provost marshal caught a company-grade officer [lieutenant or captain] or an enlisted man doing that, he would probably be drawn and quartered—or at least court-martialed.

Monday I had the car repaired and generally prepared for my drive to Germany. In the evening we went to town hoping to see a riot over de Gaulle's showdown with his cabinet. Over the radio we had heard an announcement about the mobs in the Place de la Concorde and in front of the Palais Royale, but, by the time we got there, everything was quiet. All of the lower part of the Champs Élysées and the Place de la Concorde were blocked off (the subway stops were also closed). Only American or British personnel were allowed to pass.

I love you and miss you. I wish I could stop seeing the world.

Frankfurt, Germany
November 25, 1945
Dear Folks:

This letter is being written just after making a trip to Creglingen [the city from which my mother's father emigrated]. This morning about ten o'clock Heine and I started out for Creglingen in the Horsch limousine (Colonel Lee's looted German car). After a short stop in Würzburg, we arrived at Creglingen about four o'clock in the afternoon. It was a very interesting ride.

The beautiful countryside between Würzburg and Heidelberg has not been affected very much by the war. Some of the towns have a sort of Hansel-and-Gretel picturesqueness about them. One of the many useless jobs in this job-creating Army of Occupation of ours is the checking of every person or vehicle that goes down the main roads. One of the eighteen times we were checked was just outside of Creglingen. Luckily, Creglingen has been spared by the U.S. Army. The nearest soldiers are those at the check point about a mile outside the city. The nearest unit is the

15th Tank Battalion at Rothenberg, where they have the military government office for the area and an enlisted men's club, where we found a dance attended only by frauleins.

When we drove into the city, we attracted considerable attention with our big automobile and my taking pictures of every store or sign that I thought might possibly be of some interest to Popi [*my grandfather*]. Not being able to speak any German, I was afraid the trip would not be much of a success, but luck was with me. While I was running around with my camera a lady said in perfect English, "Will you take my picture?" My answer was very simple, "Do you speak English?" The answer was in the affirmative.

After talking to the lady a short while, I learned she was a displaced person from Estonia who has lived in Creglingen for four years. After telling her that I came to see the home of my grandfather and granduncle, she took me to the burgomaster, who was not in. She then took me to the church accountant to find out where Popi's family lived. The church accountant immediately knew who the Sinsheimers were. He took me out in the main street and showed me their home, which, with a new coat of paint, appears to be in fine condition.

Later I was introduced to two respectable-looking, well-dressed, elderly men who knew Uncle Rudolf well. They wanted to know whether he expects to return to Creglingen now that the war is over. They remember Popi as the tall brother of Uncle Rudolf. Although I couldn't go inside, I went to see the Creglingen synagogue, which has been closed for several years. Still, it appears to be in rather good condition. It has not been desecrated with paint or penknives. [**My granduncle Rudolf Sinsheimer (1873–1955) did not emigrate until 1939. He came to the United States in 1937 to attend my bar mitzvah but returned to Germany. As a wounded World War I veteran who had been awarded Germany's highest military honor, the Iron Cross, he felt safe.**]

All in all, the town looks rather prosperous. It might have been just a pile of rocks, like so many other cities in the area. I would say it has been very lucky.

Knowing that the thing in Creglingen that Popi really wanted to know about most was the Jewish cemetery, I got the woman who spoke English to take me there. The cemetery is surrounded by a stone fence and a large iron gate, which has kept out the cows and vandals—and almost kept Obermayer out also. Although it is in very poor condition with stones knocked over, high grass, weeds, and wire all over the place, there are no signs of deliberate destruction. The cemetery appears to be divided into two sections, the front containing the old graves and the back containing the newer ones. In the back section, which in general is in better condition than the front part, I found the stone of Popi's mother, which is broken and knocked over but not defaced in any way. I could not find any other Sinsheimers in the cemetery, although I suppose some are there.

This cemetery was no different from any other. There was a nut hanging around waiting for someone like me to try to scale the fence. When he saw me, he yelled at me, shook his fist, and then crossed himself about a half dozen times. I asked whether anything was being done about the upkeep of the place and was told "no."

Frankfurt, Germany
November 29, 1945

Dear Folks:

Here we have one of the best setups in the Army of Occupation. Still, we find ourselves continually bored and regularly griping because there is nothing to do.

To describe life in Frankfurt I must first tell you something of the physical setup. Approximately 70 percent of Frankfurt has been destroyed. Of the remaining 30 percent, the Americans have taken over a little more than half. We occupy every large building in the city. We have also taken over an entire section that is fenced with double-barbed wire. It is guarded by paratroopers who check our pass every time we enter or leave.

Inside that area is the Farben building and several smaller buildings, as well as the billets in which live most of the officers and all the WACS and other women attached to the Army.

*Although there are a half dozen movies, two places where you can dance, and three where you can get something to eat, it is almost impossible to go anywhere without seeing everybody you know and all sorts of people you don't want to know. In many ways I believe the life here is similar to what you would find in the Canal Zone or some other all-Army installation that is not exactly a camp or fort. Still, you live an all-Army social life, which consists of being drunk six nights a week. [**Officers up here get a monthly liquor ration of eleven bottles.**] To date the enlisted men have gotten nothing but a promise that their allotment of liquor is being saved for the day when they are going to open a bar in their billets.*

Frankfurt, Germany
December 3, 1945
Dear Folks:

We have become very busy again as our office has gotten the "go" signal from the War Department to practically empty the U.S. guardhouses in Europe by the middle of February. Next week they are going to start evacuating prisoners to the States for the first time since V-E Day. All of this means a lot of work, but, once it is done, life in this office will become almost as lazy as that in the rest of the Army of Occupation.

I suppose there is other big news in the world these days, but the biggest for me is the news about redeployment. It continues to be good, notwithstanding the statements of General Ike and other characters who say that redeployment is knifing the military government in the back. The men who work in the public-relations office live in our billet. They have the story that the Army expects that all men with more than forty-five points will have entered the redeployment pipeline before January 1, 1946. That means that men like me—with forty-one points—should be entering the pipeline sometime in the latter part of January or the beginning of February. I have always looked rather skeptically at the news that comes out of the front door of U.S. Army public-relations offices, but the news that comes from the back door comes from other enlisted men.

Yesterday we went to Heidelberg. The University of Heidelberg still does not have any students. The buildings are being used by the Seventh Army for offices and classrooms. The town impresses me as being very prosperous because there is no evidence of bomb craters or rubble. The stores have unbroken glass windows with standard window displays.

Although my French is so poor that I was afraid to use it in front of anyone who knew the language, I realize what a big help even that little was. In Germany I can't even get my laundry back from the lady I gave it to several days ago. My record of never having washed my own clothes overseas continues unbroken.

Frankfurt, Germany
December 9, 1945
Dear Folks:

Since coming to Frankfurt, I'm sure that my letters have become rather dull and uninteresting. Try as I may to change them, I can't honestly make this place seem interesting or exciting. When you are as annoyed and disgusted as I am these days, neither whiskey nor kisses nor books can be very exciting or interesting.

Soon it will be announced to the public that redeployment will be drastically cut. The present speed of redeployment has reduced the efficiency and power of the closeout force and the occupation Army so much that they are not able to run the officers' bars and clubs at their usual peak of efficiency. Almost any sort of life can be tolerable if you believe you are working for a real cause. The military occupation of Germany does not seem to me to be either noble or great or good. The closer you get to it, the more you find yourself laughing at its whole tragicomic aims, outlook, and leadership.

I just tore this letter out of the typewriter as it's hardly in the spirit in which I like to write home, but on reconsidering, I decided I'd write the same letter if I tried again.

Frankfurt, Germany
December 11, 1945

Dear Folks:

Although the news about redeployment has not changed, the other news from Germany is rather good. Things are becoming a little brighter again.

Today I spoke to the clearance officer of the Nuremberg restricted area. I made tentative arrangements for a trip down there to see the trials. After many unsuccessful attempts, I finally spoke to Bob Wolf. As I hoped, he invited me down to Nuremberg for a few days. [Lt. Robert B. Wolf (1914–), a lawyer friend from Philadelphia, was a member of the staff of U.S. Supreme Court Justice Robert H. Jackson, chief U.S. prosecutor.]

As you probably don't know, the entire city of Nuremberg is a restricted area. You can enter only if you are traveling on official business. All orders reading "Nuremberg" must be approved by the clearance officer in Nuremberg. Without a good friend down there, it would be impossible for me to go.

Nuremberg, Germany
December 15, 1945

Dear Folks:

Someday years from now, when a dinner partner of mine looks at me with that stop-boring-me look, I'll pull the rabbit out of my hat. I will tell her how I watched Goering, Hess, and Jodl squirm and make faces during the Nuremberg trials. Yesterday afternoon I spent three hours watching and listening to the trials.

You probably have to prove less about your identification and background to get into the holy of holies or the swankiest club of Newport than you do to get into the trials. Unless you have a good friend like Bob Wolf to guide you through and around the security system, an ordinary human being who wanted to see the trials would leave Nuremberg more frustrated than a Midwestern businessperson in Washington.

The area for a block or two around the Palace of Justice is restricted. No civilian or soldier without proper identification can enter the area. There are guards at the gate to the Palace of Justice

```
                    HEADQUARTERS
               THEATER SERVICE FORCES
                  EUROPEAN THEATER
          Office of the Theater Provost Marshal

                                        Main-APO 757
                                        13 December 1945


              This is to certify that T/4 Herman J. Obermayer, 33783267
       of this Staff Section who will be traveling on pass (ETO AG Form 27)
       from Frankfurt, Germany to Nuremburg, Germany on 13 December 1945
       has received verbal orders of clearance from Lt. Wolf, Nuremburg
       Restricted Area Clearance Officer. The pass will be issued by
       Service Company D, Headquarters Command, United States Forces,
       European Theater.




                              ROY WILKINSON, JR.
                              Major, FA
                              Executive, C & R Division
```

All travel in the section of Nuremberg that included the courthouse, prison, and Grand Hotel (where the prosecutorial staffs were housed) was restricted. I needed advance area clearance before arranging to attend the trials.

grounds. Unless you have a pass stating your exact business, you go on to a security office, where you are checked and interrogated. Between the security office and the gate, there are two more guards, who may be either French, Russian, English, or American, depending on the day of the week. Between the security office and the courtroom you pass through about fifteen more guards, almost all of whom check your identification credentials.

They contribute their little bit to the all-for-show atmosphere you somehow feel all around the courthouse. You cannot wear an overcoat or hat into the courtroom or even carry one with you. They are afraid you might be able to conceal a grenade, weapons, etc., in your clothing. Once you're inside the courtroom (gallery), the guards watch you like hawks. They waste no time in reprimanding you if you move from one seat to another. If you stand up, they tell you to leave.

British, French, American, and Russian flags flew over the entrance to Nuremberg's Palace of Justice during the Nazi war crimes trials.

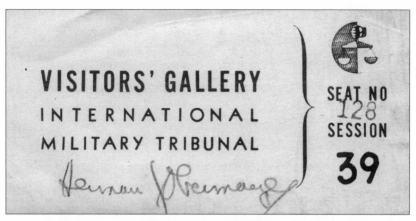

VISITORS' GALLERY

INTERNATIONAL

MILITARY TRIBUNAL

SEAT NO
128
SESSION
39

Admission ticket to the visitors' gallery at the Nuremberg war crimes trials. Gallery seats were distributed as follows: 30 to press corps members; 10 each for Russian, French, U.S., and British visitors; and 50 for court and prosecutorial staff. At Session 39, the fact that the Nazis had killed six million Jews was officially confirmed for the first time.

The gallery is almost always more than half empty. There are only 120 seats, which are distributed as follows: 30 to the press, 10 to the Russians, 10 to the French, 10 to the English, and 10 to the American commanding general in the area. The rest are distributed to various staff sections. If a seat is not being used, the guards will not let someone else sit in it, as that would leave a loophole through which some unauthorized person might enter the courtroom. On top of all this, it is impossible for a person of any nation to enter the Nuremberg area without prior clearance from the Nuremberg clearance officer.

Although the translation system, where you wear earphones and turn a dial to the language you want, is very good for conventions or the League of Nations, it is not very good for a court. The lawyers claim the translators are a little too free with technical and legal terms. While the German lawyer was talking to Judge Lawrence [British jurist Lord Geoffrey Lawrence (1880– 1971) presided at the Nuremberg war-crimes trials], it was quite evident that some of their difficulties in understanding each

*other were due to the interpreters. Personally I found it a little
confusing to watch a big man speaking who probably had a deep,
sonorous voice and then to hear a woman's voice through the earphones.*

*Goering may be a dope fiend, but he definitely doesn't give the
impression of being a fool. All through the afternoon he had a big
stack of papers in front of him, which he seemed to be working
with. I definitely got the impression that he was giving orders. He
gave advice to the other defendants. Once they read a "top-secret"
paper that had been initialed by both Admiral Keitel and General Jodl. When their names were mentioned, neither of them
showed any signs of having heard.*

*The trials were undoubtedly dramatic and interesting, but I
am not convinced they are just. When you talk about not caring
what happens to the men in the dock—whether they live or die—
and when the only important thing is that you are trying them
for posterity, I am scared. Individual rights seem to be unimportant at Nuremberg, as well as in the Army. When lawyers and
scholars and thinkers are willing to sacrifice men's lives for international morals, international law, or posterity, it is very dangerous.*

Frankfurt, Germany
December 18, 1945
Dear Folks:

*Sunday Bob Wolf and I took a trip to Rothenberg-am-Tauber,
which I passed through on my way to Creglingen. At the time I
did not realize that it is the classic example of a medieval, walled
city in this part of Europe. Although some small parts of the city
have been bombed, most of it is in perfect shape. Still, it shows
more effects from this war than from the preceding two hundred
years. A group of us (eight) went in two command cars. Of
course, we all had a good time together, notwithstanding the fact
that my being an enlisted man made things a little difficult, just
as it did all during my stay.*

*The thing that amazes me about Rothenberg and all the rest of
Germany is the enthusiasm with which the people are preparing*

Russian guard outside the Palace of Justice in Nuremberg. Guards were rotated by country on a daily basis.

for Christmas. A wreath is hanging on almost every door, even when the house is little more than a pile of rocks. The window displays, although hardly elaborate extravagances, are very well done. They show a very healthy spirit. In the freezing cold, people stand in block-long lines to buy wreaths and Christmas trees.

Frankfurt, Germany
December 19, 1945
Dear Folks:

For three days Bob Wolf went out of his way in every imaginable sense to see that my Nuremberg stay was pleasant and interesting. Of course, his efforts were made difficult because he is an officer and I am an enlisted man. In order to eat with Bob at the Grand Hotel, which is supposed to be only for officers in the Office of the U.S. Chief of Counsel and their officer and civilian friends, I had to pose as a civilian attached to the Army. I acted like a civilian and put on an act both evenings. But I didn't like it. It is not that I was afraid of being caught out of uniform. Rather, I didn't want people to think I was ashamed of being an enlisted man and wanted to pose as something else. If anything, I'm rather proud of it. It's rather annoying to think that I might have been Bob's brother or cousin, but because the rules said, "No," I could not honestly eat dinner with him. Sunday I could not eat with the group when they ate at the Hotel Eisenhut in Rothenberg. If Bob had been anything but a very good and understanding friend, I doubt I would have stayed around and taken that nonsense for three days.

All of this is rather surprising, as overall the attitude of the personnel in the Office of the U.S. Chief of Counsel is definitely not military. Like Bob, a large percentage of the men are only here in Europe on ninety days' temporary duty from the War Department in Washington. Of course, they will return there at the end of this assignment, regardless of the point system or the current whims of subordinate commanders in Europe. Almost all personnel in the office are lawyers. There are probably almost as many civilians and Navy men attached to the staff as there are Army officers. In general, that type of person is inclined to snicker at the military and the importance soldiers attach to themselves. Typical of the pleasantness of the office is that, during the coming recess, the chief counsel's office has taken over three large hotels at Berchtesgaden, and the entire office will be down there for five days—one group over Christmas, the other over New Year's. *[Berchtesgaden, known as Eagle's Nest, was Hitler's Alpine retreat near Salzburg, Austria. At times it was used as a headquarters for the German Army's high command and as the site of diplomatic meetings (just as U.S. presidents use Camp David). Hitler's house sat atop a 6,000-foot mountain and was theoretically impregnable. It was accessed through a tunnel and a 370-foot elevator.]*

Frankfurt, Germany
December 20, 1945
Dear Folks:

Today we added a German typist to our staff. Recently they have been hiring German civilians to work in the office as clerks, typists, etc. Although certain people in this section were opposed to it in principle, they finally got in step with the times.

By the time redeployment is completed, most of the clerical staffs of the big offices in Frankfurt will be German. Although I don't like the idea of accepting the Germans as our social equals—which you must do when they work in the same office with you—I believe it is much better than wasting the lives of Americans maintaining card files and running mimeograph machines in Germany.

Miss Fry [the English civilian secretary assigned to the Theater Provost Marshal's office] has been in Paris all week. I am looking forward to her reactions to the newest member of our staff. She has a holier-than-thou attitude about fraternization. She regularly asks the fellows what they would say if she went out with German men. She refused to discuss the subject after someone asked her what she thought about double standards.

During my Nuremberg trip I spent several hours walking through "old Nuremberg," which today is mostly ruins and rubble. This was another one of those tactical bombing jobs that will make good propaganda for the Germans when they get ready for the next war.

The whole bombing was done in a matter of minutes after the town refused to surrender to our troops, which were just outside. The Air Force decided to bomb old Nuremberg, which could not possibly be considered a military objective. Even in its ruined state, it is still rather interesting. All around it is a deep moat. I was surprised to find that a great many people live in the moat because down there they are protected from the wind and cold. All of the classic churches and castles in this area have been destroyed, as well as most of the stores and homes. Still, somehow, life seems to go on. Where food stores formerly stood, we now see tiny wooden booths run by the same proprietors, who sell bread and other food in the open. Before the open food booths people stand in long lines to buy things. Although this particular section of Nuremberg has been ruined, most of its beautiful suburbs have been untouched—so our officers may live in a style to which they were not accustomed.

In the evening during my Nuremberg visit, after supper at the Grand Hotel, we went to see the Rockettes at the Opera House. They were really wonderful. Someday I'd love to go see them again in NYC.

Frankfurt, Germany
December 23, 1945
Dear Folks:

The Germans in defeat seem to be making many more preparations for Christmas than are the victorious but frustrated and homesick Americans who make up the Army of Occupation. By order of General McNarney, we have a holiday from Saturday noon (December 22) to Wednesday morning (December 26), but I'm sorry to say that there doesn't seem to be any place to spend the holiday except in Frankfurt.

Due to the critical shortage of MPs in Europe, Paris has been closed as a pass area. You can go there only on duty or furlough. Neither place will cover a pass for the three-day Christmas holi-

*day. I originally asked for a pass to Brussels, but I was turned
down in this office. There is not a scheduled train from here to
Brussels, so my prompt return could not be guaranteed. Then I
asked for a pass to Garmisch-Partenkirchen in the Bavarian
Alps, where they held the 1936 winter Olympics. I was turned
down for Garmisch because it is exclusively a Third Army rest
area. The result: I am spending the Christmas holiday in Frankfurt, which I believe is the most unattractive city in Europe.*

*I would be interested in knowing just how much fuss was
made at home about General Patton's death. Over here I think it
has caused more excitement than the announcement of either
Roosevelt's or Hitler's death.* Stars and Stripes *had a tremendous headline. The radio has had innumerable memorial services. Military police units from Metz, Brussels, etc., have been
sent to Luxembourg for the occasion. Many of the sedans and
limousines attached to this headquarters have been requisi-
tioned for the funeral possession. The current wisecrack is "Will
the angels have to wear lacquered helmet liners in the future?"*
**[General George S. Patton Jr. (1885–1945), one of World
War II's most flamboyant field commanders, was killed near
Heidelberg, Germany, in a car accident on December 12,
1945. His military funeral in Luxembourg was the biggest
ceremonial event of its kind in the European Theater. Thousands of U.S. troops, as well as Allied soldiers and diplomats, participated.]**

*Daddy asked some questions about the luxury car that used to
be assigned to this division. It was a Horsch (German) limousine
with fancy upholstery and many fancy gadgets. It is still assigned to the Theater Provost Marshal, but it is no longer the
plaything of Hank and me, due to the ignorance of a sergeant in
this office. When they asked for a list of cars from this office that
would require gas and maintenance, he unwittingly included our
car. As a result, it now has a driver assigned to it who is in charge
of its upkeep.*

*Each time I see all this rubble and the remarkable spirit of the
people who live in this mess, I can't help but be astounded.*

Frankfurt, Germany
January 9, 1946
Dear Folks:

A few hours ago it looked like there might be some real excitement in Frankfurt today. At the noon mess, mimeographed sheets were distributed that said, "Do you want to go home? Attend the mass meeting tonight at WAC circle."

Everybody immediately fell for it with a typical mob, hip-hip-hurrah enthusiasm. By early in the afternoon most of the enthusiasm had died down. Word of the proposed meeting had gotten to General McNarney. [Joseph T. McNarney (1893–1972) was the **commanding general of the U.S. Army of Occupation in Germany.]** *He conceived a very wise scheme for making the plan ineffective. All officers and men were called into a meeting by their section chiefs. We had two meetings with General Wessels. We were told that the mass meetings had the full sanction of the commanding general. Still, no senior officer would be there to answer questions.*

A meeting would be organized tomorrow, to which each staff section would send representatives to discuss the problem with qualified officers. It was a brilliant plan. It took all the power out of the thing. It didn't leave the men filled with resentment, as an order forbidding them to meet would have done. Most of the officers became prisoners for the night, as the demonstration was scheduled to take place near their billeting area.

Mother's letter in which she wondered whether I would feel bad about Jean Ballenberg's engagement amused me a great deal. I am sure Mother is much too shrewd to believe that I ever really liked that girl. Still, I must admit that it does make me feel a little sad when I realize that the girls I know are marrying fellows I never knew, and I am in a position where I can do nothing but comment from afar.

Frankfurt, Germany
January 12, 1946
Dear Folks:

This has been a rather exciting week, one filled with mass meetings, conferences in the general's office, rumors, denials, rep-

rimands, and general confusion. On Thursday we had another meeting with General Wessels. He told us how wrong he thought the demonstrations about the redeployment situation were.

After the offer of the authorities to discuss the situation with the men, any future mass meetings would be considered just short of sedition. As you probably read in the papers, they had meetings in front of the Farben building both last night and the night before. There is a big sign on our bulletin board calling for another mass meeting tomorrow afternoon. There have been several rather curious signs on the bulletin board, including one that announced a plan to organize a club of men who want to be future daddies of American children. Yesterday's announcement by General Eisenhower about the return to the States of nonessential personnel overseas, I believe, should give anyone with pull the means to get out. It was published in the Stars and Stripes *as an AP release. The cable itself seems to be so highly secret that even my friends in the office of the secretary of the general staff or the public-relations office have not seen it.*

Frankfurt, Germany
January 14, 1946
Dear Folks:
Today I feel happier than any other day since I first heard that I would be assigned to Paris. This afternoon at two o'clock I heard that I was one of five men from this command who have been chosen to attend the University of Geneva for two months, beginning next week.

Sometime during the third week in December the announcement was made that several Swiss universities, including the University of Geneva, would admit American soldiers as students for two-month courses that will be taught in English. Of course, I was immediately interested not only because I want to go to school but also because there is no place in Europe where I could spend a more pleasant two months than in Switzerland. There will be 150 American soldiers in Geneva. As yet, I know very little about the courses that will be taught, except that it will be a general liberal-arts curriculum with courses in philosophy, theology, and French, among others.

CHAPTER 9

ATTENDING CLASSES AS A DIPLOMATIC PAWN

LARGE WARS have large economic consequences. A war-related, international economic dispute sent me to the University of Geneva in January, 1946. At issue was the disposition of German financial assets that were transferred to banks in neutral Switzerland.

Gold bullion looted by the Nazis from central banks in conquered nations—including Belgium and Norway—was transferred by railroad to Swiss banks, where it was used to collateralize purchases of war materiel in other neutral countries. During the conflict's waning years, rich individuals, as well as industrial behemoths like Krupp, Thyssen, Farben, and Schering, used long-established banking relationships in Switzerland to move large sums out of the Third Reich. The Allies claimed that virtually all German assets in Swiss banks belonged to the victors. They insisted that stolen funds should at the very least be returned to their rightful owners, both government and private.

The Swiss disputed these assertions. They claimed that the bullion in the vaults of a nation's central bank was the legitimate booty of a military victor. Transfers to Swiss banks by long-time customers and old friends were legitimate business transactions in a nonbelligerent nation. While a treaty covering these matters was being negotiated, all U.S. financial assets in Switzerland were blocked and vice versa.

The blocked assets caused a coal crisis in Switzerland. For centuries, Germany's Ruhr Valley had been Switzerland's chief source of heating fuel. With the Ruhr Valley occupied by British and American armies, the Swiss could not purchase the coal required to heat public buildings and private homes. Notwithstanding the importance of the Swiss-British-U.S. banking disagreement, the Allies feared the public-relations repercussions of allowing an obscure financial-diplomatic dispute to make the winter of 1945–1946 harder on the Swiss people than the war years. A quirk in international law saved the day. The accepted rules of war allow military field commanders to make arrangements with local governments for the benefit and safety of their troops that supersede diplomatic treaties and protocols. This legalism was interpreted to mean that American generals could arrange to send GIs to Switzerland on leave and also to send 750 soldiers to study at Swiss universities. The much-needed coal was the "currency" by which the U.S. Army paid for my tuition, room, and board at the University of Geneva.

My assignment in Switzerland came about because of the hauteur of Swiss bankers. It anticipated an issue that continues to block Europe's final reconciliation to the Holocaust's moral imperative. Jewish organizations are still working to secure full reparations for the descendants of certain Jews who were killed in Nazi death camps and who transferred money to secret Swiss bank accounts before their deportation. Since the identity codes required to claim these secret deposits are lost—and many families were wiped out in their entirety— Swiss banks have been profiting from these funds for sixty years. The banks will continue to profit indefinitely unless further restitution is secured for the descendants of Holocaust victims. Although large sums have been paid during the past decade to Jewish organizations representing Holocaust survivors, Stuart E. Eisenstat, former U.S. ambassador to the European Union, published a book in the summer of 2003 detailing the magnitude of still-unresolved issues.

In Switzerland the U.S. Army had no official status. Soldiers were issued visitors' visas just like ordinary tourists. Rank was not recognized. Privates, sergeants, captains, and majors were all simply American students attending the University of

Geneva. Displaying badges of rank on uniforms was discouraged. While in Switzerland, all U.S. soldiers were paid the same, regardless of rank. Only when we returned to France were adjustments made for pay-grade differentials deferred while we were in Geneva. The Swiss assignment was almost like being a civilian.

The non-GI environment also extended to living arrangements. We were housed and fed in more than a dozen individual boardinghouses in widely separated neighborhoods of Geneva. The soldier contingent met only at rare formal assemblies in university buildings. I was assigned to the Pension Sergy in suburban Flourissant. Its location forced me to take a streetcar to class each day.

Two months in a small Geneva hotel with five other American soldiers and more than a dozen permanent guests of many nationalities opened my eyes to the meaning of the term "neutral country," a favorite euphemism of diplomats. In the twenty-first century, "neutral country" describes a nation that is consistently unhelpful to the United States in international forums but claims to look at issues independently. It does not vote against the United States on *all* issues. It took only a few conversations with fellow residents at the Pension Sergy in 1946 to understand that the Swiss, although "nonbelligerent," were far more helpful to the Nazis than to the Allies. They were not neutral. In addition to being Germany's wartime foreign-exchange broker, Switzerland was home to the famed Swiss watch and camera factories that manufactured many critical timing and optical components for Luftwaffe bomber avionics. Throughout the war German and Italian businesspeople and bureaucrats vacationed at Swiss mountain resorts, which were inaccessible to British and American visitors until after V-E Day. Trains carrying troops and war supplies regularly traveled back and forth between Germany and Italy through Swiss mountain tunnels. Fronting for the German government, Swiss agents, both corporate and individual, purchased agricultural and other home-front products, as well as war materiel throughout the world. Switzerland was probably more helpful to the Nazis as a "neutral" than it would have been as a formal member of the Axis.

Because the university-training-for-coal deal was hastily struck, all of the arrangements were haphazard—from housing to curriculum to mail delivery and medical care. Still, two months in Geneva was a wonderful way to close out a military career.

In a letter Mother asked why the taxpayers should pay me to have a good time in Switzerland. The answer was that soldiers at the University of Geneva were performing one of a peacetime Army's traditional roles. We were supporting a high-level diplomatic stratagem. We were pawns in a big-time, international financial maneuver. Neither the Army brass nor the faculty cared if we learned anything. The program's sole objective was to get German coal to Switzerland. Teaching assignments were irrational and poorly organized. They were built around professors who spoke English, regardless of whether their subject fit into a structured curriculum.

Until all of the soldiers were forbidden to travel to Swiss ski resorts because of the large number of broken limbs, most University of Geneva soldiers headed for the mountains each weekend. Since the boardinghouses where we were lived were paid in advance for our meals, they supplied us with cold cuts and bread to take care of mealtime during our weekend jaunts. Because we always traveled with our sleeping bags (known as "fart sacks"), we were able to sleep in luxury hotels' servant quarters, which were almost always unheated. When we prepared our sandwiches in small restaurants where we bought coffee and cakes, we were almost always treated to hot, full-course meals. American GIs were welcome visitors in Switzerland.

By March, 1946, I had accumulated enough discharge points to be eligible for redeployment home. This allowed me to skip my scheduled return to the Army of Occupation headquarters in Frankfurt. Instead, I went directly from the Army's Swiss Leave Center in Mulhouse, France, and then to the Second Reinforcement Depot in Namur, Belgium. This time I became an unattached replacement—with great glee.

Geneva, Switzerland
January 20, 1946
Dear Folks:

This is not the land of milk and honey that exists on the other side of the ocean, but it is the nearest thing to it in Europe. What a pleasant change it is from the rubble and misery of Frankfurt. Here they have full shop windows, wonderful pastry and candy, scotch whiskey, good gin, beautiful hotels—and the world's best ski slopes only a few hours away. I feel almost like a civilian again with a visa and ration tickets in my pocket, a nice apartment in a good hotel, and no military police in the country. I live with captains and majors who are today only schoolboys like me. Incidentally, I also expect to improve my mind, assimilate a little culture, and pick up some college credits.

Thursday we traveled from Strasbourg to Mulhouse, where the Army maintains the Swiss Leave Center through which we were processed. The Swiss Leave Center is a unique place. It efficiently takes care of all the paperwork, etc., of sending hundreds of men daily into a neutral country that is not part of the U.S. Army's European Theater. The leave center is located in a group of buildings that were formerly some sort of a French Army cantonment. It is very much like the French Army installations I stayed in at Chartres and Chalons-sur-Marne.

Here the men who are going to Switzerland on leave select one of thirteen tours, change their money, attend lectures on Swiss customs, venereal disease rates, black markets, and get their visas. Although we did not have to select a tour, we had to declare the amount of clothing and other possessions we were taking with us, change our money, process records, and listen to a speech by a Colonel Webb, who is in charge of American students in Switzerland.

Colonel Webb is a Southern farmer who has been in the Army for twenty-nine years. He left all of us with the impression that he was a lot more of a Georgia farmer than either a soldier or an educator. He told us that things were very poorly organized for this first GI student group. Our Army postal service would be very poor, he warned. We might have to pay duty on our PX rations and packages from home and our currency situation would be poor. We were allowed to take only 200 Swiss francs ($46.62) with us. How we would get the difference between that and the $200 we are allowed for the two months will be worked out later.

Geneva, Switzerland
January 21, 1946
Dear Folks:

The ride from Mulhouse to Basel was uneventful and cold as hell. At Basel there was lots of confusion about the customs inspection, which all of us had to go through. We had been warned about bringing more than seven candy bars, one carton of cigarettes, and one bottle of whiskey into Switzerland.

In the Basel station while waiting for the train to Geneva, I had my first taste of Switzerland. We had lunch in the station restaurant. Even on one of the meatless days, it had a fine, complete menu and wine list (including six different kinds of Scotch). With some fine service we had a "light" lunch of hot ravioli, soup, and cherry tarts. Of course, we had to give up a ration ticket, as you do whenever you buy any food in Switzerland. We were issued three days' worth of ration coupons for extra little things when we went through customs.

From Basel to Geneva, we rode third class in one of those wonderful electric trains that are part of the Swiss National Railway System. The train departed right on schedule and arrived at every city along the way on time. Here, at the University of Geneva, the old annoying officer–enlisted men relationship no longer exists. We eat, sleep, and go to school together. On the train I played bridge with three captains, which is something I would not have thought of doing, even if asked, under other conditions. Although the directive under which these schools are set up says that no more than 10 percent of the student body shall be officers, there is considerably more than that percentage here. This is the best deal a soldier could get in Europe today. I don't suppose the men who solve the world's problems at officers' club bars could let this one pass them by.

Geneva, Switzerland
January 23, 1946
Dear Folks:

In yesterday's letter, in which I told you about the train ride from Basel to Geneva, I forgot to tell you what everyone who takes the ride for the first time mentions: the tremendous beauty of the countryside. The ride from Lausanne to Geneva along Lake Geneva with the Alps in the background reminded me very much of the ride from Reno to Yosemite along Lake Tahoe, with the Sierra Nevadas in the background.

Early Saturday morning Red Murray **[my roommate, a private from Pittsburgh, who had completed his freshman year at Yale]** *and I went downtown to try to buy secondhand ice skates. We erroneously figured that, living opposite the only rink in Geneva, we would have an opportunity to skate at least once every day. Everyone, as usual, was very cooperative and helpful. We bought the skates, only to learn that they don't have as much ice in Geneva as they do in Philadelphia. It would have been better to rent skates. Although the purchase of our skates annoyed us, our first purchase in Switzerland did not. While walking down the main street, we passed a liquor store that was filled with all the best whiskies, wines, and liqueurs. We bought a bottle of good Scotch for the first time in Europe. All the items were about one dollar more expensive than they are at home, but after seeing only black-market alcohol for a year, it was very good.*

Saturday afternoon the first meeting of the entire soldier-student body was convened. We selected our courses and curricula. The list of courses offered was really quite unusual. Most of the courses are taught only one or two hours a week. They do not seem to be designed like our American curricula, with credit points of paramount importance. All courses are taught in English by Swiss professors, the great majority of whom lectured in the States before the war.

After attending a lecture at a foreign university, you cannot use the library to do a little extra research on the subject. **[At the University of Geneva, virtually all of the reference books, the card index, and the readers' guides were in French.]**

*This makes the attending of lectures a race to take copious notes,
which is really not too good. Although there is really not a wide
selection of courses offered, I worked my roster out so that, among
other things, I do not have classes on Friday. This will allow me
to see something of Switzerland and its ski slopes. I particularly
tried to select courses that I could not take in the States and that
would give me typical Swiss and European ideas about America,
England, English writers, etc.*

*I selected the following courses: Intermediate French (3 hours a
week), Theory of International Organizations (1 hour), Experi-
mental Psychology (1 hour), History of French Literature
(1 hour), Educational Psychology (1 hour), Raw Materials and
World Problems (1 hour), John Milton (2 hours), Shakespeare in
French-Speaking Countries (1 hour), Psychology of Development
(2 hours), and America and Europe (1 hour). At this point it
looks wonderfully interesting.*

Geneva, Switzerland
January 28, 1946
Dear Folks:

*Early Friday morning two men from my boarding house and I
left for St. Cergue with our bedrolls, blankets, and forty-odd sandwiches. We hoped to spend a cheap weekend in the Alpine ski resort nearest Geneva. While riding from our boardinghouse to the
train station, we met an American who had been in the Army
in the last war. He has spent the past twenty years here in the
Geneva area. We explained to him what we were looking for at St.
Cergue. As luck would have it, he told us that for seventeen years
he ran the first-aid station at St. Cergue. He knew everybody up
there. He then bought us a couple cups of coffee and gave us letters
of introduction to the men who run the restaurants, ski slopes,
train station, etc. He explained that we had only a little money to
spend and wanted to go skiing. His letters worked like charms.*

*Without saying a word we were shown to the Auberge de
Jeunesse, which is a sort of Swiss youth hostel. There they made a
big fuss over us. We were the first American soldiers to visit them.
They showed us rooms where we could sleep on straw for 1 franc*

(23¢) a night or on mattresses and box springs for 1½ francs a night. We proved ourselves typical free-spending Americans. We slept on mattresses.

Geneva, Switzerland
February 3, 1946

Dear Folks:

My teeth have been bothering me again. I went to a Geneva dentist who removed another inlay. While on the subject of medical care, I might as well tell you something of our medical setup in Geneva. There is one medical corps officer attached to the Army resident-staff detachment in Bern. This organization administers to the medical needs of Army personnel in Switzerland outside the military attaché's staff [at the U.S. Embassy]. In Geneva, the Army sends us to a Dr. Demolé, who speaks perfect English and is considered one of the best doctors in Geneva. There is a pharmacy in Geneva where medicines that have been prescribed by Dr. Demolé are filled and charged to the Army. Dr. Demolé sent me to the dentist. I assume the Army will pay the bill. Overall I would say that we have a very good medical setup.

One of the many things about Switzerland that makes you feel that you are far away from the Army is the food. We receive the same food rations as Swiss civilians and the same issue of ration coupons. The Army gives our hotels enough to cover our meals, and we get to use the rest of our meal and confection coupons for sandwiches, chocolate bars, and so on. If we are away for a meal and give the pension notice, we get enough coupons to cover the meal we are missing. When we go away for a skiing weekend, etc., they always pack a lunch for us or give us all the necessary stuff to make our own sandwiches when we picnic. Monday, Wednesday, and Friday are meatless days, so we have had lots of fancy cheese dishes. Sometimes before we leave we get some of the famous Swiss meal "fondue" (several kinds of cheese, kirsch [a cherry cordial], vin blanc, and bread).

Army meals have a lot more meat, but they never include fresh milk, fresh butter, fancy desserts, or sweetbreads and mushrooms, as we had last week. We are always amazed at the way tearooms

A diplomatic dispute with the Allied Powers rendered Switzerland's traditional source of coal—Germany—unavailable during the 1945–1946 winter. Logs were piled outside the League of Nations' Palace in Geneva, where all of the buildings were heated that winter by wood.

and cafeterias never serve sandwiches or bread with a cup of coffee or a milk shake but always serve elaborate pastries, éclairs, or napoleons instead. This is the case not only in big city tearooms but also in places in small towns that look like they ought to have "Diner" or "Sloppy Joe's" signs out front. In the cafeteria (no seats; customers eat standing up) of the Grand Passage, the biggest department store in Geneva, you can always get the chocolate products of Swiss firms, whose names are almost as well known in the States as they are in Switzerland (Nestlé and Suchard). [Land-locked Switzerland prepared for food rationing even before the outbreak of hostilities in 1939. After the fall of France in May, 1940, when the country became totally surrounded by Axis powers, it instituted strict rationing of food products, including coffee, tea, cocoa, cheese, eggs, meat, and bread. For two days each week, the consumption of meat was prohibited. Regular food-ration coupons could be exchanged for special "blue coupons," which could be used for restaurant meals. People were encouraged to develop private truck gardens, and industrial companies bought or rented large plots of land so their employees could grow their own vegetables on individual, subdivided plots.]

Geneva, Switzerland
February 5, 1946
Dear Folks:

Both the American and Swiss civilians go out of their way to meet us. They make a big fuss over us, regardless of rank, which is, of course, much different from the arrangement we had in France. The officers' life in Paris was a continual round of parties and balls. The French never seemed to understand that a commission is no indication of culture, background, or respectability. Enlisted men might be able to give them something more than their money in the Rue Pigalle [a Paris neighborhood of strip joints, cheap bars, and brothels].

Here all of us have been invited to one reception or party after

The League of Nations' Palace in Geneva, Switzerland.

*another. My first experience with American civilians was two
weeks ago when I took a train to Berne for a few hours. On my way,
a man came over and spoke to me in English. Before we were done,
I found out that he was an employee of the Standard Oil Company
of New Jersey. He invited me to spend a night with him at his home
in Zurich. As I told you in an earlier letter, we only had our cheap
setup in St. Cergue because we met an American civilian on the
trolley while going to the station. Last week at St. Cergue, two
women came up and introduced themselves to us. They were the
Swiss representatives of the YWCA and the American Friends Service Committee. In Lausanne another woman spoke to us and told
us about her daughter at Vassar and her marriage in Cleveland.
It's very nice to have respectable women speak to you as men and
friends and not as scum, potential customers, or charity cases, as
always seems to be the case in Red Cross clubs. Thursday night the
American committee is having a reception for us.*

Geneva, Switzerland
February 6, 1946
Dear Folks:

*Although life here is full and active, I am not very impressed
with our academic setup at the University of Geneva. While I expect to tell Dean Neidlinger at Dartmouth how much I learned
here and that I should certainly get as much credit for this work
as I did for the summer semester in 1942, the Army authorities
here do not believe that most good colleges will give us credit for
this work. [**Dartmouth granted me—and most veterans—a
lump-sum credit for our wartime military service. Quasi-
academic experiences like the ASTP and University of Geneva
classes were given consideration when establishing the amount
but were not broken out.**]*

*The biggest difficulty here is language. Although all of the
teachers speak fairly good English, there are only a few English
books in the library. Most of us are totally lost as soon as we leave
our lectures. A prerequisite of fluent French would have barred
me from coming to Geneva. Still, I believe it would have made the
courses much more worthwhile for those who did come. Another*

great difficulty is that there was no screening as there was in the ASTP's STAR units. The only prerequisite was a high-school diploma, with the result that there is such a wide difference in the academic backgrounds of the men that only half of each class should be taking the course they are attending. To this I might add that I do not think that most of the lectures are of the caliber of those I heard at Dartmouth or Central High. With almost 40 percent of the term behind me, I do not feel that I have learned a great deal in the classes. However, don't think that I am bitching. I am sure that I could not spend my time more profitably or pleasantly anywhere else in Europe today.

One of the things I have particularly noticed is that I haven't heard anyone say a good word about the Jewish refugees who spent the past years in Switzerland. In St. Cergue this is particularly true. They have a large, elaborate hotel (which used to be English) that was used as a refuge for the past seven years. It has been occupied successively by Jews, Poles, Russians, and today by Swiss nationals who could not get out of Germany during the war. We never asked what the people thought of the various refugees, but they always volunteered information. They didn't like the Jews and were glad when they left. We were told this by at least five people. Some also told us that, although they didn't like the Russian government, they much preferred Russian refugees to Jews. Although you can't draw any real conclusions from this sort of thing, there is undoubtedly evidence of some sort of embryonic anti-Semitism. Although in a French city like Geneva you are not too aware of it, all of us who have been in Switzerland for a few weeks are fully aware of just what sort of "neutral" Switzerland was during the first four years of the war.

Geneva, Switzerland
February 11, 1946
Dear Folks:

I've finally fallen in love. I'm not sure whether it is skiing or snow-capped mountains that I love, but I'm sure that I spent one of the most wonderful weekends of my life at Gstaad. The sight from the top of the mountains was tremendous. Although you can see pictures of the Alps, a person who has not skied down them or climbed them to the very top cannot fully appreciate their beauty.

Not only is Gstaad surrounded by beautiful mountains with good ski runs, but it also has that very pleasant atmosphere you expect to find in fancy English resorts. Before the war it was almost an English colony. Although today 150 GIs and a very few Englishmen are on leave there, its clientele is still very nice and young. At present the most important English guest is "Monty" **[British war hero Lord Bernard Law Montgomery of Alemain],** *who is staying there as a civilian. A few miles away in the same valley King Leopold of Belgium and Agha Kahn are vacationing.*

After a beautiful ride, Red Murray and I arrived in Gstaad Friday morning about 10:30. We immediately went to the tourist bureau, which is run by the Cunard-White Star Line. We explained that we had brought our own blankets and food and wanted a very cheap room where we could throw down our bedrolls. Luck was with us. The person working there arranged for us to have a room in the servants' quarters of the Hotel Victoria, in the center of town, where we had two soft beds and access to hot water for three francs (70¢) a night.

After renting skis and boots at a special reduced price for GIs on leave, we spent the afternoon skiing down the Wassergrat, one of the easier runs. The run is about three-quarters of a mile long, and you go up it in a chairlift, which in itself is a real experience. In the evening we visited a few of the bars in Gstaad. We heard the singer who is widely advertised in this country as the "Little Swiss Dinah Shore." She is quite good. Her voice resembles Dinah Shore's in many ways. Here, even more than in the other parts of Europe, everybody knows American movie actors and bands. You regularly hear them singing the American songs that are popular this winter ("Sentimental Journey," "Atcheson, Topeka, and the Santa Fe"). Most people say they learned the songs from the radio (Armed Forces Network Munich-Stuttgart). **[Dinah Shore (1921–1993) was one of the 1940s' most popular singers. She had her own radio and TV show and also starred in films. "Blues in the Night" was her biggest wartime hit.]**

Hotel Victoria in Gstaad, where I stayed in unheated servants' quarters
when I went skiing. Only sleighs—not cars—were allowed on the roads in
winter.

Geneva, Switzerland
February 12, 1946
Dear Folks:

Last Thursday night the American community gave a reception for the GI students. It was a very nice affair. As things developed at the party, we have dates Monday and Tuesday of next week to have drinks at the homes of the two Dartmouth men who work in the consulate. One is the vice consul, George Phillips, who came over here about a year ago with his wife. The other is a fellow by the name of Crosby, who was discharged from the Army as a captain in August and before the war taught English at the American University at Beirut, Lebanon. All of these people have very interesting war stories to tell, so different from the average GI–Ernie Pyle–John Hersey sort of stuff. [John Hersey's (1914–1993) 1944 bestseller, A Bell for Adano, described GIs during the Sicily Campaign (1943).]

The relative value of the American dollar here in Switzerland is really quite a shock after you have been in countries where it sells on the black market for five to ten times its value. Here you get only 60 percent of the value of the dollar when you buy Swiss francs through unofficial channels. The GIs who come here on leave can change only 255 Swiss francs through official channels. Since that will not buy them as many watches and pastries as they want, they look for things to sell to the Swiss. This is rather difficult. Most of the things we want to sell them are obtainable here but are usually of inferior quality—no pure-wool goods, no "big four" (Camel, Lucky Strike, Old Gold, and Chesterfield) American cigarettes, and few rubberized raincoats like the GI ones. The black market has already been flooded by the 200,000 to 300,000 soldiers who have been through Switzerland on leave.

The only things that can be sold with ease today are dollars (2.5 francs to the dollar; the official rate is 4.29) and British pounds (seven francs to the pound; the official rate is about 17). The jewelers buy them. Then they sell them to people going to the States or people who are speculating in dollars at a small profit. With Swiss assets blocked in the United States and England, the

Swiss are limited in the amount of cash they can take out of the country. Of course, they are glad to be able to buy our money cheaply. I tried to cash some of my traveler's checks at the American Express office the other day but was told that because I'm a soldier in Switzerland, they could do nothing for me. This business of blocked assets and selling the dollar is the sort of "high finance" that civilians at home never think about, but something that every soldier in Europe knows about.

Yesterday I told you what a good time Red and I had in Gstaad. Three of our friends who were going to meet us up there went to Zermatt instead. They had an avalanche, which forced them to stay for a week, move into the best hotel at government expense, and go skiing.

Geneva, Switzerland
Valentine's Day, 1946
Dear Folks:

In one of Mother's recent letters, she asked what language I spoke here in Geneva. I can speak only one. Almost everyone you meet can speak a little of that, as well as two or three others. Every announcement of any importance is written in French, German, and Italian. An important announcement means "no spitting" and "no smoking" signs in trains, instructions on how to open train windows, the markings on currency, the names and instructions on Swiss-manufactured Colgate shaving cream and toothpaste. However, this is the largest French-speaking city in Switzerland. It is probably much more like the prewar French cities than any other city in the world.

You are always interested in what newspapers and magazines I read and what access I have to libraries. The only American publications (European editions) that are regularly sold here in Geneva are Newsweek *and the* New York Herald-Tribune, *both of which can be purchased here the day after they are printed in Paris. I buy* Newsweek *regularly because my* Time, *like my mail, which is forwarded through Army post office channels, arrives irregularly. I have not seen a copy of* Stars and Stripes *since I left Mulhouse and have not missed it a bit. They have an*

American reading room in Geneva, but it is far from where I live. Several weeks ago we rented a radio, so we regularly hear the Armed Forces Network's news broadcasts from Munich, which keeps us up to date on the half-truths, propaganda, and nonsense that the Army of Occupation headquarters puts out about redeployment and so on. Although we are far away from the big Army installations in Europe, we get much more up-to-date news than do most soldiers in Germany and Austria.

Geneva, Switzerland
February 16, 1946
Dear Folks:

Two years ago this week we heard that the ASTP was closing. This weekend we learned that the coal-for-college-students program is closing up at the end of the present semester. The reasons for the closing of the Army's Swiss university experiment are fairly obvious. All of the U.S. papers have headlines about redeployment and demobilization. None of the men here were very surprised at the reports. This news makes me feel doubly lucky to be attending the one and only "U.S. Army extraordinary session" at the University of Geneva.

Saturday morning I returned to Geneva from Gstaad via Montreaux, which is called the Riviera of Switzerland. While there I visited the Chateau of Chillon, about which Byron wrote his famous poem. If I had to be a prisoner, I could think of no more beautiful place to be imprisoned. The chateau is built just over the edge of Lake Geneva, and from the windows you look out over Lake Geneva to the snow-covered French Alps. If you look out the windows that face the Swiss Alps, which rise behind the chateau, you are surprised to see a complicated arrangement of pillboxes, tank traps, cleared minefields, and so on. Montreaux holds a commanding position over Lake Geneva. Although the Swiss were neutral, they were prepared to raise hell with anyone who attacked them. All through the mountains between Gstaad and Montreaux, you see fortifications of all sorts. This makes me think how much more useful the "democracy-loving" Swiss would have been as allies than as neutrals.

Geneva, Switzerland
February 25, 1946
Dear Folks:

In Daddy's letter, he asked me about the packages that he sent to me at Frankfurt and the regular mail to Switzerland. I will not receive the packages as long as I am in Switzerland because the Army and the Swiss have not been able to agree on how duty should be charged on packages that were sent overseas to Army post-office addresses. They were probably forwarded from Frankfurt to Mulhouse and are waiting for me at the Swiss Leave Center there. As for the regular mail sent here, it will arrive eventually.

Last week we received the bad news that the Army is requiring the University of Geneva to examine us in all of our courses. Although this will somewhat complicate the next two weeks and make me a little more diligent than I might have been, I am rather pleased. This way it will be easier for Dartmouth to give me credit for the work I did here.

Geneva, Switzerland
February 28, 1946
Dear Folks:

It was wonderful talking to you on the phone last night. The connection was so good and everything went off so smoothly that I could not help feeling that we were not really so far apart. Tuesday night I spent several hours by the phone expecting the call. At about 12:45 the operator called and asked whether I was expecting a call from Philadelphia. I answered "yes" and for some unexplainable reason expected that it would come through that night. I waited until two o'clock. Then I went to bed but got up again at 5:45 and called the operator (a very difficult job with my French) to find out whether the call had come through while I was asleep. Then she explained to me that the call at 12:45 A.M. was just to notify me of the call last night, but the operator didn't speak very good English. Fearing an all-night stand last night, I went to bed at 10:30 P.M. and set the alarm for 12:00, but everything worked out so well that you may have heard the alarm ringing while we were speaking. It won't be too long until I'll be calling from New York.

One of the first questions you asked over the phone was about money. If you have interpreted the discussion of money in my letters as not-too-subtle hints, I'm sorry. I don't need any money! Since I stopped traveling from Camp Pickett to Philadelphia every weekend, I have been able to live very well on my Army pay and have even saved a few dollars.

Geneva, Switzerland
March 7, 1946
Dear Folks:

Shortly after six, we took the train for Wengen and went through some of the most beautiful country in the world—along Lake Thun to Interlachen and then up into the Bernese Oberlands to the base of the Jungfrau. We were warned that it was almost impossible to get a place to stay at Wengen, so like big shots we got out of our class and, through American Express, made a reservation at the cheapest hotel in Wengen, only to find when we got there that they took a dim view of eating all of our meals in our room from the sandwiches we had prepared in Geneva. We stayed at a joint that American Express has never heard of, but where we didn't have to buy any meals from the hotel. We also decided that on all future trips we would travel with our sleeping bags and sleep in the unheated servants' quarters of hotels.

Geneva, Switzerland
March 9, 1946
Dear Folks:

I am more embarrassed to write this letter home than I have been to write any letter since coming overseas. I have taken a certain amount of pride in the fact that I had a good time whenever there was a possible chance to. And I still have not been forced to ask for money from home or withdraw any from the bank that I did not repay.

Since Switzerland was a neutral country, U.S. soldiers attending Swiss universities did not receive regular mail through the Army's postal system. Letters and packages addressed to their APO addresses were held at the Army's leave center in Mulhouse, France. This is the first mail call there.

However, yesterday, I got myself involved in an uncomfortable situation. I borrowed money, not from my family but from the Sickles family [Philadelphia family friends in the watch-importing business, who had introduced me to Adolphe Newman, a Swiss watch exporter]. Every time I see Mr. Adolphe Newman he asks if he can lend me some money. I have always refused—until Thursday. Then I asked whether he could cash my traveler's checks or the enclosed money order, which I bought in Frankfurt. He told me to return yesterday, when he would then tell me what he was able to do with them. The banks here in Geneva would not handle either of them. They say money orders are only for U.S. internal use. Traveler's checks can be cashed only after entry is made on an American passport and after the number of the check and the passport are sent to the American Embassy. He insisted that Mr. Sickles would not want me to be short of money. Although I was embarrassed and objected, he *gave me 200 francs, which he is going to charge to the Sickles's account. Enclosed is a postal money order for $75, of which I hope you will send the Sickles about $47. Send the remainder to my account at the Dartmouth National Bank.*

I borrowed the money from Mr. Newman because Red and I expected to go to Davos and ski down the twelve-mile long Parsenn, which is supposed to be the finest ski run in the world. **[Walter Prager was a ski instructor at Davos before he came to Dartmouth as chief ski coach.]** *However, the people who run the Swiss college program for soldiers got chickenhearted and issued the following order yesterday. Its wording is so strong that we decided not to violate it.*

1. Effective this date, because of the high accident rate, American Army students in Switzerland are prohibited from skiing.

2. Any accident sustained while skiing will be considered as resulting from direct violation of orders and will be classed as *not* in the line of duty.

The whole thing is very annoying for many reasons, the chief one of which is an unconscious resentment of authority that can prohibit you from skiing or skating or drinking. The fact that a skiing accident is not in the line of duty is doubly annoying when you realize that, according to the Army, soldiers contract venereal disease in the line of duty.

CHAPTER 10

RETURNING HOME

MY JOURNEY HOME officially began at the Second Reinforcement Depot in Namur, Belgium, a huge, nineteenth-century Army garrison with dozens of four-story brick barracks that had been upgraded with indoor plumbing, heat, and showers. As on previous reinforcement depot assignments, I did little at Namur except eat, sleep, read books—and await further orders.

Next stop was a "cigarette camp." Before Camp Lucky Strike was fully operational, seven similar (but smaller) tent cities were built near Le Havre. On my homeward trip I was processed through Camp Philip Morris, a mid-sized camp built for thirty-five thousand soldiers. In 1945 and 1946 three million soldiers were processed through "cigarette camps" going either to or from the European Theater.

Other than the fact that it was also a tent city named for a cigarette brand, Camp Philip Morris in March, 1946, bore little resemblance to Camp Lucky Strike a year earlier. At Philip Morris all of the tents had wood floors, electric heaters, electric lights, and beds with mattresses. Some even had doors. The roads were asphalt or concrete. Three hot meals were served daily on steel trays in mess halls. Throughout the camp the latrines had flush toilets and showers, and we had access to enlisted-men's clubs, PXs, barbershops, and movie theaters with first-run films. Where secrecy, mystery, and rumor were part of Lucky Strike's mystique, a large, illuminated twenty-foot-long shipment schedule listed when ships would leave port, as well as the anticipated arrival time of boats from the United States.

Soldiers were prepared for their return to the United States at "cigarette camps." These camps were upgraded after V-E Day to include enlisted men's recreation halls, paved roads, tents with floors, and showers. I was processed at Camp Philip Morris, outside Le Havre.

A billboard-sized, troop movement and departure schedule near the enlisted men's recreation hall at Camp Philip Morris was updated many times each day.

This ship was cracked in two by a mine in Le Havre harbor. On April 1, 1946, almost a year after V-E Day, it still had not been cleared away. Troops at the port of embarkation said the ship was part of the first convoy to enter the port in January, 1945. My troopship had been part of that convoy.

Troopship travel is never luxurious or fun. Still, there was a vast difference between crossing the North Atlantic in peacetime and doing so when German U-boats challenged Allied control of the sea lanes. I returned on the *Colby Victory,* one of a special class of troopship built in 1945 and 1946 to hasten redeployment. Designed to sleep 1,597 men, it had few, if any, empty spaces. We still slept in four-high racks suspended from pipes, but we were able to sit down at meals and roam the decks freely both day and night. There were no restrictions on smoking, leaning on railings, or using flashlights. Most nights a movie was shown on the aft deck.

The warm welcome the *Colby Victory* received when it entered New York harbor was totally unexpected—and a happy finale to soldiering. By then the war had been over for seven months. Battle-scarred warriors and long-serving soldiers had been brought home months earlier. We were unexceptional, nonvalorous, routine GIs who had earned the right to return home after long service in the European Theater. I expected to disembark unceremoniously at an obscure Army wharf.

Instead, New York greeted us as heroes. A tugboat with a five-foot high banner across its wheelhouse shouting "Welcome Home—Well Done" escorted the *Colby Victory* through the harbor. Each ship we passed saluted us with its whistles and foghorns. When we passed near the Statue of Liberty, the *Colby Victory* used all of its horns and whistles to blow a salute, and the returning soldiers spontaneously began singing "God Bless America." As we approached the Army's Staten Island pier, a band played martial music. A colonel stood at the end of the gangplank and saluted each soldier individually as he stepped onto U.S. soil.

I was formally discharged at Fort Dix, New Jersey, on the afternoon of April 10, 1946, a few hours before my family was scheduled to celebrate the Passover Seder, the world's oldest celebration of freedom and the anniversary of the ancient Jews'

A five-foot high banner saying, "WELCOME HOME—WELL DONE," was attached to the wheelhouse of the tugboat that met the *Colby Victory* troopship in New York harbor. All ships in the harbor saluted the *Colby Victory* with whistles and fog horns as we passed them.

successful revolt against Egyptian tyranny. My military career ended with participation in a solemn—but uniquely significant—religious ceremony. The entire family, including my grandparents and distant cousins, was gathered for the festivities. After being greeted with cheers and hugs, I requested that the service be delayed briefly until I could properly participate—in civilian clothes.

Namur, Belgium
March 17, 1946
Dear Folks:

It's almost all over now. I'm really on my way home. In my pocket I have orders which read "relieved of assignment to units indicated and transferred . . . to Second Reinforcement Depot, Namur, Belgium, for processing and return to the Zone of the Interior." With orders like that, the only thing left to speculate about is how long it takes to get processed (usually one to two weeks) and how rough the trip across the ocean will be.

My two months in Switzerland were both pleasant and profitable. If I were leaving Geneva for any place except Philadelphia, I would be rather downcast. Due to the language barrier and the

Parade yard at the Second Reinforcement Depot in Namur, Belgium. The arrow points to my room.

ever-present feeling that Geneva was only a stop on the way home, I didn't leave as many good friends behind in Switzerland as I did in Williamsburg, but I certainly left a piece of my heart there.

Tuesday evening I went to a reception given by the mayor of Geneva for the U.S. Army students at the University of Geneva. There were drinks and food and stuffy speeches. All the politicians of Geneva were there, telling us about the similarities of our governments and our ways of life. They also inquired whether we thought we would get home and be demobilized before America and Russia went to war.

It seems that every time I meet Swiss people they ask that same question. Although I think about it, like everybody else, I find the "neutral interest" of the Swiss in wars, their profits, and our "grande armée" very annoying. One of the interesting things at the reception was that some of the officials wore their uniforms, which consisted of Lord Nelson hats, big chains around their necks, and red-and-gold affairs that looked like a smock-dress combination.

Thursday afternoon we had graduation exercises in the University of Geneva auditorium. They were good, except for Colonel Webb, who made one of those inappropriate, chauvinistic speeches which would be tolerated only by a group of drunks on the Fourth of July. An American sergeant who was a Harvard junior when he was drafted spoke for the American students in French. The president of the University of Geneva student body spoke to us in English. Major Brown presided. The rector of the university and the head of the Institute of International Affairs each delivered short speeches. The whole affair was short and dignified and left everybody with a nice taste in their mouth.

Thursday night Red and I went out once again with Mr. Dutoit **[a clerk at a Swiss auto club who was a participant in the American Club of Geneva's program to entertain GIs.]**, *who had arranged for us to meet two English-speaking girls and go dancing with him and his wife. Although we were not too impressed with the girls, we had a nice time. Mr. Dutoit certainly went out of his way to be nice to us and to make our stay in Geneva pleasant. When we arrived at Gare Cornavin at 6:00 A.M.*

*Saturday morning, he was waiting there to say good-bye to us.
Nobody less than my parents could get me up at 6:00 A.M. to go to
a railroad station to wish me bonne chance and bon voyage.*

*Friday was a very full day beginning with the sale of my golf
balls, books, extra clothes, and so on, which I do not intend to carry
halfway around the world on my back. I'm quite a collector of
junk, as long as my equipment travels by truck or train, but when
I carry it all on my back, I even count the extra razor blades.*

*The number of women who came to the station to say good-bye
to all those "atomic-loving" American soldiers was amazing. The
train platform was crowded with smugly smirking soldiers and
weeping women, plus the entire chorus from the Palais d'Hiver,
Geneva's roughest nightspot.*

Namur, Belgium
March 20, 1946
Dear Folks:

*I'm back in the Army again. Back to the spit-and-polish,
peacetime Army where you have nothing useful to do all day, but
you are kept more or less alert waiting for whistles, bugles, and
formations. If we were sober, all of us would hate it, but most of us
are thoroughly drunk with the idea of getting home and away
from all of this nonsense. Nothing makes any difference now.*

*Saturday in Mulhouse I received two packages which you sent
to me in Frankfurt but which were held in Mulhouse because the
Army and the Swiss could not agree on which Swiss customs
regulations applied to packages sent to soldiers through Army
postal channels.*

*Since coming here we have gone through the same processes we
went through before we came overseas. We were made to throw
away our extra clothing. Then we were issued new required equipment for all that we had lost, worn out, or just didn't want—
without no questions asked. Our records were checked. They lectured us on military courtesy, and we had our money converted.
They lost my immunization record and gave me an extra typhoid
shot just to make the books balance. Now there is almost nothing
to do but sit and wait until we move to a cigarette camp at the*

port. Since they are planning to close the Port of Antwerp on March 31, rumors say that we will move to the port next Tuesday or Wednesday (26th or 27th). Then we should board the boat within forty-eight hours.

Namur, Belgium
March 22, 1946
Dear Folks:

We're still doing nothing but waiting, hoping, and trying hard not to believe all of the rumors that float around a place like this. In many ways, this is the easiest life imaginable. There is very little that you are forced to do but get up in the mornings and stand in line for an hour before meals. But at this point in the game, no life could be much harder. The information about our departure for a port the middle of next week has almost passed the rumor stage. If we do not waste more than the usual forty-eight hours there, I have a good chance of being home for Seder.

After Swiss food, Army chow represents a real change, but in many ways a good one. We no longer have attractive Swiss waitresses, tablecloths, and fancy food. Instead, we have coffee ladled from a fifty-gallon ash can by a German. The rest of our food is thrown onto our mess kits, but the food is good. We get meat every day and have real American Army breakfasts with fruit, cereal, powdered eggs, and coffee. We can get seconds on coffee with supper.

After eight months in the Military Police department, I finally drew my most distasteful MP duties: town patrol. Namur is an Army town similar to Blackstone, Va., or Fayetteville, N.C. It has a curfew. MPs patrol all of the streets and enter all of the cafés every fifteen minutes or half hour. Due to the reduction in MP units all over the continent, there are not enough regular MPs to pull this detail. Officers and men who are passing through the depot act as auxiliary MPs. With one officer and another enlisted man, I patrolled a block with about five cafés. Because all of us are going home soon, we were not anxious to get into any fights. We did a good patrolling job—to the extent of six free beers, a free steak, and two plates of chips.

Men leaving Camp Philip Morris for the pier at Le Havre on April 1, 1946.

Namur, Belgium
March 24, 1946
Dear Folks:

Tomorrow morning bright and early the trip to the port begins. Although on the map Namur and Le Havre seem close to each other, we have been told that the trip will probably take us two days and one night [approximately 250 miles]. My orders now read Fort Dix, N.J. After we reach the staging area at Le Havre, it is only a matter of waiting until there is a boat for us.

Although Belgium is quite a change after Switzerland, it is much nearer normal and more like the States than any other European country I have visited. Food, including steaks, eggs, and patisserie can be bought almost anywhere without points. Most household equipment can be bought in the stores.

Camp Philip Morris, France
March 30, 1946
Dear Folks:

This will be the last letter I will write you as a soldier. Within thirty-six hours I will be boarding the Colby Victory *and taking what I hope will not be my last look at Europe for a while. With good luck I will speak to you before you receive this letter.*

Good-bye to Red Cross coffee and doughnuts at the pier at Le Havre.

Boarding the *Colby Victory* troopship for the trip home.

My welcoming family in Philadelphia.

Camp Philip Morris, where I have been for the past five days, is just outside Le Havre, but because of the strained relations between the Americans and the French in Le Havre, none of us are allowed to see the city or leave camp. [Almost two months earlier, on February 6, 1946, tense Franco-American relations merited coverage in the New York Times. *It reported, "Disorders among United States 'redeployables' in Le Havre has resulted in a curfew being imposed. The town is now out of bounds to American troops."]*

A week, a month, a year ago the change from military to civilian life seemed very easy. Now as the big day is really just around the corner, I am beginning to realize that it will not be so easy to decide what I will wear, what I will do, and who I will tell to go to

hell. I am sort of shocked at the strong, habit-forming, mental opi-
ate the Army is. Today it is easier than ever to understand why
regular Army officers think and live the way they do. Thank God,
it is almost all over, and I can throw off the shackles and try to be
a man again. I should be freed just before or during Passover.
What could be a more fitting time to celebrate liberation?

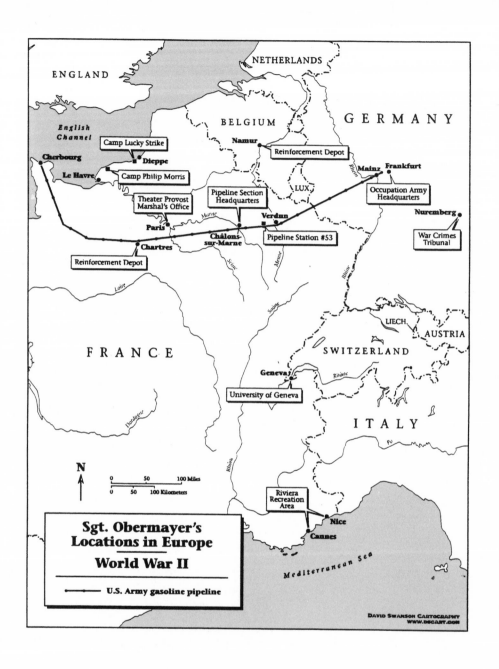

ENGLAND

NETHERLANDS

English
Channel

BELGIUM

GERMANY

Cherbourg

Camp Lucky Strike

Dieppe

Namur

Reinforcement Depot

Mainz Frankfurt

Le Havre

Camp Philip Morris

LUX.

Occupation Army
Headquarters

Theater Provost
Marshal's Office

Pipeline Section
Headquarters

Verdun

Nuremberg

Paris

Marne

Chartres

Reinforcement Depot

Châlons-
sur-Marne

Pipeline Station #53

War Crimes
Tribunal

Seine

Loire

LIECH.

AUSTRIA

FRANCE

SWITZERLAND

Geneva

Rhône

University of Geneva

ITALY

Po

N

0   50   100 Miles
0   50   100 Kilometers

Riviera
Recreation
Area

Nice

Sgt. Obermayer's
Locations in Europe

Cannes

Mediterranean Sea

World War II

U.S. Army gasoline pipeline

DAVID SWANSON CARTOGRAPHY
WWW.DSCART.COM

Epilogue

NOT UNTIL I had crossed the biblically ordained threshold of threescore and ten years did I fully understand the formative role of my Army service. As life's shadows lengthened I better appreciated the disproportionately large part the years 1943 to 1946 had played in the development of my character, personality, and sense of values. Many of my contemporaries share similar feelings about their own war years. And most of us gained this insight late in life.

I was a low-level enlisted man in an eleven-million-person Army. For three years I wrote home about small people, tedious assignments, and minor events that came my way. From a personal perspective that reflected the biases and understandings that were part of my upbringing, I chronicled happenings that were part of the twentieth-century's cataclysmic event. Until very recently I did not think that my war stories were worthy of discussion at family conclaves, let alone publication in a book.

The odyssey of my Army letters is revealing. I did not know until 1962 that they had been lovingly saved. They came into my possession, along with my baseball pennants, canoe paddle, political buttons, Eagle Scout sash, and college textbooks, when my parents moved from their suburban home to an apartment. All of these memorabilia were immediately stored in my attic. I was busy raising a family and editing and publishing daily newspapers in New Jersey and Virginia. I had no time for nostalgia.

In 1947 I wrote an article for a Dartmouth literary magazine urging ambitious students not to join any of the various veterans' organizations that were actively recruiting on campus.

Victory on life's battleground depended on looking forward, not backward. Affiliation with trade unions, professional societies, and service clubs could advance a career, but the American Legion or Veterans of Foreign Wars could not. Veterans' groups lobby for veterans' benefits. Their interests are narrow. But with maturity, I came to appreicate their unique role in reminding future generations of the debt they owe to those who sacrificed when their country called them.

Approximately a decade after my discharge, I was unhappy with my job as classified-advertising manager of the *New Orleans Item.* I prepared what I believed was a strong résumé with details of my academic and career achievements, but no mention of my Army service. I discussed it with my father-in-law, an active reservist and World War I and II veteran. He urged me to rewrite it. Without full information about my military service, it was incomplete, he said. I saw my soldiering years as a career-path distraction. I had acquired no job-related skills. I could not yet see the forest for the trees. I was unwilling to assign value to the experience of putting my life on the line as part of a great, worldwide crusade.

Early in life my father taught me that a good way to understand my feelings about abstractions—politics, religion, art, love—was to commit my perplexities to writing. This would force me to organize, analyze, and prioritize. It still does. This habit is manifest in my war letters. A desire to organize and prioritize my thoughts was a large part of my motivation to write home about religion, art, and leadership. Committing ideas to writing was also a component of the parental discipline in our home. Often, when I got into shouting matches with my sister, who was two and a half years younger, we would be sent to our respective rooms to prepare lists of the matters in dispute. Later we would be told to exchange lists and to read them aloud.

My quandary about being a patriotic American soldier while supporting the creation of a Jewish nation-state in Palestine was probably the issue about which I wrote most often. Did it represent a dual loyalty? By war's end I had resolved my dilemma. I became a Zionist. I concluded that the existence of a Jewish homeland in the Middle East did not conflict with America's interests or values. With the passage of time, it has become increasingly apparent that the bond that ties Israel to the United States is based more on shared standards of conduct and mutual goals than on realpolitik or military opportunism. In 1975, my wife, Betty Nan, and I, along with our four daughters, rented the home of Israel's chief justice, Aharon Barak, and spent a nontourist month in Jerusalem. We did our grocery shopping at the local supermarket and shared intellectual evenings with contemporaries who were pursuing active careers in academia, business, and government. We acknowledged that on a nontourist trip it was appropriate for teenaged daughters to spend their afternoons meeting boys at the local pool rather than viewing ancient artifacts in museums.

My letters home make it clear that as a teenager I already had strong convictions about politics and economics. I feared big government's coercive power and believed that under most circumstances, there is an inverse relationship between regulation and personal liberty. Fears about the unintended consequences of large-scale, state-directed wealth redistribution regimes made me unenthusiastic about many of the most widely acclaimed post-war social programs. If the franchise had been extended to eighteen-year-olds, as it was thirty years later, I would have voted against FDR and the New Deal. These tendencies were predictive of a lifelong interest in the philosophy of Friedrich A. Hayek, the Nobel laureate who was called "Thatcher's guru" by London tabloids, described as the "world's foremost free-market theorist" in American periodicals, and termed a "classical liberal" in scholarly journals.

My middle years were full. For three decades I successfully owned and edited small daily newspapers that were important factors in their local communities. As part of my job—it was also my pleasure—I became a Rotarian and a Chamber of Commerce activist, as well as a trustee of a historical society, library, art museum, Boy Scout council, synagogue, and hospital. I believed a community newspaper—and its editor and publisher—should play an active leadership role in support of public causes in which it believed. Chronicling and interpreting each day's events was just one part of its job. At the same time, Betty Nan held leadership positions in several community organizations, including the Jewish Foundation for Group Homes and Virginia's largest synagogue, which she served as president for two years.

As long as my name was at the top of a newspaper masthead, I never contributed to a political campaign or attended a politician's fund-raiser. At the same time, my newspapers always editorially endorsed candidates (of both major parties) in general elections and took positions on the myriad referendum issues that appear on Virginia ballots. After the sale of the *Northern Virginia Sun,* I affiliated myself with the Republican Party and testified before the GOP platform committee in 1992.

Business and professional travails were made less painful—and the joy of achievement enhanced—because I enjoyed a happy home life. For nearly fifty years I have been married to Betty Nan Levy, whom I adore. We met in her native New Orleans, where she was a sales executive in a family-owned jewelry store. We have shared a lifetime. But even more importantly, we have been immersed in each other's successes and failures, joys and sorrows, achievements and frustrations. We have raised four daughters, and I continue to have close, loving relationships with all of them, as well as my ten grandchildren.

In my middle years the present was demanding and rewarding. When I recalled my time in the Army—which was not often—I thought of it as just one of many character-forming, boyhood experiences, such as college, Boy Scouts, summer camp, and religious school. During this same period, the United States was involved in an unpopular war in Southeast Asia. Vietnam dominated the news for a decade. All things military were held in low esteem. This attitude carried over to lack of interest in World War II.

A generation after Saigon's fall, interest in the earlier conflict increased dramatically. For nearly three years Tom Brokaw's Greatest Generation books and Stephen E. Ambrose's *Citizen Soldiers* appeared at or near the top of the *New York Times'* best-seller list. Their storytelling skills made the World War II service of people like me interesting, even fascinating. Although the names were different, I felt I knew many—perhaps most—of the men whose wartime experiences they chronicled: friends, classmates, neighbors, and close relatives.

From 1971 to 1988, I wrote a weekly column for the *Northern Virginia Sun*. I commented on a wide variety of topics, personal as well as general. No subject was off limits. Over the years I wrote dozens of columns on education, social mores, my family, the environment, politics, and religion, but I did not write a single column about my Army experiences—and only a few about U.S. military preparedness. My war years were a closed chapter. In 1989, when I began an eight-semester stint teaching at the University of Maryland's College of Journalism, I had not yet examined the treasure trove that existed in the moldy boxes of letters.

Between 1990 and 2002, Betty Nan and I accepted eighteen State Department assignments to advise Eastern European newspaper executives on converting state-owned media enterprises into profit-making businesses. Several newspapers we consulted with are now exemplars of a free and independent press. Others have failed. The experience gave us an understanding of just how difficult it is for lifetime Marxists to adjust to capitalism's realities. Most of these assignments began with my host reading my résumé to the staff. Virtually without exception, the former apparatchiks were more interested in asking me about my Army days than about my forty years of experience in profitably managing daily newspapers. The wounds of war were still only partially healed for them. Many of World War II's bloodiest battles were fought on their soil and in their neighborhoods. Intuitively they prioritized my résumé; career details were less significant than my participation in an overarching historic event. As in most good pedagogic relationships, the teacher learned as much as—and probably more than—the students.

Reluctantly I attended my fiftieth class reunion at Dartmouth in 1996. My roommates had died. Most of my closest friends were unable to attend. I anticipated a white-haired, gimpy version of the twenty-fifth: singing football songs, guzzling beer, overstating professional achievements, chit-chatting with preppie wives, and listening to fund-raising appeals. To my surprise, I had a good time. Conversation focused less on college than on our mutual war experience, of which college was an integral part. We knew we had shared something more profound than being at a particular educational institution at the same time. As our class meeting was drawing to a close, a classmate rose to announce that the Defense Department had recently authorized a special medal for men who participated in the Normandy Campaign. He was sure many of us were eligible, and he had the necessary forms. A half dozen men, all of whom had completed successful careers, lined up to apply for a decoration they would never wear.

In 2002, Betty Nan and I spent a week visiting Normandy's cemeteries and memorials. That experience convinced me that preparing these letters for publication was more than an ego trip. Possibly the most interesting battle-area museum is at Arromanches, the site of the artificial harbor constructed by the Allies to support the invasion. Veterans are admitted free and are asked to wear a large lapel sticker. The sticker stands out. Total strangers walked up and shook my hand. Most said nothing. A few said, "Thank you." None asked what battles I had participated in, what decorations I had won, or what rank I had achieved. I had participated. That was enough.

Our Normandy trip included a visit to the site of Camp Lucky Strike, where I spent one of the most unpleasant months of my life. To locate the site, we called on the tourist bureau in St. Valéry-en-Caux, a nearby resort with a current population of forty-five hundred. The village's promotional packet includes a French-English brochure describing its World War II role. No great battles were fought there. No Resistance leaders were born or died there. Still, the town's historian spoke with pride about St. Valéry-en-Caux's important contribution: Its citizens helped build the U.S. Army's single largest reinforcement facility in Europe—Camp Lucky Strike.

The trip's emotional high point was the American cemetery at Omaha Beach. Its simple eloquence is overwhelming. Almost none of the nearly ten thousand young Americans buried there had chosen to assault a mined and booby-trapped beach below heavily fortified cliffs. Random selection put them there. Most of them were my age, too young to have acquired the vocational or professional skills that might have earned them safer jobs. Cemetery superintendent Gene Dellinger says the average age is between nineteen and twenty years (on D-Day I was nineteen years and eight months old).

My transfers—from a combat infantry division to an airborne engineer battalion to a combat engineer unit and finally to a pipeline company—were the result of shifting tactical and strategic needs. I never knew why my assignments abruptly changed. I did not know when the next move would be ordered. But I did know that as long as I was a soldier, there would be regular—and unexplained—changes in my status. Sooner or later my next assignment would be one where the odds were against my ever returning home.

As Betty Nan and I walked hand in hand to the precipice overlooking the beach, I became tearful.

"What are you thinking?" she asked.

"There, but for the grace of God, go I."

Acknowledgments

ALTHOUGH I have written for publication most of my adult life, this is my first full-length book. Before formally acknowledging the friends, colleagues, and family who helped make this book a reality, I reviewed authors' statements of appreciation in several dozen recently published military memoirs. They were formulaic, almost stereotyped. Editors, agents, and researchers were thanked for their help. At the end came a tribute to a long-suffering, understanding spouse.

I am deeply grateful to many people whose friendship and wisdom aided me in this task. For *Soldering for Freedom*, however, the typical order in which assistance and counsel are acknowledged must be reversed. From the first day I considered writing a book, to the approval of the final galley proofs, my wife's role has been indispensable. Betty Nan is a smart woman. Further, she is a skilled, demanding editor whose critical pen has changed picture captions, chapter headings, and footnotes, as well as parts of the book's basic text. Almost five decades of marriage have given her a critical—and loving—insight into my thought processes and perspective.

Three years before I considered developing a book around my 1943–1946 correspondence, I discussed donating my wartime letters to the Eisenhower Center for American Studies in New Orleans. Assistant director Annie Wedekind convinced me the letters were of historic value. She advised me that the center, a major World War II archive affiliated with the National D-Day Museum, would be delighted to make my letters part of its permanent collection. Without her initial encouragement I would never have reread and organized my World War II correspondence. Annie was succeeded by Kevin

Willey, a talented research-institute executive and archivist. Kevin has become a friend whose help and support has been invaluable. All of my World War II letters and most of the photos have been donated to the Eisenhower Center, or its affiliate, the National D-Day Museum, New Orleans. This book represents approximately one-third of the total.

In the summer of 2002, I submitted a sampling of my letters to the Texas A&M University Press along with some general ideas about how I thought a unique World War II book could be developed. Before our first meeting, the acquisitions editor, Jim Sadkovich, developed an outline of a book constructed around a teenage soldier's letters to his parents. He visualized a book that would be both salable to the general public and contain important new historical facts. Without Jim's creative mind, generous encouragement, and mastery of his craft, this book would still be aborning.

Portions of the book were read by three friends who are professional editors: Andrew Glass, Gary Rosen, and Patricia Hass. Each suggested important revisions. Each one challenged my assumptions and helped me see my own handiwork with a fresh perspective as the book evolved.

Heather Crocetto and Barbara Van Woerkon, research librarians at the National Press Club's Friedheim Library, have helped from the beginning. Their professional expertise and cheery manner made researching obscure, but important, facts pleasant.

I cannot overstate my gratitude to Catherine B. Wilson, who devoted hundreds of hours to typing and retyping the manuscript. She has learned to read my handwriting—which has not improved with age—and to accommodate my often unreasonable time demands.

Friends Del Fidanque, Marjory Ross, Amy Schapiro, Al Leeds, and Eric Dezenhall, who have expertise in various aspects of book publishing, have generously shared their knowledge of a field in which I am a novice. Bob Madani and Reza Hajiha of Advanced Photo in Falls Church, Virginia, put life and vitality into sixty-year-old photos taken with a primitive camera. David Swanson, a professional cartographer, artfully recorded each stop on my soldier's European odyssey.

Each of my four daughters has aided and encouraged me in the years between the book's conception and completion. My second daughter, Roni Atnipp, has been particularly helpful. After completing a successful television career, both on camera and as a producer, she became a book consultant. She has excellent editorial judgment and no hesitancy in telling her father when she believes he is wrong.

I am grateful to have been able to discuss this all-consuming project with loyal friends and devoted family. Each has made a subtle contribution to the finished product. Relaxed conversations in the glow of comradeship and love convinced me that this book is a valid contribution to the history of World War II.

INDEX

207; Passover, 143, 146–47; resistance deaths, 227; V-E Day, 134–35, 159–63; V-J Day, 201
Holland, 205, 221
Holland, Bob, 120
Hollywood, California, 140
Holocaust, xiii, 216, 231–33, 259
Horsch limousine, 196, 241–42, 255
horse racing, Paris, 188
hospitals, U.S. occupation, 131
Hotel Ecosse, 177
Hotel Raphael, 211
Hotel Ruhl, 189, *219*
Hotel Victoria, 271, *272*
Hotel Wagram, 207

I. G. Farben building, 234–35, 239, 243
ice skating, Switzerland, 264
incarcerated soldiers, 187–88, 189
Indiantown Gap, Pennsylvania, 56–58, 67–68
inoculations, 54–55, 286
insurance, troopship conversation, 113
interpreters, Nuremberg trials, 249–50
Iraq comparison, xiv, 130
Israel trip, post-Army, 295

Jack-o-Lantern, 234
Jackson, Joe, 172
Jackson, Robert H., 230, 231, 246
"Jacobowsky and the Colonel" (Behrman), 173
Jacobson, _ (at birthday celebration), 206–207

jerry cans, 131–32, *138, 176*
Jersey Central Station, 90
Jewish faith. *See* Jews/Judaism; worship services; Zionism (comments about)
Jewish Welfare Board, 35
Jews/Judaism: concentration camps, xiii, 216, 231–33, 259; Disraeli biography, 48–49; Hebrew class, 175; holidays/celebrations, 8–9, 35, 143, 283–84; refugees, 216–17, 236–38, 270. *See also* worship services; Zionism (comments about)
Joan of Arc, *116*
Jodl, Alfred, 246, 250
journalism. *See* newspapers
Jubecourt-en-Argonne, 132–33, 168
Judaism. *See* Jews/Judaism; worship services; Zionism (comments about)
Julius Caesar (Shakespeare), 146

Kahn, Paul, 34
Keitel, Admiral, 250
Kennedy, Edward, 166–67
Kilday, Paul J., 206
Kipling, Rudyard, 194
Kleinstein, Sergeant, 178

Lake Geneva, 264, 275
Lamar, Hedy, 117
landing craft infantry (LCIs), 89
language-aptitude tests, 12, 19, 20
Larkin, General, 209
latrines: ASTP period, 13–14; Camp Lucky Strike, 110; Camp

refugees, 216–17, 236–38, 270

Reims, France, 172–73, 176, 177

reinforcement depots: overview, 99–100, 187, 228; Camp Lucky Strike, 99–105, 108–20, 298–99; Camp Philip Morris, 280, *281,* 288, 290–91; Chartres, 104–105, 106, 120–24, 292; map, *292;* Namur, 261, 280, 284–88

religion comments. *See* philosophical comments

Remagen, Germany, 160

Reno, Nevada, 140

reparations, Holocaust victims, 259

Republican National Convention, 37

Resnikoff, Chaplain, 41, 42

Rhineland Campaign, 106, 108, 117, 160, 165

Rhine River, gasoline pipeline, 106, 125

rifle training, 62, *63*

Riveria Recreation Area, 189, 217–24, *292*

Rockettes, 254

Rome analogy, 95

Rooney, Mickey, 214, 237

Roosevelt, Franklin D., 6, 74, 147, *148–49,* 150, 152, 295

Rosen, Gary, 302

Rosenbluth, Joe, *112*

Rosenwald, Lessing J., 21–22, 156

Rosh Hashanah services, 9, 35

Ross, Marjory, 302

Rothenberg, Germany, 234, 242, 250, 252

Rothman, Snuffy, 117

Rothschild Synagogue, 200

Rouen, France, x, 105–106, *107,* 114–16

Rufus L. (Indiantown Gap friend), 58

Ruhr Valley, Germany, 258–59

Rwanda, 233

sabotage: gasoline pipeline, 125–27, 129–32, 135; troop train, xiii–xiv, 100–101, *103*

Sadkovich, Jim, 302

Saint Margaret's Church, 31

saluting regulations: Nice, 190, *225–26;* Paris, 178, 185, 208–209; Red Ball Highway, *181;* Riems, 172; Switzerland, 259–60

Saturday Evening Post, 21, 142

Saxe, Jo, *112*

Schapiro, Amy, 302

Schaubel, Major, 48, 57

Schoenfeld, Lieutenant, 23

schooling. *See* classroom studies (ASTP period); education

Sciota, Illinois, 168

"scoop" group, newspapers, 167

scouting (youth), 60–61, 183

scrap metal, 211

security measures: Frankfurt, 238–39, 241–42, 243; Nuremberg trials, 246–47, 249; troopship travel, 86–87. *See also* censorship

segregated troops, 15–16, 95, 124

sergeant stereotype, 64–65

Seventh Army, Heidelberg, 245

Shakespeare, William, 48, 146

synagogues: France, 147, 149–50, *151,* 200, 222, 224; Germany, 242; Virginia, 296. *See also* cathedrals, France; worship services

Taplinger, Gordon, 179, 180
tea dances, Riviera Recreation area, 219
tearooms, Switzerland, 266–67
telegrams (cable service), 112
telephone service, 171, 224, 227, 276–77
Temple University, 44
tetanus inoculations, 54–55
Thayer, Ernest Lawrence, 213
theater. *See* movies/shows
theater provost marshal's office: overview, 187–88, 189; St. Cloud letters, 191–98, 203–204, 227–28
theft, 129–30, 132, 135, *182*
37th Infantry Division, 16, 44
3310 Service Unit (STAR), letters from, 18–24
*3321*st Service Unit, ASTP letters from, 24–50
Time, 153, 192, 274
Tokyo, 203
Tomb of the Unknown Soldier, 227
"Tommy" (Kipling), 194
training. *See* Army Specialized Training Program (ASTP); basic training period; William and Mary, College of
train sabotage/crash, France, xiii–xiv, 100–101, *103*

train travel: France, 176, 177, 217, 236–37; Germany, 236–37; Switzerland, 263–64, 277, 285–86; United States, 18, 57, 90, 94
traveler's checks, 274, 278
Trip Over the News, 93, 96–97
troopship travel: overview, 15, 86–89, 282–83; letters during, 89–98
Truman, Harry, 216
Turner, Lana, 117
Twenty-Second Corps, 196
typhoid inoculations, 54–55, 286

U-boat zone, 86–89
"Uncle Tom" code, 10
United Nations Relief and Rehabilitation Agency (UNRRA), 199, 216
University of Geneva. *See* Switzerland
University of Heidelberg, 245
University of Maryland, 297
UNRRA (United Nations Relief and Rehabilitation Agency), 199, 216
Up Front (Maudlin), 208
USO shows, 135–36
USRRA (U.S. Riveria Recreation Area), 189, 217–24, *292*

vacation trip, childhood, 6
Valentine's Day, 45, 274–75
Van Woerkon, Barbara, 302
V Corps, 196, 240
V-E Day, 134–35, 159–63, 206–207

venereal disease, 55, *68, 158,*
185–86
Verdun: ammunition depot, 132;
FDR's death, 147, *148–49,*
150, 152; German propaganda,
169–70; hospital, 131; map,
292; prophylactic station, *158*;
synagogue, 147, 149–50, *151*;
V-E Day, 161–63
Versailles, France, 198
veterans' organizations, 293–94
"victory girls", 140
Virginian Military Institute
(VMI), 43, 44
Virginia Polytechnic Institute
(VPI), 12–13, 18–24
V-J Day, 201, 203, 206–207
V-mail, 140–41, *154*
Voir magazine, 200
von Runstedt, Gerd, 97
VPI period, 12–13, 18–24
V sign, France, 147

WACs, 194, 234, 239, 243. *See
also* girls/women *entries*
wages. *See* pay (wages)
waiting times: Chalons, 183–84;
demobilization period, 280,
286–87; training period, 19,
48, 49; troopship preparations,
89–90; VPI period, 19. *See also*
reinforcement depots
Walker, Danton, 27, 28
war bonds, 32, 45, 199
war crime tribunals, xv, 230–33,
234, 246–47
Ward (fellow trainee), 29–30
War Labor Board, 74

war progress overview: at ASTP's
closure, 17; during Camp
Lucky Strike period, 111, 117;
during Camp Pickett period,
55–56, 67; before conscription,
6, 10; at troopship landing, 88;
on V-E Day, 135
washing facilities. *See* bathing
facilities; laundry facilities
Washington, D. C., 31–32
Washington Times-Herald, 28
Wassergrat ski run, 271
weather: Camp Lucky Strike, 100,
102, 104, 110, 113, 119; Frankfurt period, 235; Le Havre, 4,
89; Nice, 218; Pumping Station,
157; training period, 19, 57
Webb, Colonel, 262, 285
Wedekind, Annie, 301
weekend passes. *See* passes/
furloughs
Wengen, Switzerland, 277
Werfel, Franz, 173
Wessels, General, 237, 256, 257
Wiesbaden, Germany, 201
Wildflecken camp, 237
Wilhelm, Sergeant, 203
Wilkinson, Roy, 191–92, 203–
204, 208, 209
Willey, Kevin, 301–302
William and Mary, College of:
overview, 13–14, 16; departure,
56–57; letters from, 24–49
Williams, Ted, 172
Williamsburg, Virginia, 24, 45.
See also William and Mary,
College of
Williamsburg Inn, 16, 43